Stress Management

Lessons *from the* **Savior**

Stress Management

Lessons *from the* **Savior**

Karen Shores, PhD

CFI
An imprint of Cedar Fort, Inc.
Springville, Utah

ISBN 13: 978-1-4621-3899-9

Published by CFI, an imprint of Cedar Fort, Inc.
2373 W. 700 S., Springville, UT 84663
Distributed by Cedar Fort, Inc., www.cedarfort.com

Library of Congress Control Number: 2020950086

Cover design by Courtney Proby
Cover design © 2021 Cedar Fort, Inc.
Edited and typeset by Rebecca Andersen

Printed in the United States of America

10 9 8 7 6 5 4 3 2 1

Printed on acid-free paper

Dedication

This is dedicated to my eternal companion, Mark R. Shores, who is preparing a place for us on the other side of the veil, and to my precious tiny angel grandchildren, Alexa, Parker, and Kyson. All have taught me new and creative ways to be stressed as well as new, precious, tender, and peaceful ways to feel loved.

And most of all, I dedicate all of this work to my Savior, the true author. These are His lessons. These are His principles. I dedicate this book, my life, my heart, and all I have to Him.

Contents

Acknowledgments

My sincere gratitude goes to all of those family and friends who have contributed their time, expertise, and wisdom to this work—especially Regan Shelby, Peggy Stowe, Ingrid Rauter, Diane Wells, Pamela Wolslager, and Peggy Barulich. Thank you from the bottom of my heart. I love you all.

Introduction

"When I heard that the director of Brigham Young University Education Week had received many requests for a stress management class, I happily offered to provide one. I had taught stress management classes for nearly thirty years. Learning the newest, latest, and greatest approaches to stress management had become a passion of mine, partly because I had experienced a great deal of stress in my own life and partly because I wanted to provide my students with the most useful tools I could find to help them manage *their* stress.

Through the years, I collected many articles and conducted extensive research concerning stress management. I noticed—as I listened to general conference and studied my scriptures—that there were many scriptural references and quotes that validated the growing list of principles of stress management that I had collected. With that in mind, I decided to title my Education Week class "Stress Management: Lessons from the Savior."

For weeks, I worked on putting the class together, praying before I sat down to work. However, I was totally frustrated that I couldn't get the class material to come together correctly. Something was wrong. It felt *off*. Initially I thought I was just having trouble trimming down so much material. That wasn't it. Then I thought I was just struggling trying to make the material fit into the four separate one-hour classes. Students can pick and choose which classes they wish to attend, so each daily class must stand alone but fit into a whole series. With the constant shuffling of students, I wanted to make sure that the material for each day could stand alone and provide value but still fit into that overarching series theme. This can often be a big challenge, so I thought that must be why I was struggling. It wasn't.

It didn't take long to recognize something that I had experienced periodically in life: A stupor of thought.

Wow! How did I miss that?

I thought I knew principles of stress management; I was busy writing down what I knew, researched, and taught for years. To address the stupor of thought, I decided to stop the process and spend a few days in fasting and prayer to find out what the obstacle was. When I received the answer, I was humbled beyond belief. I had named the class "Stress Management: Lessons from the Savior," but truthfully it was really "Stress Management: Lessons from Karen Shores with Scriptures Thrown in to Validate It." At that moment, I threw away all the previous material and started over with no preconceived ideas about where I would be led.

The very next morning, I was awakened at 4:30 a.m., hearing a clear principle in my mind and my heart. I quickly got out of bed and began to research the principle, pull together materials, and write everything as quickly as I could. The same thing happened the next morning, and the next, and the next. It was every morning at 4:30 a.m. for two and a half weeks. Now, those who know me know that I would generally growl at someone awakening me at 4:30 a.m. But when being taught so profoundly by the Spirit, I found myself falling asleep at night eagerly anticipating the next lesson. I was deeply saddened when the wake-up calls ceased.

Education Week finally started, and I was thrilled to be presenting what the Savior had taught me in the wee hours of each of those mornings. Each evening during Education Week, it was my routine to go over the presentations for the next day. I checked my PowerPoint for flow and to correct any typos. Then I would make sure to get a good night's sleep.

On the evening before the last day of class, I did my normal routine of reviewing the next day's material, saying a prayer for a good night's rest and for the Spirit to help me on the last day. I crawled into bed feeling calm and grateful that things had gone so well up until that point. At 3:30 a.m., I was awakened in a familiar way. I heard a prompting, instructing me to add two principles to the last day's presentations. One principle went to each class I was teaching—one principle was for The Healing Powers of the Spirit, Mind, and Body and the other principle was for Stress Management: Lessons from the Savior. So I crawled out of bed, picked up my laptop, and opened the first presentation. I scrolled down to the bottom of the PowerPoint and began to type. However, I was quickly stopped. The principle needed to be added to the beginning, not the end. I was told that the principle needed to be at the beginning so that I did not run out of time and end up rushing through its explanation. I moved it to the beginning.

As I opened the stress management PowerPoint, I began to insert the new principle at the beginning, unconsciously thinking the instruction would be the same. It was not. This time, I was instructed to put the principle at the end. It needed to be the *last* principle the students heard. As I stopped to process the instructions I had received and the real message of this new principle, tears welled in my eyes. The Savior deeply loves all of His children, and each message reflected the depth of His love, including the last thing that he wanted His children in that class to hear. It is the last principle in this book.

CHAPTER 1

What Is Stress?

"What classes are you teaching at Education Week this year?" the caller inquired.

"I'm teaching two classes" I said, "The Healing Powers of the Spirit, Mind, and Body and Stress Management: Lessons from the Savior."

There was silence on the other end of the phone. Was she still there? Was she waiting for another class title? Did she want me to elaborate on the topics? "That's it," I added, "only two classes this year," I said, in case she was awaiting some further information.

There was a long, uncomfortable pause. Just as I began to ask if she was still there, she started to speak, very slowly and deliberately.

"Don't take this personally," she said, "I mean, I don't want you to be offended by this but . . ." My mind raced to recall a time when I had ever heard anything positive following an opening like that. Nothing came to mind.

"I took a stress management class before and it didn't help at all, so I won't be wasting my time attending your class." The tone in her voice was escalating from the friendly voice that began the conversation to a voice filled with tension and anger. "Besides," she continued, her voice quivering from the anger and tears she was clearly holding back, "there is only one cause of *all* of my stress and *I can't do anything about him!*" Her last comment was filled with anger and punctuated with defiance. She quickly said she had to go and hung up the phone.

I was so deeply saddened by the call for two reasons. The first, of course, was that she was obviously hurting, angry, and overwhelmed by her stress, and I wanted to be able to help her. The second reason was that she mistakenly believed that since she couldn't eliminate the trigger of her stress, she had *no power at all* over her stress. That idea is fairly prevalent and simply *not* true. There are many things that we can do to manage, minimize, or even cope better with our stress even if we cannot eliminate its cause. The Savior has provided many lessons for us on how to do just that.

Like my friend, you may have been to a stress management class or attended a lecture on ways to de-stress your life. Perhaps, you have read an article that provided a list of things to do to reduce your stress. Maybe you have heard a television clip giving you ten tips to a stress-free holiday. You may have felt the same feelings that my friend felt—that none of it did any good or it was a waste of time. At the very least, you probably didn't feel a lot of stress relief from reading the articles, listening to the television suggestions, or attending a class on stress management. As a matter of fact, it might even have felt like all of the stress-reduction suggestions made your stress worse. After all, the list of *things to do* to relieve stress just added to your list of *things to do*. Don't they know that the reason you are stressed is because you already have *too many* things to do?

Before we go any further, it might be a good idea to define the word *stress* so we are all on the same wavelength. Even though we use the word often and we think we are really clear about what it means, it will help if we have a common definition to refer to. Actually, stress comes in two seemingly opposite forms. There is a good stress (yeah, hard to believe, isn't it?) called *eustress*. I have defined eustress as the physiological response to changes in the environment or events that you perceive to be good.

Eustress is the type of stress you feel when something good is occurring. Perhaps you are getting married, having a long-awaited baby, excited to start a new job, anticipating a pay raise, taking a long-awaited vacation, chasing a great opportunity, or even enjoying the thrill of a new roller coaster ride. Eustress is a change in the environment or an event that requires some adjustments on your part, *but* because you perceive it to be a good event, it can cause you to feel excited, happy, invigorated, motivated, and rejuvenated. Eustress is a good thing and can actually *improve* your health.

The other kind of stress, the bad stress, the stress that overwhelms you is the stress that most of us are referring to when we say we are highly stressed. This negative stress is called *distress*. I have defined it as the physiological response to changes in the environment or events that you perceive to be negative, dangerous, and/or a threat and that invoke fear.

That means that when you perceive a threat, you will feel stressed. Some of those events that cause a threat could be having a fight with a spouse, dealing with financial problems, enduring job-related pressures, or living through the terrible-two temper tantrums of a toddler. Threats can be physical, mental, emotional, social, spiritual, or financial. These threats—especially when you cannot see any way to reduce the threat—can lead to intense stress. This kind of stress can cause you to feel anxious, nervous, frightened, scared, helpless, hopeless, burned out, fatigued, frustrated, and physically drained. Another widely used definition of stress developed by professor and psychologist Richard S. Lazarus is "a condition or feeling experienced when a person perceives that 'demands exceed the personal and social resources the individual is able to mobilize."[1] In other words, we feel stressed when things are out of control. This is the type of stress that we are going to address. This is the type of stress that needs managing. It is the type of stress for which the Savior teaches us so many lessons.

Our goal in life should not be to get rid of all of our stress but to have more of the *right kind* of stress. We want more eustress, the thrill of the roller coaster ride, and less distress, frantically trying to out-swim a shark.

For those who are visual learners, it might help to have a visual model of what the stress process looks like.

Change/Event + Perception (Thoughts) + Physiological Response =

STRESS

---

1. American Institute of Stress, Definition of Stress, 2012, http://www.stress.org/Definition_of_stress.htm. See https://www.ncbi.nlm.nih.gov/pmc/articles.

Another way to look at this process is by using a simple equation:

$$A + B + C = D \text{ (STRESS)}$$

Where A = the change/event, B = your perception, C = your physiological response, and D = Stress.

$$A + B + C = D$$

A	B	C	D
Change in environment/ event/situation/ thought	Perception (Thoughts)	Physiological Response	**STRESS**

My friend and many others assume a different equation: A = D or that the event = stress. She thought that if you have a difficult event in your life, you have inescapable stress. She thought the *event causes the stress*. Not true. It is only the trigger.

Consider this: If there is a negative event occurring but we aren't aware of it, we don't feel stress. The stress comes when we become aware of the event, and our brain tells us that the event is bad, dangerous, or a threat. Haven't you seen people who have the same events in their lives as you do but they don't seem to act like they are stressed? I used to think that those people weren't really human, just angels dressed as humans to give us some hope for the future. In truth, those people merely perceived the event differently, therefore they responded differently.

My friend is not alone in her feelings of being overwhelmed by her stress. She is not alone in feeling that she can't do anything to stop her stress or that she is powerless over her stress. It might even be fair to say that you share her exact same feelings. If you are reading this book, chances are high that you are dealing with a great deal of stress in your own life. You might even feel like you are experiencing much more stress than other people seem to experience. You may feel like no one else understands how crippled you are because of the intense stress that you are carrying.

Well, the truth may come as a big surprise. *Many* people around the world, especially Americans, are going through the same intensity of stress that you are. The New York American Institute of Stress shows us some very profound facts regarding the prevalence of stress.

1. The United States has the most stressed population in the world. In spite of the fact that we live in a land of great freedom and wealth, we are more stressed than other populations in the world that struggle with high amounts of disease, high infant and child mortality rates, no clean drinking water, and high rates of hunger and poverty. Why would that be?

2. Ninety percent of American adults experience high levels of stress at least one to two times per week. Ninety percent? We are definitely not alone in our stress. That means almost all of us experience high levels of stress frequently and fairly consistently.

3. Fifty-seven percent of American women feel excessively stressed much or most of the time. *Wow!* Over half of the women in America are feeling excessive levels of stress much or most of the time. That doesn't say "kind of stressed," or "a little stressed," it says there are *excessive* levels of stress much or most of the time. That means there is very little time when women feel calm, peaceful, and relaxed.

4. One million employees miss work every day due to stress. As we will see in chapter three, there are myriad physical, mental, emotional, social, and spiritual symptoms that develop as a consequence of chronic stress. Many of those physical and emotional symptoms are debilitating enough to cause workers to feel like they cannot go to work.

5. In the United States, we spend over $800 million on antianxiety medications each year. It is important to note that stress feels like anxiety and can even mimic the symptoms of anxiety disorders so well that it is often hard to tell the difference between feelings of high stress and symptoms of anxiety disorder.

6. Twenty-five percent of American adults are subject to crushing levels of stress nearly every day.[2] *Crushing levels.* That means for 25 percent of us, stress is so intense that it makes us feel like it is difficult to function, to continue to carry the load, to breathe. Carrying crushing levels of stress leads quickly to negative health effects and complete exhaustion. Did that percentage of crushing levels of stress surprise you? 25 percent of American adults? That means one of every four people in the United States feel crushed beneath the weight of their stress. One in four and they are driving next to us on the freeway.

No, we are definitely *not* alone in the stress that we feel. As a matter of fact, it looks like the very low-stressed individuals are the unique ones. Though it might be comforting momentarily to know that others understand and can even empathize with our crushing levels of stress, it also means that we are living in a kind of national pressure cooker where the tension and stress levels are so high that on any given day we have witnessed some people erupting in explosive anger or crumbling under the crushing weight. It is likely to continue.

Are stress levels increasing? Many have suggested that it feels like stress levels are steadily increasing. That certainly could be the case. Though stress in not new. People of all ages have dealt with stress.

Woven through the centuries are some common stressors: finding and obtaining food, water, and shelter, challenges with weather, illnesses, death of a loved one, economic challenges, political turmoil, wars, and much more. Periodically there have been some major stressors unique to a particular generation, a specific country, or a certain race or religion, such as World War I, World War II, the pandemics of 1918 and 2020, the Black Plague, ruthless dictators, the Holocaust, slavery, the Civil War, and the Mormon pioneers fleeing persecution. There have been some extremely troubling, fearful times throughout history, times of intense stress when groups of people have been pushed past their limits. Our day is no different. We are living in the last days, and prophecies

---

2. Survey from the American Institute of Stress (https://www.stress.org/stress-research/) and surveys from American Psychological Association (*http://www .apa. org/news/press/releases/stress/2013/infographics.aspx*).

tell us that the last days will be filled with increased challenges and difficulties. These events could definitely increase our stress.

What do the scriptures tell us of the events in the last days that will likely increase our stress levels?

"Nation shall rise against nation, and kingdom against kingdom: And great earthquakes shall be in divers places, and famines, and pestilences; and fearful sights and great signs shall there be from heaven" (Luke 21:10–11).

"And in that day shall be heard of wars, and rumors of wars, and the whole earth shall be in commotion, and men's hearts shall fail them… And the love of men shall wax cold, and iniquity shall abound…they perceive not the light, and they turn their hearts from me because of the precepts of men…And there shall be earthquakes also in divers places, and many desolations; yet men will harden their hearts against me, and they will take up the sword, one against another, and they will kill one another" (D&C 45:26–33).

Let's take a closer look at the specifics in those scriptures and how they are impacting our stress levels.

INCREASED GLOBAL CONFLICT

"Nation shall rise against nation, and kingdom against kingdom" (Luke 21:10). "And in that day, shall be heard of wars and rumors of wars" (D&C 45:33).

Does an increase in wars and rumors of war increase our stress level? Absolutely! Stress comes from feelings of fear, danger, or threat. Wars and rumors of war keep us at a perpetual level of threat. As we watch the unrest and conflict throughout the world, we certainly hear the rumors of war and witness increased outbreaks of war. The global unrest can be very unsettling, increasing our underlying stress levels. In Luke 21:9, we are given some further guidance: "When ye shall hear of wars and commotions, be not terrified: for these things must first come to pass; but the end is not by and by."

MORE NATURAL DISASTERS, FAMINES, AND PESTILENCE

"And great earthquakes shall be in divers places, and famines, and pestilences: and fearful sights and great signs shall be from heaven" (Luke 21:11). "And there shall be earthquakes also in divers' places, and many desolations" (D&C 45:33).

Does it not seem that there are progressively more earthquakes, tornados, hurricanes, floods, drought, tsunamis, fires, and other natural disasters? Indeed! According to the United Nations report, natural disasters have nearly quadrupled in number between 1970 and 2017. These natural disasters are more frequent and are occurring in places where they have not occurred before. In their wake they leave injury, death, and destruction. Natural disasters and extreme weather conditions have certainly plagued people from the beginning of time. The challenge here is that these events are increasing in number and therefore increasing stress levels.

Pestilence is a deadly and overwhelming disease that is highly contagious, virulent, and infectious. We have seen a number of diseases and illnesses that could fit into this category, including the COVID-19 pandemic, HIV, SARS, the bird or swine flus. For many, stress levels increased dramatically as the pandemic of 2020 spread around the world. The pandemic of 1918 killed millions of people around the world. It spread rapidly and killed quickly.

INIQUITY ABOUNDS

"And the love of men shall wax cold, and iniquity shall abound" (D&C 45:27). "For they perceive not the light, and they turn their hearts from me because of the precepts of men" (D&C 45:29). "Yet men will harden their hearts against me, and they will take up the sword, one against another, and they will kill one another" (D&C 45:33).

Is there any question that iniquity abounds today? It only takes listening to the evening news, watching one reality show on television, or listening to the words of songs on the radio to know that iniquity has crept in and taken up residency. Traditional values, morals, principles, and character have eroded away to the point that Isaiah foresaw:

people would "call evil good and good evil and put darkness for light and light for darkness" (Isaiah 5:20).

Little by little, and yet faster and faster, that which is good is being labeled as old-fashioned, ridiculous, fuddy-duddy, or "so yesterday," while that which is evil is touted as new, creative, progressive, modern, and current.

It is not unusual for people standing firm in their values and morals to be mocked, bullied, ridiculed, publicly humiliated, laughed at, or even shunned by family and/or friends. On the other hand, there are thousands of examples of men following the "precepts of men" turning away from God-given principles, behaviors, morals, and values. The precepts of men become so fashionable, convenient, and prominent in the media and in our culture, that we begin to think that holding firmly to God-given values leaves us totally alone in the foxhole.

Rick Warren summed up the concept rather succinctly: "A lie doesn't become truth, wrong doesn't become right, and evil doesn't become good, just because it's accepted by a majority." This shifting of principles in our world causes life to become very stressful. The lines that once differentiated moral and immoral, integrity and deceit, love for others and self-centeredness, have become blurred. These blurred lines make it progressively more difficult to stand fast in gospel standards. Principles and values are the things that should be stable and solid, the things that we should be able to hold onto firmly in order to survive all the other changes.

FAILING HEARTS

"Men's hearts shall fail them" (D&C 45:26). "Surely, men's hearts shall fail them; for fear shall come upon all people" (D&C 88:91). "Men's hearts failing them for fear" (Luke 21:26).

Are men's hearts failing them? Yes, and at an alarming rate. We can interpret "hearts failing" in two ways. The first is the physical heart. Heart disease is currently the number one leading cause of death in the United States, and it is in the top ten leading causes of death throughout the world.[3] In addition, heart disease is one of the most prominent chronic diseases we face, affecting the quality of life for millions of people. Stress is one of the big risk factors for heart disease. As our stress increases, the risk of heart problems increase.

The second "failing heart" can occur when our hearts fail from pain, grief, sorrow, loneliness, despair, divorce, wayward children, fear, lack of hope, debilitating depression, or loss of faith. All of these emotions have increased as well. Suicide rates have increased. Drug use, to cover emotional pain, is at epidemic levels. Depression is rampant, and the number of people who believe in God is dropping. Our hearts are, indeed, failing us.

SURFEITING AND CARES OF THIS LIFE

"And take heed to yourselves, lest at any time your hearts be overcharged with surfeiting, and drunkenness, and cares of this life" (Luke 21:34).

Surfeiting is not a common word. I had to look it up. It means to overindulge, consume too much or to excess. Surfeiting in regards to food is no surprise. Two-thirds of Americans are overweight and one-third are obese. We didn't get that way from restraint in food consumption.

Are we overindulgent in drunkenness? Again, no surprise there as we look at the increase in sales of alcoholic beverages, the number of drunk driving citations, accidents, hospital visits for severe alcoholism, and the increase in violence, crimes, and abuse of family members due to alcohol. In addition, research shows alcoholism causes damaging effects on relationships, long-term damage to children of alcoholics, higher unemployment rates, and a plethora of other challenges. All of these increase stress.

This scripture could also be referring to other forms of intoxicants and mind-altering drugs, prescribed or illegal. Drug addiction has become a major concern in our culture. Lives are destroyed as the addictions become so pervasive that individuals steal from their own

---

3. "Deaths and Mortality," Centers for Disease Control and Prevention, https://www.cdc.gov/nchs/fastats/deaths.htm.

families to get money for their drugs. Addictions change the chemistry of the brain to the point that the addicted individual becomes more concerned about their next dose of drugs than they do about food, shelter, or their own safety.

Putting aside food, alcohol, and drugs, there are hundreds of other ways that we surfeit: shopping, pornography, television, social media, gambling, sex, gossip, entertainment, appearance, money—this list could take up the whole page.

When our "hearts are overcharged" with indulging to excess in any of these worldly ventures, we give the target of our indulgence our full focus and priority and increase our own stress in many different ways.

CARES OF THIS LIFE

And what are the "cares of this life"? Stop and think for one moment about the many stresses in your life. How many of those are "worldly cares"—things that have little eternal value or import? There are thousands. As a matter of fact, it is likely that *most* of the things that we do during the day and the things that we worry about at night are "cares of this life." Every night before I go to sleep, I make a list of the things that I need to do the next day. Besides going to work and taking care of children, most of the other things on the list are "cares of this life," sadly. The list includes things like make an appointment with the dog groomer, fix the broken light in the car, put away the Christmas stuff, get stamps at the post office, order the filter for the refrigerator water dispenser, find a new container for the craft supplies, etc. All are cares of this life.

What is the difference between those things that are necessary and those things that are unnecessary cares of this life? Our ancestors were generally focused on the necessities of life: food, clean water, shelter, safety, health, family, and community. We still need the same food, water, shelter, safety, and health for our families. Truthfully, most things beyond that list of necessities slip into wants instead of needs. We want bigger, better, newer, and more; homes, walk-in closets, cars, clothes, technology, big screens, appliances, and tons more entertainment.

It takes only a quick look at our typical day to see all the "cares of this life." Many cares of this life swarm through and around social media. In one of my classes, I asked students to track how many hours per day they spend on social media. The numbers are staggering. The average time the students spent was at least seven hours per day. Other research indicates that the average American spends at least three to five hours per day on social media. When checking social media daily becomes a time-consuming priority in life, we have let our hearts be overcome with "the cares of this life."

"MEN WILL HARDEN THEIR HEARTS AGAINST ME" (D&C 45:33).

The current research indicates that the number of people who believe in God is declining at a fairly rapid rate. The number of people who consider themselves to be religious or spiritual is also on a dramatic downward slope. Men hardening their hearts against God is now commonplace. Using God's name in vain is so prevalent that it has become "the norm." Many people blaspheme God even as they proclaim that He does not exist. Many people are angry with God for their trials, for not getting what they want when they want it, or because they want life to be easy. An angry heart is a hardened heart. For all who live with an angry family member, you know immediately how much stress that causes in your home. A world filled with angry, hardened people leads to bullying, contention, dispute, violence, war, murder, and complete disregard for human life.

"AND THE LOVE OF MEN SHALL WAX COLD..." (D&C 45:27), "...AND THEY WILL TAKE UP THE SWORD, ONE AGAINST ANOTHER, AND THEY WILL KILL ONE ANOTHER" (D&C 45:33).

Whether we use swords, guns, knives, brass knuckles, or our automobiles while we feel road rage (not swords but certainly deadly steel), the resulting death or injury is still the same.

Not only do we see this scripture play out in the casualties of war, but it also occurs on our streets, on our roads, in our schools, and in our neighborhoods. The number of murders, rapes, gang fights, drug wars, brutal assaults, and domestic violence against spouses, children, and aging parents is increasing rapidly. This increasing violence is clear evidence of "the love of men waxing cold."

When we see innocent people massacred at a movie theater or a shopping mall, or innocent children shot in their schools, or our sweet, wise, elderly family members abused in nursing homes, or innocent women and children kidnapped and sold into human trafficking, it deeply disturbs our sense of safety, security, and peace. These trends throw us into a constant level of fear, danger, and threat. Though we probably don't walk around every day in a highly conscious fear for our safety, that underlying fear and threat of danger lingers as a constant addition to our stress levels.

THE WORLD IS IN COMMOTION

"And the whole earth shall be in commotion," (D&C 45:26) "and all things shall be in commotion" (D&C 88:91).

Commotion is defined as a state of confused and noisy disturbance, tumult, ruckus, furor, agitation, and disorder. These verses are referring to the "noisy disturbance" and interruptions in the whole world in the last days. On a very small scale, have you ever tried to get work done on the computer but were interrupted by email alerts, Instagram notifications, text messages, and advertising pop-ups while the house phone, cell phone, and doorbell were all ringing? It causes quite the frustration figuring out which message, alert, notification, or bell gets your attention first. And that was just a personal small-scale example. When we look at all the commotion in government, healthcare, technology, economics, and media, that commotion turns quickly into ruckus, furor, agitation, and disorder. The year 2020 seems to be the poster child for the word *commotion*: pandemic, earthquakes, hurricanes, tornados, locust, killer bees, economic crisis, unemployment, presidential election, riots, looting, destruction of buildings and statues, massive fires on the West Coast, and even an arctic storm. That is what commotion means.

We are subjected to commotion constantly: bureaucracy, red tape, politics, crowds, deceitful sales people, escalating prices, changes in health care insurances, new laws, and continuous maintenance and repairs of cars, homes, appliances and computers as well as children needing to go in fifteen different directions for school, sports, music lessons, and scouting. All of the things that swirl around us at tornado-wind speed qualify as disturbance and agitation and commotion.

I recall an elderly aunt telling me many years ago that she was having trouble keeping up with all the mail, newspapers, advertisements, and magazines that were delivered to her home. "I am getting so far behind," she bemoaned. "I just can't read all of it." She was genuinely distressed and overwhelmed. "Why do you have to read it all?" I inquired. "Can't you just skim through it to see if there is anything you really need or want to read and throw the rest away?" "Oh, *no*," she replied. "They wouldn't send it to me if it weren't important." Her distress was real. She believed that the plethora of useless information was somehow of critical importance. Sadly, we are bombarded daily by so much mail, email, advertisements, newspapers, television news, magazines, social media, and official-looking documents delivered to us, that it is getting harder and harder to sort through it all to discern what really deserves our attention.

While wading through the commotion, it is hard not to be distracted by the multitude of demanding material and people trying to grab our attention. We not only have the same mountain of written materials delivered to our homes as did my sweet aunt, but in addition we have constant advertisements thrust at us on television, billboards, business signs, pop-up ads, intrusive phone calls, and salespeople at our front door. If my little aunt were still alive, her heart would be "failing" from the sheer overload of the unimportant information masquerading around as critical and expedient.

Another Factor That Leads to Commotion Is Change

Recall that the definition of stress (distress *and* eustress) is "the physiological response to changes." Change is an integral component of stress. This means that when we are experiencing rapid, intense, and pervasive changes in our lives, it leads to escalating levels of stress.

Change itself is neither good nor bad. It can be both or neither. Change is required for growth and progress. We must have change to have bright, yellow daffodils in the spring where we planted a bulb in the fall. Without change, there would be no antibiotics to help your body fight infection. Without change, there would be no babies, butterflies, or gorgeous leaves changing colors in autumn. Change can bring hope, healing, and growth. Conversely, it can also bring injury or despair. It can be exciting or an annoyance. Some kind of change is required to resolve or improve an ugly, difficult situation, though the difficult situation was caused by something that changed to begin with. Change makes life better and it makes life worse. It is not change itself that causes stress to escalate, it is the type, *speed*, and intensity of change that is responsible for the escalating stress.

All changes—whether we perceive them to be good or bad—require *some adjustment* on our part. Yes, even good changes require some adjustments. Those adjustments take time, concentration, problem-solving abilities, reorganizing, and getting used to the new way of life. Plus, each change causes other things to change as well in order to accommodate the first change. This means that one change generally causes a chain reaction of change and adjustment.

For example, perhaps you have been lucky in landing a great new job. That's only one change, but in addition to learning the new job, you change your work location, the people with whom you work, your working conditions and processes, when you get paid, the route you take to work, the clothing you wear, the hours you start and stop work, what errands fit in on your way to and from work, your health insurance, your benefits, and many more details. One change truly leads to a chain reaction of many more changes and adjustments.

It takes time to adjust to *each and every change* in the very long chain reaction and settle into a new comfortable routine. If changes occurred very slowly in life, we could handle one isolated change with its subsequent chain reaction of events and still have plenty of time to enjoy some normalcy, stability, and relaxation before the next change occurs. That is the way life used to be for previous generations—changes came slowly and generally only one at a time. Life had a slower pace, less complexity, and more time to adjust to the few changes that occurred. Prior to 1950, major changes in technology occurred an average of once every *fifty years*. That gave individuals, as well as the entire culture, plenty of time to internally process what the change meant, make all the necessary adjustments, incorporate the new process/technology into their lives, acclimate to the change, and establish routine and comfort with their new daily routine. In other words, people had ample time to adjust.

We no longer have the luxury of ample time to adjust. We no longer have fifty years in between technological changes. We no longer have the option of dealing with one change at a time. Gone is the comfort of slow acclimation and the enjoyment of a calm and stable routine. As a matter of fact, we are adjusting to *many* changes every day, in *many* areas of our life, *all at the same time.* Today things change so rapidly that even as you walk out the front door of a computer store with the newest, latest, and greatest computer, there is an even newer technology coming in through the back door. Your brand-new computer is obsolete before you ever get it set up. This rapid change occurs in every part of our lives: technology, social media, medicine, transportation, economics, insurance, food safety, pollutants, and how we pay for things. Before we get to adjust to something that has changed, it has changed again.

COMMOTION FROM CONSTANT CHANGE AND LACK OF ROUTINE

Let me briefly explain why constant change and lack of routine increases stress. Things that are routine are things that we can do without much thought or concentration. When we do something repetitively, it becomes a routine that no longer demands our concentration, focus, problem-solving, or decision-making capacities. When things become routine, it helps us function more easily and frees up our brain to focus on the things that do require our attention. It is extremely difficult to give focus, concentration, and thought to every single thing we do.

To understand the impact of routine, let's think back to a time when you had to learn something new that required your undivided concentration and coordination, such as learning to drive a car, learning to play the piano, or learning a new language.

Let's go through the process of learning to drive a car with a manual transmission. The first attempt at learning to drive was probably extremely frustrating, though probably extremely comical to those watching, and stressful to the teacher and owner of the car. Learning to drive required concentration, focus, attention, coordination, and more patience than you thought you possessed. Your left foot, right foot, left hand, and right hand all had different jobs to do, but they had to coordinate all of their different efforts to function perfectly at exactly the same time. As your right foot pressed slowly down on the gas pedal, your left foot had to ease up slowly on the clutch until you found the exact spot where the car would move forward smoothly. It is likely that your first attempt to do this caused the car to jolt forward and then die. It is also likely that your second attempt ended the same way…and the third and the fourth and the fifth.

In addition to trying to coordinate your feet, you had to add in your hands, shifting between the different gears with your right hand, steering the car with your left hand…and, oh yeah, let's not forget checking the rearview mirror, looking over your shoulder for traffic, and using your turn signals or windshield wipers. Many gave up learning to drive a manual transmission car because it required too much concentration, coordination, and practice.

The first day of learning was shockingly awful and probably included a few swear words. The next day was still awful, but at least you were braced for the challenge. The third day, you gained some comfort in the awkwardness, but you were still not able to make the car go forward smoothly for more than ten feet in a totally empty, massively large parking lot. Will you ever be able to get out of first gear? Is there any chance you can put it all together and finally make it safely onto a deserted street? You continue to practice and practice. Finally, you can put it all together and can at last make the car go forward smoothly in a straight line. Once the car rolls smoothly, you must learn to manage frequent starts and stops, right-hand turns, left-hand turns, lane changes, traffic signals, the presences of other cars, anticipating the moves of other drivers (Is that even possible?), following directions to where you are going, figuring out how to parallel park, dealing with construction and changing weather conditions, adjusting the radio, *but not* texting and driving. It's a lot to learn and coordinate. It takes *constant* concentration, coordination, and focus to learn. You are certain this complicated process will never become "routine."

Now, jump ahead five years. You drive the kids to school, stop at the store and at the post office and then go to work. What were you thinking about as you were driving? Coordinating the gas pedal and the clutch? Shifting gears? Probably not! More likely, you were driving safely; you were totally aware of traffic while you were singing with the radio and thinking about what you needed to buy at the store. Driving isn't complicated anymore. As a matter of fact, you probably never once thought about shifting gears or pushing down the clutch. It has become *routine*, an automatic process. The previous all-consuming concentration and practice has developed extremely efficient muscle memory and nerve pathways up to and throughout your brain. Horace Mann said, "Habit is a cable: We weave a thread of it every day, and at last we cannot break it." Those habits become routine with automatic pathways to your brain that allow you to drive more safely because you are able to pay attention to the road rather than concentrating on the mechanical details of the process. You drive easily because the process of driving has become second nature, comfortable, and routine. Habits make life routine enough for us to function. Julie Henderson suggested, "Habits are the shorthand of behavior." We need that shorthand in order to function.

So it is with all the changes in our lives. Every time there is a change in life, it requires our constant focus and deep concentration as we adjust and practice enough to make the change a new routine. Once a process is routine, our brain is free to shift to other matters or learn other new things, or raise children, or spend time with our family and friends. As more things become automatic, the easier our everyday activities become.

Unfortunately, every change causes you to return to concentrating on something that used to be a routine process, but because it changed, you now have to focus on it again to fix it, adjust to it, and make it into a new routine. Every time your cell phone breaks and you need to get a new updated version, you spend many hours, or sometimes many days, figuring out how to do all the things with the new phone that were routine on your old phone.

We function best when we have only one change at a time with ample time to adjust, acclimate to that change and make it a no-brainer. However, our world is changing so rapidly that we constantly deal with more than one change at a time, in more than one area of our lives, in rapid succession with no time to acclimate. We become overwhelmed.

Our culture is moving faster and faster with progressively more complex changes and demands on our time. Just consider how complex and time-consuming it is to file a tax return, wade through medical bills and figure out what the insurance has paid, help children do their "new math" homework (What is wrong with the old math? Does new math give you different answers?), protect ourselves from identity theft (Who knew someone could or would want to steal your identity?), or just flip through the ever-changing menu of five hundred television stations. The speed of change in our lives contributes dramatically to our stress levels. The most important thing to remember here is the first step in the stress process is that something changed. The more change, the more stress. The faster things change, the faster our stress escalates.

However, let's remember that change is an eternal principle. We try to change to become more Christlike. Change is progress. Change leads us forward. We just need to control the types of changes in our lives and make those changes in manageable ways.

In 1918, James E. Talmage said in an LDS General Conference address: "Have you never read that all things should be in commotion in the last days? This is the day of shaking, when everything that can be shaken shall be shaken, and only those things which are established upon an eternal foundation shall endure."[4]

---

4. James E. Talmage, in Conference Report, 1918.

We are definitely being shaken: physically, mentally, emotionally, socially, financially, morally, and spiritually. All of the prophecies of the last days are in the process of being realized. In the Joseph Smith translation of the book of Matthew, it states that the commotion of the last days will parallel the commotion of "the days of Noah" (Matthew 24:37). This means there will be continued and increasing changes, adjustments, commotion, danger, turmoil, disturbance, disorder, and fear—also known as constantly increasing *stress*.

Obviously, the scriptures indicate that we are feeling the effects of the last days, and those effects dramatically increase our levels of stress. We see the wars and rumors of wars. We witness the natural disasters. The news constantly reports evidence that the love of men has waxed cold and iniquity abounds. We often feel that our hearts may fail us as the whole earth swirls in commotion, surfeiting, drunkenness, and the cares of this life.

President Howard W. Hunter counseled us to not worry ourselves sick about the trials and difficulties of the world in these last days:

> Inevitably the natural result of some of these kinds of prophecies is fear, and that is not fear limited to a younger generation. It is fear shared by those of any age who don't understand what we understand. But I want to stress that these feelings are not necessary for faithful Latter-day Saints, and they do not come from God. To ancient Israel, the great Jehovah said: "Be strong and of a good courage, fear not, nor be afraid of them: for the Lord thy God, he it is that doth go with thee; he will not fail thee, nor forsake thee... And the Lord, he it is that doth go before thee; he will be with thee, he will not fail thee, neither forsake thee; fear not, neither be dismayed" (Deut. 31:6, 8). And to you, our marvelous generation in modern Israel, the Lord has said: "Therefore, fear not, little flock: do good; let earth and hell combine against you, for if ye are built upon my rock, they cannot prevail... Look unto me in every thought; doubt not, fear not" (D&C 6: 34, 36). Such counsel is laced throughout our modern scriptures. Listen to this wonderful reassurance: "Fear not, little children, for you are mine, and I have overcome the world, and you are of them

that my Father hath given me" (D&C 50:41). "Verily I say unto you my friends, fear not, let your hearts be comforted; yea, rejoice evermore, and in everything give thanks" (D&C 98:1). In light of such wonderful counsel, I think it is incumbent upon us to rejoice a little more and despair a little less, to give thanks for what we have and for the magnitude of God's blessings to us, and to talk a little less about what we may not have or what anxiety may accompany difficult times in this or any generation.[5]

LESSONS FROM THE SAVIOR

Now, let's get to the most important question of the book: What are the stress management lessons from the Savior? The word stress is *not* in the Topical Guide. Stress is not one of the subjects in Gospel Doctrine classes. Has the Savior left us without guidance and wisdom on a topic that is overwhelming and crippling so many of us? Given the magnitude and prevalence of stress in the world, is it possible that our Heavenly Father is completely unaware of the stress in our lives? Is it possible that a loving, omnipotent, omniscient Heavenly Father who knows the end from the beginning was taken by surprise that His children are overwhelmed and even crippled by the stress levels that we are experiencing? *No*, He has not left us alone. He has not withheld His wisdom from us on how to deal with stress. Quite to the contrary, there are hundreds of scriptures on stress and an abundance of messages from the prophets and apostles, counseling us on how to manage our stress. We just need to know where to find them.

In order to better understand why we have not been able to see the many scriptures and messages for us regarding stress, we need to go back in time, for just a moment, to the beginning of the 20th century. Prior to 1932, the word stress was defined as the amount of pressure or tension it would take for a structure to crack. The word stress was used to identify the strength and structural stability (or lack of it) of buildings, bridges, walls, and other structures. It was not used to describe people. In 1932, Hans Selye, often referred to as the Father of

5. Howard W. Hunter, "An Anchor to the Souls of Men," *Ensign*, October 1993.

Stress, began to use the term *stress* to explain the same phenomenon in humans: How much pressure or tension does it take for human beings to crack?[6]

Prior to 1932, human beings definitely experienced stress, they just referred to it in different terms. The terms they used were: problems, trials, challenges, difficulties, adversity, afflictions, etc. When we understand the different terminology used, it becomes easier to see that there are hundreds of lessons from the Savior on how to manage stress. So, let's start the process of learning what they are.

6. Mark Jackson, "Evaluating the Role of Hans Selye in the Modern History of Stress," National Center for Biotechnology Information, 2014, https://www.ncbi .nlm.nih.gov/books/NBK349158/.

CHAPTER 2

Lesson 1:
Stress by Design

Sometimes, it is hard to believe that the Savior knows or understands our stress. Did the Lord *really* know how much stress we would have in our lives? Did He leave us to figure out how to deal with stress on our own? Did the fact that we have so much stress in the world come as a surprise to Him? No, not only is He *not* surprised by our stress, the truth is that He planned the world and our lives to have stress in them *on purpose*.

LESSON #1: WE HAVE STRESS IN OUR LIVES BY DESIGN

Right from the very beginning, we see evidence that stress was intentionally designed to be part of our lives. When Adam and Eve were cast out of the Garden of Eden, they were told: "Cursed shall be the ground for thy sake: in sorrow shalt thou eat of it all the days of thy life. Thorns also and thistles shall it bring forth to thee...by the sweat of thy face shalt thou eat bread" (Gen. 3:18; Moses 4:23–25).

Did you notice the words cursed, sorrow, thorns, thistles, and sweat? Those words don't sound like we should plan on clear skies and smooth sailing. They are words that indicate that we are meant to have some difficulties, challenges, tough times, and trials. In addition, once we understand that the word *stress* is synonymous with words like trials, tribulations, adversity, and affliction, we find that there are many other scriptures that attest to the fact that having stress in this mortal life *is* by design. *No one is exempt* from this process. Stress was built into the design of mortality—it is a requirement of the mortal experience.

The scriptures make it abundantly clear that stress is not just a passive experience but has been given to us on purpose. "I give unto men weakness that they may be humble" (Ether 12:27). "Nevertheless, the Lord seeth fit to chasten his people; yea, he trieth their patience and their faith" (Mosiah 23:21).

From these two scriptures, we see clearly that the Lord has intentionally planned and given to us the very weaknesses that lead to a portion of our stress. Additionally, He sometimes gives us trials, chastening, and experiences that will try our patience and our faith. Most of those trials feel like stress.

As we further search the scriptures looking for evidence that stress is given to us by design, we find another principle that is intricately tied to stress: the principle of opposition in all things. We are told: "For it must needs be that there is an opposition in all things" (2 Nephi 2:11). To illustrate that further, we can turn to an oft quoted section in Ecclesiastes to read a vivid description of what opposition means: "To everything there is a season, and a time to every purpose under the heaven: A time to be born, and a time to die, a time to plant, and a time to pluck up that which is planted, a time to kill, and a time to heal, a time to break down, and a time to build up, a time to weep, and a time to laugh, a time to mourn, and a time to dance... a time to get, and a time to lose...a time to keep, and a time to cast away, a time to love, and a time to hate, a time of war and a time of peace" (Ecclesiastes 3:1–4, 6, 8).

This scripture confirms that we are intended to have times of joy, peace, happiness, laughter, clear skies, and smooth sailing—the things we wish we had *all* the time. But the other half of each couplet contains experiences that we definitely don't want to have, experiences that we likely see as stressful: a time to weep, to mourn, to lose, to break down, to cast away, or to die. It is clear that the eternal principles and design for our lives include times of ease and times of stress.

Now, just because the world and our lives were designed to have stress in them, does not mean that *all of our stress* is God-given. As a matter of fact, most of our stress is a function of living in this world and is not specifically God-given. In his book *All These Things Shall Give Thee Experience*, Elder Neal Maxwell stated that there are three causes of trials, adversity, and stress in our lives and only one of them is God-given.

First, Elder Maxwell suggested that a big cause of our trials (stress) is one which we don't want to believe. A great deal of our stress comes from *our own weaknesses and mistakes*. That's hard to hear. Many of us wish to blame all of our stress on someone else or on some outside inescapable source. We don't want to believe that the very stress that is crushing us comes from a situation we created ourselves. That would be absurd! We certainly wouldn't put ourselves through something so difficult, so stressful, and so challenging. Well, we wouldn't do it consciously. Nevertheless, much of our stress *is* created by our own choices, our own weaknesses. We, like all other people in the world, make mistakes, break commandments, mix up priorities, and fail to follow the wise counsel given to us by the prophets and the scriptures. Often, we bemoan the horrendous stress in our lives when that very stress is the consequence of our own poor choices and decisions.

The second cause of stress, according to Elder Maxwell is that we live in an imperfect world with imperfect people. The world is imperfect. Pipes break, storms take down utility poles, snails (or crickets) eat our crops, earthquakes shake down entire cities, animals and humans get sick or injured, it rains unexpectedly on an outdoor reception, ice forms on the roads where we need to drive, and the elements deteriorate our roofs. An imperfect world leads to many possibilities for stressful days. Just this past summer, I spent many hours of hard work clearing a wonderful place in my yard for a garden. I pulled the weeds (one of the imperfections of the world from my perspective), tilled the ground, fertilized it, and planted a wonderful variety of vegetables. I watered those seeds and plants, pulled the weeds, and spent a great deal of time nurturing my little garden. One day when I went out to pull some weeds, the little plants—which were looking so healthy just a couple of days before—were gone. All that was left of my little plants were bare stems. Nearby I found some extremely fat, sluggish snails trying to drag themselves out of sight.

Even though many of the processes of the world (snails eating my garden) are part of the circle of life, some of those processes make our lives more stressful.

In addition to the imperfect world, we live in a world *filled* with imperfect people. People who were given their own set of weaknesses, who make mistakes, who break commandments, who can be unkind, who steal from you or destroy your property, or who choose to drink and drive. Many of the trials and stresses in our life come from the actions of others. At some point in your life, you have probably had someone make a mistake on a bill or in a bank account or on an order you placed for supplies or services. It may have caused you a great deal of stress trying to get it corrected. Does it ever feel like all those imperfect people are just waiting for you to drive by so they have a target for their mistakes? Elder Dieter F. Uchtdorf summed up this principle by saying, "The people around us are not perfect. People do things that annoy, disappoint, and anger. In this mortal life, it will always be that way. Nevertheless, we must let go of our grievances. Part of the purpose of mortality is to learn how to let go of such things. That is the Lord's way."[7]

The third cause of stress, a very small portion, according to Elder Maxwell comes from God-given trials and chastening. These are times when the "Lord seeth fit to chasten his people; yea, he trieth their patience and their faith" (Mosiah 23:21). Elder Maxwell reminds us that we tend to think that the majority of our stress is God-given when the truth is *very little* of our stress is God-given.[8] Now, wait a minute. Isn't the first lesson of stress management that we have stress by design, and doesn't that mean that our stress is God-given? Yes and no. Just because God designed the world to be a place where stress, trials, challenges, and adversity exist, and a place where we can be tried and tested, *does not mean* that each and every trial, challenge, or time of adversity that we experience was specifically designed by Him to be a personal trial for us.

One of the first steps to managing our stress requires that we practice gut-wrenching honesty about the real source of our stress. Is our stress from the imperfect world, from imperfect people, from an imperfect self, or is it truly God-given?

---

7. Dieter F. Uchtdorf, "The Merciful Obtain Mercy," *Ensign*, April 2012, 7.
8. Neal A. Maxwell, *All These Things Shall Give Thee Experience* (Salt Lake City: Deseret Book, 1979), 29–32.

Elder J. Christopher Lansing affirms the suggestions of Elder Maxwell by saying, "Some crises we bring on ourselves through disobedience to the laws of God or man. Some come upon us through no fault of our own."[9] The tricky part is deciphering the difference. Further complicating the trickiness of deciphering the difference is that generally our stress comes from a combination of sources, not just from one source. We mix some of our own weaknesses with the weaknesses of others in an imperfect world to create the stress that we feel.

STRESS BY DESIGN? REALLY? WHY?

When I realized that we have stress by design, the first thing that popped into my semi-rebellious mind was: *Really? By design? This is intentional? Why?* I would have preferred the scenario of clear skies, smooth sailing, and only the happy events listed in Ecclesiastes. However, stress *is* by design, and I really wanted to understand why. As I prayed and searched for those answers, I discovered that there are indeed many reasons why we have stress in our lives, and why we have stress by design.

1. For Thy Sake

Part of the answer to the *why* question begins by simply going back to the very first scripture we read about the thorns, thistles, sweat, and cursed earth. Let's go back to that scripture and look at it again, but this time at different words: "Cursed shall be the ground for thy sake" (Gen. 3:18; Moses 4:23-25).

The Lord told Adam and Eve that the reason He was cursing the ground was for their benefit. The weeds, the thorns, the thistles, and the hard work were intricately tied to the things that would be for their good. The thorns come with roses. The hard work brings food and shelter. Each struggle has its opposite beauty. The struggles of a life in this world ultimately lead us back to the beauty of eternity with our Father in Heaven.

Joseph Smith learned the same lesson in regards to the reason for his trials while he was in liberty jail. (This is a very generous term for the dug-out, sub-level dungeon that wasn't even tall enough for

---

9. J. Christopher Lansing, "Enduring Well," *Ensign*, January 2014.

Joseph to stand up straight in.) In D&C 122, Joseph pleaded with the Lord for answers, for comfort, and for peace from the overwhelming trials, persecutions, and afflictions he was subjected to. In response to his heart-wrenching petition, the Lord consoled and comforted Joseph with these profound words: "Know thou, my son, that all these things shall give thee experience, and *shall be for thy good*" (D&C 122:7). Again, in D&C 98:3, the Lord reiterated the same concept in response to the persecution of the saints in Missouri: "All things wherewith you have been afflicted shall work together for your good."

Trials, struggles, afflictions, and stress are for our good and for our sake and for our benefit, but what exactly do those hardships do that make them good for us? Neal A. Anderson answered that question for us in a conference talk given in April 2014. He quoted from an article about trees and wind that reads: "In nature, trees that grow up in a windy environment become stronger. As winds whip around a young sapling, forces inside the tree do two things. First, they stimulate the roots to grow faster and spread farther. Second, the forces in the tree start creating cell structures that actually make the trunk and branches thicker and more flexible to the pressure of the wind. These stronger roots and branches protect the tree from winds that are sure to return. You are infinitely more precious to God than a tree."[10]

Stress does the same thing for us that wind does for the trees. It helps our roots grow faster, driving them deeper and farther into the ground, and it helps strengthen and refine us in ways that will help us deal with future life events.

Douglas Malloch wrote a poem entitled "Good Timber," which sums up the analogy of the trees and stress in our lives:

> The tree that never had to fight
> For sun and sky and air and light,
> But stood out in the open plain
> And always got its share of rain,
> Never became a forest king
> But lived and died a scrubby thing.
> The man who never had to toil

---

10. Neil L. Andersen, "Spiritual Whirlwinds," *Ensign*, April 2014.

To gain and farm his patch of soil,
Who never had to win his share
Of sun and sky and light and air,
Never became a manly man
But lived and died as he began.
Good timber does not grow with ease:
The stronger wind, the stronger trees;
The further sky, the greater length;
The more the storm, the more the strength.
By sun and cold, by rain and snow,
In trees and men good timbers grow.
Where thickest lies the forest growth,
We find the patriarchs of both.
And they hold counsel with the stars
Whose broken branches show the scars
Of many winds and much of strife.
This is the common law of life.[11]

For us, as it is for trees, the storm changes us. Haruki Murakami wisely stated: "When you come out of the storm, you won't be the same person that walked in. That's what the storm is all about."[12] Going through the storms of life, we learn that there is no growth in the comfort zone and there is no comfort in the growth zone.

"Adversity will surface in some form in every life," says Marvin J. Ashton. "How we prepare for it, how we meet it, makes the difference. We can be broken by adversity or we can become stronger. The final result is up to the individual."[13]

President Thomas S. Monson explained this principle further, saying, "Our Heavenly Father...knows that we learn and grow and become stronger as we face and survive the trials through which we must pass. We know that there are times when we will experience heart-breaking sorrow, when we will grieve, and when we may be tested to our limits. However, such difficulties allow us to change for the better, to rebuild our lives in the way our Heavenly Father teaches

---

11. Douglas Malloch, "Good Timber."
12. Haruki Murakami, on Twitter December 16, 2015.
13. Marvin J. Ashton, "Adversity and You," *Ensign*, October 1980, 2.

us, and to become something different from what we were—better than we were, more understanding than we were, more empathetic than we were, with stronger testimonies than we had before."[14]

Elisabeth Kübler-Ross, well known for her work on grief, reflected that "the most beautiful people we have known are those who have known defeat, known suffering, known loss, known struggle, and have found their way out of the depths. These persons have an appreciation, sensitivity, and an understanding of life that fills them with compassion, gentleness, and a deep loving concern. Beautiful people do not just happen." She recognized that challenges and struggles do for us what the wind does for the sapling. Humans experiencing stress, challenges, and struggles learn to grow into what we were created for, to become like our Father in Heaven.

Helen Keller, one of those beautiful people who became great through personal struggle, said, "Character cannot be developed in ease and quiet, only through experience of trial and suffering can the soul be strengthened, ambition inspired, and success achieved."

Finally, Elder David Bednar said, "Many of the lessons we are to learn in mortality can only be received through the things we experience and sometimes suffer. And God expects and trusts us to face temporary mortal adversity with His help so we can learn what we need to learn and ultimately become what we are to become in eternity."[15]

Now, given a choice, we would likely choose to *not* have wind, weeds, thorns, thistles, sweat, and hard work as part of our lives. Many people would likely choose to *not* have stress, trials, struggles, affliction, and grief. We likely would choose instead a life of ease and comfort like Adam and Eve experienced in the Garden of Eden. We might choose all of the pleasant things from the Ecclesiastes list of options and choose *none* of the painful ones. We might even choose to have an earthly experience with *no* pain, suffering, or stress at all.

Wait! Did that first sentence of that last paragraph say "given a choice"? Yes, we *were* given a choice. But a life free of pain, suffering, and stress is *not* what we voted for. We know that there was a War in

---

14. Thomas S. Monson, "I Will Not Fail Thee, Nor Forsake Thee," *Ensign*, November 2013, 87.
15. David A. Bednar, "Accepting the Lord's Will and Timing," *Ensign*, August 2016.

Heaven—a war about whether we wanted our lives to be controlled by Satan, forced to do correct things and live without choices *or* if we wanted the agency to choose for ourselves what we would do on this earth. We knew when we voted to come here that the only way for us to know if we *really* wanted to be on the Lord's side was by being presented with myriad choices between right and wrong, good and evil, wisdom and foolishness. We knew we would have a variety of experiences, good *and* bad, and that those experiences would serve to teach us, refine us, and help us become more like God.

As we saw the entire plan laid out in front of us, in the pre-existence, we did not harbor any naiveté that any of us would have only a life of ease and comfort. We knew that like Christ, we would need to learn by the things which we suffer (Hebrew 5:8). I often have to remind myself that I made the choice to come here when I had *all* the facts and saw the whole picture clearly, because from this earthly perspective, I would certainly vote for a few less trials and *much* less stress.

Sometimes it is hard to see how our stress, our trials, our grief, and our afflictions lead us to a good outcome. But think back to a time of stress earlier in your life. Did you learn something from it? Did the experience help you make better decisions after that? Were you able to help another person who had a similar experience? François Auguste René Rodin stated, "Nothing is a waste of time if you use the experience wisely."

The prophet Lehi in a blessing to his son, Jacob, said, "In thy childhood thou hast suffered afflictions and much sorrow, because of the rudeness of thy brethren. Nevertheless, Jacob…thou knowest the greatness of God: and he shall consecrate thine afflictions for thy gain" (2 Nephi 2:1–2). Our trials and afflictions, and thus our necessary stress, can ultimately be for our gain, for our sake, for our good.

2. Humility—Remember Him

Another reason we have stress by design is that in order to hear the word of the Lord, we need to be humble. When we are humble, we are teachable. When we are not humble, but instead, hardened and arrogant, we are *not* teachable. Afflictions and stress work together to humble us so that we are able to listen and heed the counsel of the

Lord. There are many scriptures that help us see this principle: "Many were softened because of their afflictions, insomuch that they did humble themselves before God, even in the depth of humility" (Alma 62:41). "For he beheld that their afflictions had truly humbled them, and that they were in a preparation to hear the word" (Alma 32:6). In the book of Helaman, the Lord tells us very directly, why a life of ease and comfort is detrimental to our lives and why trials and stress are critical to our progression and salvation. "Yea, and we may see at the very time when he doth prosper his people, yea, in the increase of their fields, their flocks and their herds and in gold, and in silver and in all manner of precious things of every kind and art: sparing their lives and delivering them out of the hands of their enemies: softening the hearts of their enemies that they should not declare wars against them: yea, and in fine, doing all things for the welfare and happiness of his people: yea, then is the time that they do harden their hearts and do forget the Lord their God, and do trample under their feet the Holy one—yea, and this because of their ease and their exceedingly great prosperity. And thus we see that except the Lord doth chasten his people with many afflictions, yea, except he doth visit them with death and with terror and with famine and with all manner of pestilence, they will not remember Him" (Helaman 12:2–3).This scripture is extremely clear. When our life is too easy, when we are given everything we want, we do not remember the Lord. Instead, we get complacent and hardened. Think of the times when you have been closest to the Lord, were they not the times when you were in the most pain, the most distress, the deepest trial? Isn't that the time when you have been the most humbled and have found yourself turning to the Lord for peace and comfort and answers? Conversely, don't we get just a little laxer in our efforts to stay in tune with the spirit when everything is going perfectly in life?

3. Know the Bitter to Appreciate the Sweet

There are still more lessons that the Savior has taught about why we have trials and stress in our lives. These scriptures suggest that we need to know the bad things in order to savor the good things. "For if they never should have bitter, they could not know the sweet" (D&C 29:39). "They taste the bitter that they may know to prize the good" (Moses 6:55).

As much as we would like to just "prize the good" and leave the bitter out of the equation, it doesn't work that way. The bitter teaches us precious lessons about the sweet and the good in life. We become more grateful for what we have when we have been through a time of going without. How sweet is it to feel healthy when you have just experienced a savage flu? How savory does plain old oatmeal taste after you have been starving for months? How grateful are we when we finally find a job, any job, after being unemployed for an extended period of time? When we experience the bitter things in life, we have a deeper appreciation for even the most mundane events. If you want to feel the greatest peace and joy, it is necessary to feel pain and sorrow. Certainly, surviving trials and troubles makes our return to the mundane much sweeter.

Confucius aptly sums up the tutorial of learning through bitter experience: "By three methods we may learn wisdom: First, by reflection, which is the noblest; second, by imitation, which is easiest; and third by experience, which is the bitterest."

As with most things in life, experiencing the bitter does not always lead to an appreciation of the sweet. There are those who choose to focus on staying bitter, learning lessons of cynicism, pessimism, and resentment. Learning to appreciate the sweet and prize the good is a choice. But it is *our* choice to make.

4. Refined and Strengthened

The trials we have in life can either strengthen us or destroy us. We choose. When faced with adversity, challenges, or trials, we can curl up in a little ball, cry, whine and become bitter, angry, and cynical, or we can dig deep into our soul and muster up the courage to face the trial.

More commonly, we do a little of all of them: First we wither and shrink for a time, believing that the trial is too great to handle and we just don't have the strength. Sometimes, we even wallow in this pitiful state, feeling sorry for ourselves. After all, this trial is too big, it isn't fair, and it is far greater than any trial that anyone else has ever had to go through. And then, after we have cried for a while, hopefully we remember to turn to the Lord for help. We pray, pour our hearts out and then listen for the guidance and counsel that helps us summon up the strength to go on. How we respond to the adversity, the trial, is *our* choice.

Each of the challenges in life helps strengthen us and prepare us to be able to face future trials. Elder Robert D. Hales said, "The purpose of our life on earth is to grow, develop, and be strengthened through our own experiences."[16] With each challenging experience, we can become stronger, wiser, and more refined. Little children can't possibly jump into learning advanced algebra or calculus before they have learned to count. They must learn to count, then add, then subtract, multiply, divide, learn fractions and decimals—all in order. We need to remember that we are little children in God's eternal plan. We learn "line upon line, precept upon precept, here a little and there a little" (2 Ne 28:30; D&C 128:21; Isa 28:10).

Another result of experiencing trials and afflictions is that this process refines us. "For, behold, I have refined thee, I have chosen thee in the furnace of affliction" (1 Nephi 20:10). We can better understand what is meant by being refined in the furnace of affliction by understanding the process of refining silver as mentioned in Malachi 3:3: "He will sit as a refiner and purifier of silver." Doug Lyon relates a story of the silversmith and how silver is refined. The silversmith holds a piece of silver over the fire and lets it heat up. He explains that in refining silver, one needs to hold the silver in the middle of the fire, where the flames are hottest, in order to burn away all the impurities. The silversmith must sit there, holding the silver, keeping his eyes on the silver the entire time it is in the fire. If the silver is left in the flames for a moment too long, it would be destroyed. How does the silversmith know when the silver is fully refined? "Oh, that's easy," he answers, "it is fully refined when I see my image in it."[17] Our trials are indeed a refiner's fire, burning away our impurities in a process that helps us become more like the Savior.

5. Blessings

A final lesson from the Savior about why we have stress by design is found in D&C 58:4: "For after much tribulation come the blessings.

---

16. Robert D. Hales, "Waiting Upon the Lord: Thy Will Be Done," *Ensign*, November 2011.
17. Doug Lyon, "Refining," May 11, 2008.

Wherefore, the day cometh that ye shall be crowned with much glory; the hour is not yet, but is nigh at hand."

In the same way that we must work *before* we receive a paycheck, we must show that we are willing to submit to the refining experiences of affliction and stress that the Lord provides for us before we can receive the blessings.

There is no question that it is often extremely difficult to even imagine how some of the intense trials and challenges that we face could ever be seen as blessings. That is because it generally takes time before trials or challenges can emerge into a state of being a blessing. Sometimes, the experience itself is a blessing. Sometimes, the experience changes our direction or path in life. Sometimes, the experience teaches us what we need to know to appreciate what comes next. Sometimes, the experience helps us see the errors in our behaviors so we can change them and make our life and the lives of those around us better. Whatever the blessing turns out to be, it often requires the stress or the trial to bring it to fruition.

Yes, life was designed, from the beginning, to have stress in it. If there were no changes in our lives that led to stress, we would become like a stagnant pond. Stagnant ponds become filled with dirt, scum, algae, decaying plants, toxic bacteria, molds, mildew, and viruses. The stagnant pond attracts mosquitoes, insects, rodents, reptiles, and other disease-carrying pests. The water in the stagnant pond becomes unfit for human use. It would cause serious illness if ingested and has no ability to clean anything. Standing near that pond sends shock waves of repugnant odors through our nasal passages and leaves us vulnerable to the bites of all those disease-carrying pests.

However, if we take that same water and send it down a raging river filled with rocks and boulders, causing the water to be constantly moving, tossed, turned, churned, and beaten against all the obstacles in its way, the water becomes purified. The water that is subjected to the "trials" of racing down a rock-filled river becomes clean and usable for drinking or washing.

Stress prevents us from becoming the filthy water in that vile, stagnant pond. It purifies our lives. The purpose of stress is to keep us constantly moving, growing, progressing, improving, and energized as we are beaten against the rocks of life. Stress, if we allow it to, can provide the avenue to keep us humble and in tune with the spirit so the Lord can bless our lives and ultimately lead us into the beautiful soul that we are.

CHAPTER 3

Lesson 2:

Our Bodies Were Created to Deal with Stress

Just as our world was created by design to have stress in it, our bodies were created physiologically with automatic systems in place that help us to respond to stress and actually perform better when we have moderate amounts of stress in our lives. The creator of our bodies knew, right from the start, that we needed to have stress in our lives to refine us, teach us, strengthen us, and help us grow. Therefore, our bodies needed to be created in such a way that we would be able to respond to that stress.

How do we know our body was designed to respond to stress? That's easy, next time you perceive yourself to be in danger or threatened, pay attention to what your body does automatically, without any intentional thought from you. Or, better yet, think back to a time when you felt threatened, frightened, scared, or in danger. If your memory needs a jolt, just pick a time when you experienced something from one of the most common fears list: being asked to speak in public, seeing a spider climb up your bedroom wall, grabbing a stick in your yard and finding out it was a snake, looking over the edge of a very high cliff, preparing for take-off on your flight to an unknown destination, or being in a tiny enclosed space. What did your body do automatically?

While teaching stress classes, I tell my students on the second day of class, that we are going to have a pop quiz, and that it is going to be an oral pop quiz. Immediately, I see many responses that their body's perform automatically: Their faces go pale or bright red or splotchy, their hands start to shake or they get sweaty palms, their shoulders tighten and pull up, their jaws stiffen, they drop their heads and avert their gaze, they often gasp or appear to be holding their breath, and many admit to feeling very nauseated.

The first question on the pop quiz is: "What is your body doing right now?"

The answers:

"My heart is racing or my heart stopped for a second."

"I started breathing faster."

"My stomach started to get nauseated."

"My hands started to get sweaty."

"My whole body tensed up. I got really antsy, nervous, and jittery."

Pop quiz question two: "Why did you tell your heart to speed up?" or "Why did you want your hands to be sweaty?" or "Why did you drain all the color from your face?"

Of course, they all answer the same way: "I didn't!"

No, they didn't. Well, yes, they did, just not consciously. All of those reactions are automatic physiological responses to stress. Why does this happen? In order to understand the process, we need to take a quick, simplified look at how our brain works. Don't worry, this isn't a neuroscience class. As a matter of fact, this will be so simple that neuroscientists *shouldn't* read it.

We have two distinct operating systems in our brains. One system we will call the *cool response* and the other we will call the *hot response*. The cool response is the normal, calm, rational, functioning level that should be where we spend most of our day. This operating system is where our brain functions when we are calm, peaceful, rational, thinking, making decisions, reasoning, planning, or doing normal daily activities.

The Hot Response system—also known as the *reptilian response*, the *instinctive response*, or the more familiar *fight-or-flight response*—is the operating system our brain is using during times of stress, danger, threat, or fear.

When we are functioning in the cool response system, we are using most of our brain, accessing memories and thoughts, responding to the information that is coming in through our senses (see Figure 1), and especially using the bracketed section in the front of our brain behind our forehead called the *frontal cortex*. This section is also known as the executive decision-making center, or the place where we plan, think, reason, strategize, project consequences, and process ideas logically. This should be where we spend most of our waking hours.

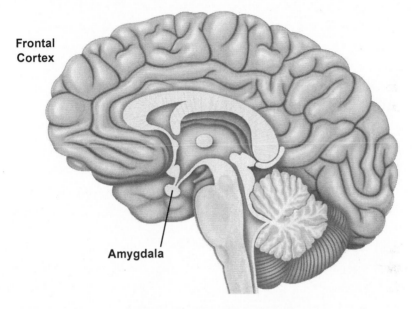

Frontal Cortex

Amygdala

Figure 1: The Limbic System

The second operating system in our brain, which is responsible for the hot response, is located predominantly in the *amygdala*. If you look at Figure 1, you can see the amygdala is a tiny, round section in the middle of the brain, near the base. This tiny section of the brain is where we process our basic instincts, including fear, danger, and threat. For lack of a better way to describe this system, let me just compare the amygdala to a scanner. Its job is to constantly scan the information that is coming in through our senses to see if any of the information is indicative of danger—the smell of smoke, a car running a red light that is about to broadside you, or an unusual creaking noise in the house at 3:00 a.m. When the amygdala registers danger, it immediately sends out a signal to the body to respond quickly to the threat, danger, or fear. This automatic response is known as the alarm phase of stress or the fight or flight response.

The signal that your amygdala sends out alerting the body to prepare to run or fight is almost like a little blueprint of instructions of what your body needs to do immediately. In truth, that little blueprint is a very complex mixture of more than 1,400 known chemical changes that occur in the body almost instantaneously to prepare you to either fight or run. Since your body doesn't know yet which activity you will choose, it prepares your body for both, gratefully so. You might get the chance to choose to either run or to fight, but other times you may need to do both. If you were to encounter a very hungry-looking tiger in the jungle, you might instinctively run, but when the tiger catches you, you may end up having to fight and then run—then fight and then pray for the safari guide to tranquilize the tiger quickly so you can run again.

Before we go further, it is important to note that some of our thoughts and experiences re-set the amygdala to be hypersensitive. Experiences like war, abuse, trauma, constant danger, being a victim of crime, etc. can program the scanner to register events as danger that other people would see as normal life. This is known as post-traumatic stress disorder (PTSD). If you had been in the midst of war with bombs and guns going off all around you, you would probably learn to respond quickly, defensively, and aggressively to protect yourself when there are any loud sounds, as innocent as those sounds might be. You can also train your brain to have a hypersensitive scanner by harboring negative, distorted thoughts. The good news is just as you can re-set your brain to be hypervigilant, you can also train your brain to calm down. It takes concentrated time and effort, but it can be done.

With two operating systems at our disposal, sometimes we mistakenly click into the wrong system, or we use a system that is inappropriate for the situation. Obviously, we rarely react calmly to a perceived danger or threat. That means we generally do not mistakenly have a cool response to a hot situation. If a car is coming at you head-on, you don't calmly pause to think through all of the potential reactions that you might consider and *then* think through each of the potential consequences of each of those reactions. Nope. No time. By the time you pause to think, the crash has already occurred. The amygdala's job is to scan for danger and react immediately to protect your life. You slam on the brakes, swerve, make three lanes out of two, or even run off the road as a basic survival instinct. Often the amygdala registers danger and responds so quickly that you find you have reacted and the situation has resolved before you even register what happened. It is highly unlikely that we would mistakenly use a cool response in a hot situation.

However, we often mistakenly react hotly to a cool situation— a nonthreatening event—because we perceive it to be a danger or threat. Natalie Goldberg reminds us that "stress is an ignorant state. It believes that everything is an emergency. Nothing is that important." How does that happen? Why would we respond hotly to something that is neither dangerous nor threatening? The answer is two-fold. First, our brain may not differentiate between physical threat (the car approaching us head-on), emotional threat (fight with a spouse), or internal threat (infection). To address the second aspect, let's go back to the definition of stress that we used in chapter one: The physiological response to changes in events or the environment that you *perceive* to be a danger, threat, or fear. Part of stress is based on our *perception* of a situation whether internal, physical, or emotional. And that perception is different and unique for each individual. Remember what I said previously, PTSD can re-set the amygdala to be a hypervigilant scanner.

The cool events to which we respond hotly are often events that threaten our ego, or our desire to look good in front of other people, or to be "right." Think about why you may not like to speak in public. Is there a chance you will die from opening your mouth in front of other people? Unlikely. Is there a chance we will say something that might damage your ego or your desire to look intelligent? Yes. For some people, this fear is crippling. I have had students drop a class because they were required to give a presentation. A great many people have this fear. Another example is that we might react hotly to a boss who asks us a question in the middle of a staff meeting. You might be thinking *What if I answer it wrong? Will everyone laugh at me? Am I going to look stupid? Will my coworkers think I am incompetent? Will I get fired?*

Perhaps our perceived fear is a result of something as simple as whether we are wearing the "right" piece of clothing to an event. *Is the attire appropriate? Is it the latest fashion? Does it look good on me? What will other people think?* The perceived fear or threat is only a threat to our ego, not to our safety.

Obviously, the list of potential events that could cause a necessary hot response is long enough. When we add all the fear of looking good, being right, protecting our ego, climbing the success later, and keeping up with the Jones, we add to our own list of events that cause stress. Our goal is to minimize stress, not increase stress. We need to calm down the amygdala, not re-set it to respond hotly to cool events. We can do that by examining and fixing our internal irrational fears, by developing healthy self-esteem and self-confidence so that our egos are not so frequently threatened, and by analyzing why we perceive cool events as a danger or a threat to us or why a cool event causes us fear, thus causing ourselves more stress.

The hot response (fight or flight) can save our lives when it kicks in to protect us from real threats. Our body was designed by our Creator to respond quickly and effectively to dangerous, threatening situations. This physiological response is critical in situations of violence, struggles against harsh variations in nature, physical threats, and natural disasters. Unfortunately, when we consistently use a hot response when there is no real threat today, we find ourselves in a state of chronic stress where the hot response not only doesn't save our life, but it damages our health.

The Fight-or-Flight Response

Let's take a minute to look at what physically occurs during the hot response or fight-or-flight response. When the mind/body perceives a threat, any threat, the automatic physiological response kicks in. The physiological response to stress is a series of 1,400 known physicochemical responses that prepare us to run or fight. To avoid sheer boredom and an additional volume of this book, we won't review all 1,400 of those chemical changes, only the top twelve. We will look at how these changes help us sprint into action when we are threatened as well as how they can help us in times of real physical threat. However, under chronic stress these prolonged chemical changes can cause damage. "When you get a

Wall Street broker using the responses a cave man used to fight the elements, you've got a problem," said Peter Knapp, a Boston University psychiatrist.[18]

According to some of the smartest men I know, whom I call dear friends, Dr. Keith Karren and Dr. N. Lee Smith in their book *Mind/ Body Health: The Effects of Attitudes, Emotions, and Relationships*, the following physical responses occur in the fight-or-flight response to stress. I explain the responses below by quoting portions of their text and inserting additional information in my own words.

1.   "The adrenal gland pumps out the stress hormones cortisol and catecholamines." These stress hormones are the messengers to the rest of the body that there is a potential danger or threat to the individual. These chemicals trigger the body to prepare for fight or flight. "In the right quantities, these are essential for life, but in excessive amounts they can impair the immune system and reduce healing, making it difficult to fight off even a minor cold. Too much cortisol over a prolonged time causes lymph glands to shrivel, bones to become brittle, and blood pressure to rise: it can even cause blood sugars to spike into diabetic ranges."

2.   "The thyroid gland pumps out thyroid hormones which accelerate metabolism and enable fuels to burn faster to give energy for fight or flight. It does the same thing to us today as it did for the primitive people: but, because we're not usually engaged in life-or-death physical battles, it produces a different set of symptoms: insomnia, shaky nerves, heat intolerance, and exhaustion. This is why some people lose weight under stress."

3.   "The hypothalamus releases endorphins, powerful natural painkillers that enabled primitive people to fight or flee even when injured. However, chronic, relentless stress depletes endorphins and can in turn aggravate headaches, backaches, and even arthritis pain. Located in the part of the

---

18. Claudia Wallis, "Stress: Can We Cope?" *Time*, June 6, 1983, 48–54.

brain that connects thinking to peripheral body processes, the hypothalamus also releases the brain's key chemical initiator of the stress response, corticotrophin-releasing hormone (CRH) injected into the midbrain, CRH causes anxiety and up-regulates the nervous system to over-respond to stimuli. People who continue to obsess about past trauma or perceived abuse continue to secrete high amounts of CRH, and they continue to scan for danger and over respond to stimuli. This over responsiveness triggers many common medical disorders."

4. "Release of sugar (glucose) into the bloodstream is followed by a boost in insulin to metabolize it, something that provided primitive people with "fuel for the sprint" or a burst of short-lived energy. That same scenario today can cause either high or low blood sugars. Continuously high insulin levels can cause weight gain and lead to elevated blood pressure and lipids (cholesterol). This insulin resistance (induced by stress hormones) can lead to the "metabolic syndrome" that puts you at high risk for cardiovascular disease."

5. "Cholesterol is released into the bloodstream, mostly from the liver: it takes over where blood sugar left off in supplying sustained energy to the muscles. But today's man or woman under chronic stress doesn't generally need more cholesterol to sustain energy, so the cholesterol is [dangerously] deposited in the blood vessels."

6. "The heart begins racing, a physiological response that pumps more blood to the muscles and lungs, carrying more fuel and oxygen to the muscles—something primitive people needed when under duress. Blood flow to the muscles of the arms and legs increases 300 to 400 percent when a person is stressed. The result today is high blood pressure: left unchecked, it can lead to stroke, heart attack, or kidney problems."

7. "Breathing rate increases, providing greater oxygen supply. While usually helpful, the increased demand on the lungs can be problematic for people with lung disease, such as asthma. Unfortunately, anxious breathing is usually shallow and high in the chest, which is not very efficient" and generally causes you to start feeling anxious and stressed. "When breathing is anxious, the mind becomes anxious." But try this experiment, see what happens to your mind when you "breathe slowly and more deeply with your diaphragm (relaxed breathing); in most cases, your mind will rapidly become calm. Note that just as the body's stress responses follow the mind's direction, your mind's responses also follow what is happening with your body."

8. "The blood thickens and coagulates more readily. If wounded (a stressor), thickening of the blood enabled primitive people to stop bleeding. However, when the blood turns thick under chronic stress today, the result can be heart attack, stroke, or embolism (blood clot)."

9. "Sex hormones (female-progesterone, male-testosterone) are reduced. That served an important function in primitive times: the decreased libido and fertility came in handy during times of drought, overcrowding, and decreased food supply by giving the community fewer mouths to feed, and by redirecting attention from amorous adventures to the threat at hand. Sadly, the same thing happens today when you are under stress: You may lose your sex drive, become infertile, or suffer from sexual dysfunction (such as premature ejaculation or failure to reach orgasm). Women under acute stress may have an early menstrual period: unrelenting, chronic stress may cause irregular periods or a complete lack of periods (amenorrhea)." Your body is totally not interested in creating a new life when it is busy fighting to save *your* life.

10. "Coordination of the digestive tract shuts down. In primitive people, all blood was diverted to the muscles, rendering them capable of extraordinary feats of power: the mouth went dry too. The same things happen today. Eating while under stress can result in stomach bloating, nausea, abdominal discomfort or cramping, and even constipation or diarrhea. The dry mouth problems persist too. Dry mouth is such an acute symptom of stress, in fact, that in China it's used as a lie detector test."

11. "The skin 'crawls,' blanches, and sweats. This heightened the sense of touch, provided a cooling for overheated muscles and diverted blood away from wounds. Today, it decreases the resistance of skin to electricity (the principle behind most lie detector tests)."

12. "All five senses become acute. In primitive people, pupils dilated to enhance night vision, overall mental performance was sharpened, the senses of hearing and touch were improved, and the entire body was brought to peak function."[19]

This whole process, which begins in the brain when the amygdala registers danger or threat and responds to that fear with an immediate change in 1,400 body chemicals, is the beginning of the stress response. Some would say that the only way to stop stress is to stop the amygdala from registering fear, and the only way to stop the amygdala from registering fear is to cut off the head—probably not a stress management technique that will gain much support.

Today, since our stress is less frequently caused by an immediate physical threat and more frequently caused by chronic threats to our well-being, we are more likely to suffer from chronic stress. Thus, all senses are constantly on red alert, sometimes resulting in pain from stimuli that shouldn't cause such pain, such as a headache getting worse to light, sound or smells.[20]

19. Keith J. Karren, N. Lee Smith, Brent Q. Hafen, Kathryn J. Jenkins, *Mind/ Body Health: The Effects of Attitudes, Emotions, and Relationships* (San Francisco: Benjamin Cummings, 2010), 31–34.
20. Karren, Smith, Hafen, and Jenkins, 34.

Physiological Recovery

All of these changes (and hundreds more) occur automatically when the brain registers potential danger or threat. However, when the threat is over and the danger is past, our body has another *automatic* response. It automatically returns to the cool-response state. All of the chemicals return to their normal balanced functioning levels, and the body returns to its relaxed state. This is how our body was designed by the Creator, from the beginning. This design works well in helping you deal quickly with threats and then just as quickly allowing you to return to your normal physical state when the threat is passed.

Let's go back to our previous example of having a car coming at us head-on in our lane. We see the vehicle and head lights right in front of us. The amygdala immediately registers the threat and within one to two seconds, our body is fully alert, in full fight-or-flight stance. We swerve, honk the horn, and try to make a new lane on the road to give us the space we need to avoid the accident. When the accident is averted by our quick response, we start to notice that our heart is pounding, we are breathing rapidly, our hands are shaking, and we feel extremely jittery. We may spend a few minutes in frazzled thought, reviewing what just occurred and realizing how close we came to being painfully crushed in a vehicle and experiencing excruciating, life-altering injuries or death.

As we continue to drive, the relief of our miraculous escape settles in and slowly our body begins to return to normal. After several minutes, we return to our conversations or singing to the radio or reviewing the list of things that we need to pick up at the store. The stress response kicked in when needed and resolved when the threat was gone, *all* automatically.

Chronic Stress

Due to the chronicity of stress that we experience today, many of us are just *not* getting to the automatic physical resolution phase. We are stuck in the chemistry of fight or flight. We seem to be stressed constantly. For many of us, stress doesn't *ever* seem to dissipate. We don't get to enjoy any relaxation from the constant fight-or-flight physical stress response. Our body is always tense, jittery, anxious, and running at high speed.

Many of us experience this feeling of chronic stress, as you recall from chapter one, 25 percent of American adults are experiencing crushing levels of stress almost every day, *all* day, without any relaxation phase. Why? Why are we *stuck* in the fight or flight stage and not enjoying the relaxation stage of the stress cycle? Our ancestors, even with their difficult lives, did not seem to experience the chronic stress that we experience today.

Today, especially in industrialized nations, our stress is more complex. We have situations and challenges that are not resolved quickly. Sometimes, the feeling of threat or danger lasts for long periods of time. For instance, our stress may come from financial challenges that could easily take years to resolve or could even last a lifetime. We may have persistent marital problems with frequent fighting, poor communication, and opposing priorities. And what parent could relax if their child were dealing with intense difficulties like drugs, bullying, mental health problems, learning difficulties, rebellion, or suicidal thoughts? For our aging population, as life expectancy increases, so do the number of chronic diseases. By the time individuals reach sixty years of age, they deal with an average of five chronic diseases, which can cause daily lifestyle adjustments, pain, disability, financial hardship, depression, and drastic changes in their future plans or living arrangements.

When we have *chronic* events that maintain a *constant* perception of threat, the fight-or-flight chemicals are *constantly* produced. When this happens, we shift into phase two of the stress response—the resistance phase. In the resistance phase, more physiological changes occur to help the body adapt to this chronic, prolonged stress. In essence, the body kicks into overtime. It works hard to maintain the immune system in order to keep the body in shape to deal with the prolonged assault of stress. In this resistance phase, the body's immune system is actually stronger than normal. Because the immune system is working overtime, it can cause some disorders of excess immunity, such as increased allergies or autoimmune diseases.

As long as the perception of threat remains constant, stress hormones continue to pump into the body, keeping the body in the resistance phase, thus preventing our body from returning to the relaxed state.[21] Since our stress is seemingly constant and unrelenting, our bodies don't ever get a chance to go back to their nonstressed, relaxed, cool-functioning state.

When a body is already in chronic fight-or-flight mode from chronic stress, what happens when a new stressful event arises? The same automatic process continues to occur, the body kicks out more stress hormones, which causes our physiological response levels to *escalate*.

Unfortunately, if the stress does not have a chance to dissipate, thereby breaking the physiological response, then with each new stressful event, the stress response continues to escalate, leading to those crushing levels of stress experienced by one in four adults. Obviously, with such high levels of stress hormones pumping constantly into our system, if we do not have a quick resolution the 1,400 physiological and chemical changes of the fight-or-flight syndrome begin to tax the body.

Our body has to do something to counteract the changes made by those 1,400 chemicals, which are causing a dangerously high heart rate, high levels of cholesterol, increased thyroid demands, decreased digestive juices, decreased sex hormones, and extremely high demands on the muscles to maintain the body at full alert. Our body was not meant to remain in this heightened state of alert for extended periods of time. Though the resistance phase is intended to help our body to maintain a heightened response for a while, there is a point where the body loses the ability to keep up with the demands of this heightened state, and it shifts into phase three—the exhaustion phase.

The exhaustion phase occurs when the body has met its maximum limit for compensating and resisting the chronic physiological changes of fight or flight. At this point, the protective properties of our immune system break down, potentially causing a mix of too much antibody immunity (increased allergies) and too little cellular immunity (increased susceptibility to infection). In this phase, we feel exactly what the name implies—exhaustion!

---

21. Karren, Smith, Hafen, and Jenkins, 42–43.

Physiological Effects of Chronic Stress

This exhaustion phase is responsible for a great deal of the illness and chronic diseases that we experience, as the result of those crushing levels of chronic stress. Some physiological effects of chronic stress expressed to me by many who are feeling those crushing levels of stress include muscle tension/strain, increased headaches and other pain, increased depression, increased irritability, inability to function well, lack of focus, problems in relationships, increased anger/hostility, increased illness, and inability to sleep. These are symptoms that we notice because they are annoying, uncomfortable, painful, fairly instantaneous, and known to be associated with stress.

However, there are *many* more deleterious effects caused by chronic stress. "That list includes cardiovascular diseases such as coronary heart disease, arteriosclerosis, atherosclerosis, high blood pressure, coronary thrombosis, stroke, and angina pectoris; neuromuscular disorders such as migraine headache, chronic back pain, and epileptic seizures; respiratory disorders such as asthma; immunological disorders such as colds and allergies; autoimmune problems such as rheumatoid arthritis and multiple sclerosis; gastrointestinal disturbances, including peptic ulcer disease, irritable bowel syndrome, functional nausea and vomiting, non-ulcer dyspepsia, ulcerative colitis, and gastritis; skin diseases such as psoriasis, eczema, cold sores, shingles, hives and acne; endocrine disorders such as diabetes, hyperthyroidism, impotence, and infertility; and a host of other disorders, including dental problems, chronic tuberculosis, Raynaud's disease, and some cancers. However, physicians caution that "few of these diseases are caused or triggered solely by stress, but it clearly increases vulnerability to other causes of illness." [22]

Long-term physical symptoms and damage occur when our stress is intense, constant, and does not have the chance to dissipate frequently. Most of us can handle mild to moderate amounts of stress as a normal part of everyday life. It is when our stress tips into the excessive, crushing, unrelenting stress that our bodies become exhausted and put us on notice: "We have had enough, get this stress fixed or we quit."

---

22. Karren, Smith, Hafen, and Gordon, 31–34.

The Savior created our bodies to be able to deal with stress. He created the physiology of the stress response. He created our body's ability to rapidly kick into the fight-or-flight response. He created our body's ability to sustain this fight-or-flight response for a period of time, to help us get through some long-term stress. He created our body's exhaustion phase to alert us that we need to do something differently in order to bring life back into balance.

CHAPTER 4

Stage 1 of the Stress Process:
The Events

Stage 1 of the stress process—not to be confused with the stress response—is a change in the environment, event, situation, or thought. In chapter one, we learned about the constant changes in our world. Many of those changes can lead to stress. In chapter two, we learned that we have stress by design. That means our lives will be filled with changes—some good, some bad, some wonderful, some stressful. Then we learn from those experiences. The very first stage of stress is having those new experiences. Each new experience means that something in our world changed.

Recall from chapter one that stress is a process, as represented below.

$$A + B + C = D$$

A	B	C	D
Change in environment/ event/situation/ thought	Perception (Thoughts)	Physiological Response	**STRESS**

We also learned that one of the *biggest misconceptions* regarding stress is that the first step in the stress process is the *only* step in the stress process. We think that change equals stress, or A = D. After all, we weren't stressed before the change occurred, and now we are stressed, so the change caused the stress therefore, the change *is* the stress, A = D.

However, as we gain more understanding of the stress process, we learn instead, that change is just the *trigger* for the stress process and that this process has the benefit of teaching us great things.

Since the change in the environment/event/situation/thought is the trigger for stress, obviously it is the best place to start our discussion on how to prevent, minimize, and manage stress. If we can prevent some of the changes, we will come a long way in minimizing our overall stress level.

Great Big Caution

It is critical in this discussion to understand that not all changes can be prevented or minimized. As we learned in chapter two, we have stress in our lives by design; we have stress for a reason. Therefore, it would be foolish to think that we could thwart God's plan for our growth by preventing all stress in our lives. There are situations or events that we just cannot avoid.

We all have some of those events or situations that are stressful over which we have no control. Maybe we were born with a disability or disease. Perhaps we have a child with autism or chromosome damage or ADHD. Or perhaps we lose a job through no fault of our own or have a dishonest investor steal our retirement funds so he can enjoy luxury living in the Bahamas. Accidents happen, natural disasters occur, people make mistakes, illnesses overtake us sometimes, appliances wear out, and children misbehave. Once we accept that there is a certain amount of stress that we cannot prevent or control, we can shift our energy to focus on the many stressful triggers that we *can* prevent or control. The really good news is that we can prevent or minimize a lot of unnecessary stress that we experience.

What are those changes in the environment/events/situations/ thoughts that trigger stress? What are the events that cause stress? The simple answer is anything and everything. That may sound a little exaggerated, nevertheless it is true. The events come in a very wide range of possibilities: problems in a marriage, financial challenges, family quarrels and fights, demands on our time, constant social media connection, chronic illnesses, constant interruptions, too many activities, too much to do in too little time, media telling us what we should have, do, be, wear, look like in order to be acceptable, and thousands more stress-inducing events. There are so many changes to deal with.

Characteristics of Changes

It is important to note here that not all changes are the same. We already inherently know that some changes in events are much harder to deal with than others. Each change differs in its characteristics: nature, situation, frequency, controllability, and intensity. The variations in these characteristics are responsible for the amount of stress we feel.

Nature
The nature of change describes what the change looks like. It could be an event, or a process that is slowly developing, or a situation that you are in, or it could even just be a thought that suddenly popped into your mind. *Really? A thought? How did a thought jump in here? Aren't thoughts and perceptions part of stage two of the stress process?* Yes. But they can also be "the change."

A thought can be the change when it comes in the form of an unexpected thought or memory or even a song that reminded you of someone you loved deeply who has passed away. Or maybe you had a sudden realization that today is Wednesday, not Tuesday as you had believed, and you have missed a very important Wednesday morning meeting. Whether the change in the environment is an actual event or a thought that acts as the event, the stress process is the same and results in the same physiological changes causing the same sensation of stress.

Situation
Often a "change in the environment" can be stressful or not stressful depending on the situation in which it occurs. For instance, it

started to rain today. If your area is experiencing a drought causing a desperate need for water in your garden, the change in the environment (the rain) is beneficial to you and therefore not stressful at all. However, if you had planned a beautiful, elaborate, outdoor garden wedding and it started to rain, the very same "change in the environment" (the rain) becomes a very stressful occurrence. If your city has had too much rain, causing severe flooding, rain can be a threat to life and home.

Another component of situation refers to how peaceful and calm your life is (or isn't) before an event or change occurs. For instance, you have just landed a new, wonderful job and you are totally excited to get started. If your life is stable and relatively stress free, the experience in starting the new job could be exciting, exhilarating, and very positive. However, if you are changing jobs at the same time you are moving to a new home in a new city because you are going through a divorce, adjusting to this new wonderful job might be extremely stressful.

Frequency

The frequency of the changes has a direct impact on how we respond to each separate change in our path. As you recall from chapter one, we need time to adjust to each change that occurs and incorporate those adjustments into our lives. When we do not have time to acclimate to one change before another change occurs, each successive change seems to be progressively more difficult to deal with. If there are too many changes or demands on our time, in rapid succession, we experience an overload or a complete burnout. For example, if you are going through the divorce mentioned previously, it would be wise to schedule the start date for the new job or the move date to your new home with some space in between to prevent dealing with all the changes on the same weekend.

Controllability

There are two distinct meanings for controllability. The first deals with how much control you have over the changes. Many researchers purport that loss of control is one of the biggest contributors to our overall stress. Several studies indicate that participants (humans, animals, rats, etc.) who are subjected to some type of unpleasant stimulus, over which they have *no* control, experience the highest levels of stress. When participants had just a slight warning that the unpleasant stimulus was coming so they could brace for it, they experienced slightly lower stress levels. Those who could control when the unpleasant stimulus was delivered had the least amount of stress.

While there are many changes in the environment over which we have no control (earthquakes, unavoidable auto accident, deaths of people that we love), there are "changes in the environment" that can be prevented or at least scheduled, planned, altered, or rearranged so that we don't find ourselves being crushed by the changes that lead to an overload of stress.

We can completely prevent the stress that comes from having an illegal drug addiction by not starting to take drugs to begin with. We can prevent the stress of losing a job due to constant tardiness and absences by being on time and reliable. We can prevent the stress of debt that we incur by having a budget and controlling our spending. We can prevent some of the stress we experience from medical problems that are directly related to having very poor health habits by taking care of our body. We will look at many of those preventable or anticipated changes later in this chapter.

The second component of controllability is learning when and how to take control of a stressful situation. In reality, we may not have any ability to prevent the event itself, but that is not the key element here. The important element is one's perception about their degree of control in the situation. That means if you are thrown into a stressful event, and you say to yourself, *This is terrible. I can't do anything about it. I'm stuck,* your stress level will increase more than if you respond to the exact same stress-inducing event by saying, *Wow, this is really a tough one, but I will figure it out, I always do.* Yet another way to look at those difficult situations is to proclaim it as an adventure, as my older sister does. Another way to express that idea came from Merle Shain, "There are only two ways to approach life, as a victim or as a gallant fighter and you must decide if you want to act or react."

The mere act of taking some control somewhere in the process is empowering. Taking control does not mean that you can prevent the event from occurring, but it does enable you to limit the helpless, hopeless feelings of stress, find a solution, and take charge of the rest of the process. For instance, during a massive torrential rainstorm, we feel more empowered—and therefore less stressed—when we join the teams filling sandbags, board up our windows, shore up any places where water could cause damage, or even move to higher ground than if we curl up in a ball on our bed, doing nothing and feeling hopeless.

Many studies have shown that people who have been laid off of a job (clearly a change that negatively alters your normal routine) fare better when they stand up and take control of their future by searching for a new job quickly or evaluating different options for where they want to go. There is no question that the loss of a job will cause you a great deal of stress as you begin adjusting to the chain reaction of changes that a job loss presents. The principle here is that you can minimize the impact of stress by stepping up and taking control of whatever pieces of the situation are still within your control.

No matter what the stressor may be, there is always something that you can do to gain some controllability, even if the control you take is just control over your own thoughts and reactions!

Giant Caution

This topic is about controlling situations and controlling you, *not* about controlling others. Everyone here on this earth voted against Satan's plan to compel people to do the right thing. Given that we are all here on earth, and therefore *all* chose agency, it is not likely that anyone here would appreciate having someone else try to control, force, and manipulate them. When you try to control others to do what you want, you ultimately cause a great deal of your own stress and cause more stress for others. You cause conflict instead of harmony. Others begin to avoid you, resist you, become angry at your controlling behavior, and wiggle away from under your thumb. Controlling and manipulative personalities shatter relationships; increase chances of divorce; and cause some to turn to drugs, violence, or other unhealthy behaviors. In other words, controlling behavior increases stress for everyone.

Intensity

The intensity of the change in the environment is a critical component of how much stress we feel. You have likely heard the ratings that go with hurricanes and tornados. The rating is reported in levels, which tell you the intensity of the storm. Knowing the level of the hurricane headed your way tells you how strong the storm is so you know what level of preparation to carry out.

Have you ever been notified that a family member has been in car accident? Just knowing there was an accident doesn't give you much information. The intensity of the accident could range from a fender bender that doesn't even cause a scratch or a dent or personal injuries, all the way to a totally demolished car and death of the occupants. The difference in the level of stress that you feel between the "no injury, undamaged car" and the "death of family members in a demolished vehicle" is gigantic.

The intensity of the stressor has a direct effect on the intensity of the stress that we experience. Some events are minimal, like a broken shoe lace or a bad hair day. Others are life changing, like a divorce or a house fire.

All of these characteristics of change impact how much stress we experience. And let's face it, we only have so much capacity to cope with stress before the stress begins to negatively impact our health. In order to keep us in a healthy range, we need to manage the nature, situation, frequency, controllability, and intensity of as many events as we can.

How much stress do the various events cause? The answer to that question is hard to nail down. There are so many variables, including personal likes and dislikes. If you told me that the choices for dinner at my boss's house tonight were liver or sushi, I would be stressed. It is a toss-up for which of those options I abhor the most. Some of you would have no stress at all because you love both options. Well, maybe you would feel a little stress if you couldn't have both.

How do we know how much stress each event causes us and how much stress we can safely handle before it begins to negatively affect our health?

In 1967, psychiatrists Thomas Holmes and Richard Rahe asked this question. In trying to ascertain how much stress an individual can carry before it leads to illness, Holmes and Rahe began developing a measurement of stress. The tool that they developed is called the Social Readjustment Rating Scale (SRRS), more commonly known as the Holmes and Rahe Stress Scale.[23]

This tool is meant to assist you in seeing how many events you are currently adjusting to and how much adjustment those events require. The score will help you understand how much of your stress capacity is already being used up. The tool can also help you to see which events you might be able to prevent or minimize in the future to bring down your overall stress levels. The Holmes and Rahe Stress Scale is a list of forty-three common life events that require some degree of adjustment.

To use this tool, just review the list of events and indicate which of them you have experienced in the last two years of your life. There is a number next to each event, called a Life Change Unit (LCU). This number is the weight or measure of approximately how much adjustment that stressor requires. Bear in mind that the LCU is the average amount of adjustment you may need to make. Each person's perception of the event will alter the adjustment you need to make. For instance, you may want the divorce and therefore experience relief rather than stress for this event. But if you absolutely do not want the divorce, your stress level may be higher. Add the numbers of each of your events to give you a total of how much stress adjustment you have been dealing with over the last two years. If you have experienced an event two or three times, add the LCU for each separate time the event occurred, but don't add the score every day of financial challenge nor every day of your mortgage.

The more events you have experienced, the higher your adjustment score will be, especially if the events you have experienced are difficult events. Holmes and Rahe discovered that the higher the score, the more likely it is that you will experience some illness because of it.

Note: There are different scales for different groups of people. Age and cultural differences can alter the reliability of the tool. This particular version was developed for adults. Other versions of the SRRS, that better represent your age, ethnicity, culture, and lifestyle can be found online.

---

23. Saul McLeod, "Stress and Life Events," Simply Psychology, 2010, https://www.simplypsychology.org/SRRS.html.

HOLMES-RAHE STRESS INVENTORY[24] (ADULTS)

Life Event	Life Change Units (LCUs)
Death of a spouse	100
Divorce	73
Marital separation	65
Imprisonment	63
Death of a close family member	63
Personal injury or illness	53
Marriage	50
Dismissal from work	47
Marital reconciliation	45
Retirement	45
Change in health of family member	44
Pregnancy	40
Sexual difficulties	39
Gain a new family member	39
Business readjustment	39
Change in financial state	38
Death of a close friend	37
Change to different line of work	36
Change in frequency of arguments	35
Major mortgage	32
Foreclosure of mortgage or loan	30
Change in responsibilities at work	29
Child leaving home	29
Trouble with in-laws	29
Outstanding personal achievement	28

24. T. H. Holmes & R. H. Rahe, "The Social Readjustment Rating Scale," *Journal of Psychosomatic Research* 213, no. 11 (1967).

Spouse starts or stops work	26
Begin or end school	26
Change in living conditions	25
Revision of personal habits	24
Trouble with boss	23
Change in working hours or conditions	20
Change in residence	20
Change in schools	20
Change in recreation	19
Change in church activities	19
Change in social activities	18
Minor mortgage or loan	17
Change in sleeping habits	16
Change in number of family reunions	15
Change in eating habits	15
Vacation	13
Major holiday	12
Minor violation of law	11
TOTAL	

Score Interpretation

Score	Interpretation
11–149	Low to moderate risk of becoming ill in the near future.
150–299	Moderate to high risk of becoming ill in the near future.
300–600	High to very high risk of becoming ill in the near future.

Obviously, there are many more stressful events than those forty-three included in this list. If you have experienced some traumatic events that are not on the list, you may need to factor them in as well, making a best guess at their value.

Remember, the LCUs are an *average* measure of adjustment that each event might require. Each event listed could manifest itself in hundreds of different ways, some more intensely than others.

Daily Hassles

In addition to the major events that act as triggers for stress, we have smaller events that are irritations, frustrations, and annoyances that drive us crazy because they are repeated over and over and over. These daily frustrations are called *daily hassles* and can be a major contributor to our overall stress levels and an increased detriment to our overall health. Some of the reasons that daily hassles contribute so much to our stress levels are: they are frequent, they tend to be things that we can't do much to fix or resolve, and we believe the hassle is unnecessary or due to someone else's incompetence. In a national survey that asked people to rate the most miserable part of their day, "sitting in traffic" was the leader. This is not a major change that leads to stress, but it is certainly a daily frustration.

Another tool, developed by Anita DeLongis, Susan Folkman, and Richard Lazarus,[25] measures the impact of those daily hassles. A unique quality of this scale is that, in addition to measuring the impact of the frustration, it can also measure events that act as an uplift. That means that there are some things that frequently cause frustration but at other times they bring some enjoyment or boost. Raising children comes to mind as one of those things that one minute brings joy, happiness, and satisfaction but the next minute brings anger, frustration, and stress.

There are several versions of this scale as well that address different cultural or generational populations. Some versions measure only the daily hassles without measuring the uplifts.

---

25. DeLongis, Folkman, Lazarus, "The Impact of Daily Stress on Health and Mood: Psychological and Social Resources as Mediators," *Journal of Personality and Social Psychology* 54, no. 3 (March 1988), https://www.ncbi.nlm.nih.gov/pubmed/3361420.

It is best to do this assessment at the end of the day before going to bed so you can evaluate your entire day. For each item, think about whether the topic has been a hassle or an uplift or both throughout your day. If the topic applies to neither a hassle nor an uplift, skip it and move on. For those that *do* apply to you, think about how much of a hassle/uplift the topic has been. Next to each topic are two numerical scales, the one on the left (the hassles) and one on the right (the uplifts). For each topic, circle one number on the left for how much of a hassle the topic has been during the day and circle one number on the right for how much of an uplift the topic has been for the day.

	Scale:	
	0 = None or not applicable, 1 = Somewhat, 2 = Quite a bit, 3 = A great deal	
0 1 2 3	Your children	0 1 2 3
0 1 2 3	Your parents or parents-in-law	0 1 2 3
0 1 2 3	Other relative(s)	0 1 2 3
0 1 2 3	Your spouse	0 1 2 3
0 1 2 3	Time spent with family	0 1 2 3
0 1 2 3	Health or well-being of a family member	0 1 2 3
0 1 2 3	Sex	0 1 2 3
0 1 2 3	Intimacy	0 1 2 3
0 1 2 3	Family-related obligations	0 1 2 3
0 1 2 3	Your friend(s)	0 1 2 3
0 1 2 3	Coworkers	0 1 2 3
0 1 2 3	Clients, customers, patients, etc.	0 1 2 3
0 1 2 3	Your supervisor or employer	0 1 2 3
0 1 2 3	The nature of your work	0 1 2 3
0 1 2 3	Your workload	0 1 2 3
0 1 2 3	Your job security	0 1 2 3
0 1 2 3	Meeting deadlines or goals on the job	0 1 2 3
0 1 2 3	Enough money for necessities	0 1 2 3
0 1 2 3	Enough money for education	0 1 2 3
0 1 2 3	Enough money for emergencies	0 1 2 3

0 1 2 3	Enough money for extras (entertainment, recreation)	0 1 2 3
0 1 2 3	Financial care for someone who doesn't live with you	0 1 2 3
0 1 2 3	Investments	0 1 2 3
0 1 2 3	Your smoking	0 1 2 3
0 1 2 3	Your drinking	0 1 2 3
0 1 2 3	Mood-altering drugs	0 1 2 3
0 1 2 3	Your physical appearance	0 1 2 3
0 1 2 3	Contraception	0 1 2 3
0 1 2 3	Exercise(s)	0 1 2 3
0 1 2 3	Your medical care	0 1 2 3
0 1 2 3	Your health	0 1 2 3
0 1 2 3	Your physical abilities	0 1 2 3
0 1 2 3	The weather	0 1 2 3
0 1 2 3	News events	0 1 2 3
0 1 2 3	Your environment	0 1 2 3
0 1 2 3	Political or social issues	0 1 2 3
0 1 2 3	Your neighborhood	0 1 2 3
0 1 2 3	Conservation (gas, electricity, water)	0 1 2 3
0 1 2 3	Pets	0 1 2 3
0 1 2 3	Cooking	0 1 2 3
0 1 2 3	Housework	0 1 2 3
0 1 2 3	Home repairs	0 1 2 3
0 1 2 3	Yard work	0 1 2 3
0 1 2 3	Car maintenance	0 1 2 3
0 1 2 3	Taking care of paperwork	0 1 2 3
0 1 2 3	Home entertainment	0 1 2 3
0 1 2 3	Amount of free time	0 1 2 3
0 1 2 3	Recreation and entertainment outside the home	0 1 2 3
0 1 2 3	Eating (at home)	0 1 2 3
0 1 2 3	Church or community organizations	0 1 2 3
0 1 2 3	Legal matters	0 1 2 3

| 0 1 2 3 | Being organized | 0 1 2 3 |
| 0 1 2 3 | Social commitments | 0 1 2 3 |

Total severity:_____	Total number of hassles: _____	Total number of uplifts: _____

After you have rated each topic that applies to you, add up the total number of the fifty-three events that you experience. Then add the total points for how severe those hassles are (the score on the left). Then do the same with the daily uplifts (the score on the right).

> **Score: It is preferable to have less than twenty-five to thirty daily hassles. The severity points should be no more than two times greater than the total number of daily hassles. Obviously, the higher the uplifts score, the better.[26]**

Seeing the number of hassles and their severity balanced against the number and intensity of the uplifts should provide you with some insights about what things to try to minimize in your life and which things you could try to maximize.

Obviously, there are many other topics that you could add to your list to make it your own. Some other topics that have been included in other versions of this tool that may give you greater insights are: not enough time for family, misplacing or losing things, problems with employees, troublesome neighbors, overload of family responsibilities, social obligations, difficulties with friends, inconsiderate smokers, troubling thoughts about your future, hassles from boss/supervisor, thoughts about death, concerns about getting ahead, concerns about owing money, nightmares, menstrual problems, being owed money, too many responsibilities, regrets over past decisions, feeling conflicted about what to do, concerns about inner conflicts, watching too much television, concerns about weight, decisions about having children, friends living with you, planning meals, gossip, problems

---

26. See https://webs.wofford.edu/boppkl/coursefiles/psy150/labs/SocialLab/Kanner81_Hassles%20and%20Uplifts.pdf *or* https://delongis-psych.sites.olt.ubc.ca/files/2018/03/Relationship-of-Daily-Hassles.pdf.

with divorce, too many meetings, concerns about the meaning of life, trouble relaxing, concerns about medical treatment, worry about changing jobs, general job dissatisfaction, difficulties seeing or hearing, fear of rejection, friends or relatives being too far away, wasting time, gender bias at work, being exploited, problems with aging parents, not getting enough rest, concerns about bodily functions, declining physical abilities, rising prices of common goods, not getting enough sleep, unchallenging work, concerns about meeting high standards, trouble reading/writing/spelling, neighborhood deterioration, auto maintenance, social isolation, difficulties getting pregnant, trouble making decisions, housekeeping responsibilities, concerns for job security, care for pets, concerns about retirement, being out of work, too many interruptions, unexpected company, too much time on your hands, having to wait in lines, concerns about getting a loan, concerns about accidents, feeling lonely, fear of confrontation, trouble with math, legal problems, not enough time to get things done, not enough energy, side effects of medications, inability to express yourself, silly practical mistakes, transportation problems, shopping responsibilities, prejudice/discrimination from others, home maintenance, yard work, noise, crime, traffic, pollution, pandemic concerns, and anything else you wish to add.

Wow—there are a lot of things that go on in our lives. As you can see, that is a fairly lengthy list from which you can pick and choose to make your own personal daily hassle/uplift lists. Monitoring your stress levels and your daily hassle levels and then offsetting them by the daily uplifts can help you get a better handle on things that you can do to decrease your stress, decrease your daily hassles, or decrease your stress by increasing your daily uplifts.

WHICH EVENTS CAN WE PREVENT OR MINIMIZE?

Understanding the many changing events in our lives as well as the frequent hassles and irritations that plague us will help us to better manage the first stage of the stress process—the event, the trigger. Some of the events or daily hassles can be eliminated or at least minimized in our lives. By preventing some of these triggers, we free up some of our stress capacity to better deal with other surprises.

In addition to the events listed in these tools, there are other events that we can control, prevent, minimize, or manage. Many of those preventable events come from our own decisions, weaknesses, poor choices, and broken commandments. We can definitely control, prevent, and minimize some of those events.

Lili de Hoyos Anderson suggested that "understanding stress is not a guaranteed way to free ourselves completely from it. But when we try to understand why there is stress in our lives, we can take steps to keep it from being a powerful negative influence. By considering stress in three categories—the stress of sin, worldly stress, and the stress of refining ourselves—we can learn to understand the impact of stress on our lives. This understanding affords us choices: we can choose to stop being victims of our situations and to start acting according to eternal, spiritual values."[27]

CHOICE AND CONSEQUENCES

Choice

Recall our discussion on the War in Heaven? It was about one principle: agency, the freedom to choose. Lucifer objected to letting all of God's children have agency to choose. He wanted to "destroy the agency of man" (Moses 4:3). Agency is so important that one-third of God's children were banished from His presence because they wanted to require everyone to do what is right. However, the opportunity to choose for ourselves, to choose what we want to do and who we want to be is the only way we can learn, grow, and progress. Of course, our Father in Heaven wants us to use that agency to choose to keep His commandments, to "be anxiously engaged in a good cause, and do many things of (our) own free will" (D&C 58:27), to love and serve our fellowman, and to choose to listen to and follow the promptings of the Holy Spirit. The important part is that He wants us to choose not be compelled.

It is important to understand that when we feel like we are deeply entrenched with a "lack of choice," our stress level will increase. When we are in an intolerable situation and feel like we are stuck, our stress

27. Lili de Hoyos Anderson, "The Stress of Life," *Ensign*, February 1994.

level spikes. When we don't see any choices that lead us back to our normal routine, we tend to feel helpless and hopeless to resolve the mess we are in. Feeling helpless and hopeless are both components of high stress.

We often see people throw up their hands in frustration and proclaim, "I don't have a choice," when the truth is, we just don't see choices we like. A lack of good choices is not the same as a lack of any choices. If we truly have no choice, our stress level skyrockets.

Recognizing that we have choices, even if they aren't "good choices," begins to decrease that soaring stress level. Obviously, we are still going to feel some stress as we feel forced into disregarding wisdom, beliefs, values, or standards in the choice we have to make. We may not have choices that lead us back to where we want to be or choices that coincide with our wisdom or preferences but we do still have some choices.

William James warned against being crippled by the lack of good choices by saying, "When you have to make a choice and don't make it, that in itself is a choice." Sadly, not making a choice puts one right back into the skyrocketing stress.

This is where we can choose to step up and take control of a situation that we don't like.

This is where we might even create new choices that didn't exist until we decided to take control of our situation. This is where we can begin to minimize the level of stress we experience.

We can find wisdom regarding our choices. In *Harry Potter and the Chamber of Secrets*, J. K. Rowling wrote, "It is our choices...that show what we truly are, far more than our abilities."[28] It is very simple, just knowing that we have a choice or can create a choice decreases our stress level.

Consequences

While we are free to make our own choices, we are not free to choose if or what consequences we will pay from that choice. Dr. Phil McGraw has often said, "When you choose the behavior, you choose the consequence." Totally true! Consequences follow as a natural result of the choices we make.

---

28. J. K. Rowling, used in her book *Harry Potter and the Chamber of Secrets*.

If we go back to the examples in controllability, we see the consequence of skipping work or going in late can lead to loss of a job; overspending leads to debt, which may be too much to ever pay off; a lifestyle of eating unhealthy food, no exercise, smoking, drugs, or heavy drinking are risk factors for most chronic diseases. Often the consequences of our choices cause significantly more stress than any other stress we are dealing with. Sadly, the stress from consequences of our behavior also carries with it the stress of knowing that what we are experiencing is our own fault.

Our choices make us who we are. Our choices determine the consequences that we must bear. Our choices can increase our stress or decrease our stress.

CHAPTER 5

Thoughts and Perceptions

"For behold, he knows all thy thoughts, and thou seest that thy thoughts are made known unto us by his Spirit" (Alma 12:3). "But this much I can tell you, that if you do not watch yourselves, and your thoughts, and your words, and your deeds, and observe the commandments of God, and continue in the faith of what ye have heard concerning the coming of our Lord, even unto the end of your lives, ye mush perish" (Mosiah 4:30). "For our words will condemn us, yea, all our works will condemn us...and our thoughts will also condemn us" (Alma 12:14).

The second stage of the stress process is *thoughts and perception*. Recall the equation in chapter one regarding the definition of stress: $A + B + C = D$.

A is the event. B is our *thoughts/perception*, and C is the physiological response.

$$A + B + C = D$$

A	**B**	**C**	**D**
Change in environment/ event/situation/ thought	Perception (Thoughts)	Physiological Response	**STRESS**

Our perception comes directly from the thoughts in our brain. The scripture, "As a man thinketh in his heart, so is he" (Prov. 23:7), is much more profound than most of us know. Our thoughts have power. Through many years of research, we have discovered that the mind, the body, and the spirit communicate and interact with each other constantly. Our thoughts impact our bodies and spirit. Our spirit impacts our thoughts and body. Our bodies impact our mind and spirit. That is because the mind, the body, and the spirit are intricately connected. The wellness of one impacts the wellness of the others.

Our thoughts can cause physical manifestations. This is evidenced by how the mind, perceiving stress, changes the chemistry in the body almost instantaneously, causing the body to experience an abundance of physical changes—rapid heartbeat, jitteriness, anxiety, nausea, headaches, muscle aches, sweating palms, etc.

Conversely, the body can cause mental and spiritual changes. For instance, if we have been physically ill for a long period of time, our mind and spirit can become depressed, sluggish, negative, despondent, and sullen.

The Lord has counseled us to pay attention to our thoughts. We are taught to "let virtue garnish thy thoughts unceasingly" (D&C 121:45). We are also instructed that our thoughts should *not* be filled with doubt and fear: "Look unto me in every thought: doubt not, fear not" (D&C 6:36). Fear is part of the definition of stress, yet we are counseled to look unto Christ in every thought and *fear not*.

These scriptures are critical counsel regarding our thoughts. Recall the War in Heaven that we discussed earlier, the war over the principle of agency that was so critical that it caused God to cast out one-third of His children for standing firmly against agency. Agency is critical. We must make choices in life every day, choices that lead us either toward or away from our eternal exaltation. Making these constant choices requires us to think through options, figure out the pros and cons, balance the costs and benefits, factor in the impact on others or on our future while trying to align our thoughts with the Savior's. Using our *agency* wisely requires us to think. Using our agency wisely depends on us having accurate, rational, principled thoughts. We cannot make wise choices with a distorted thought process. We cannot make wise choices when our thoughts are irrational, illogical, negative, and filled with faulty information. Using our precious gift of agency is dependent on the wisdom, clarity, and Christlike qualities of our thoughts.

Just as our thoughts and perceptions are critical to our agency, they are also critical to our reactions to stress. It is not the stressor but your perception of the stressful trigger that is important. Epictetus reminded us that "it's not what happens to you, but how you react to it that matters."

Yes, the event is the *trigger* to stress, however you do not feel stress when an event/change occurs until you *know* about the event and you have a short time to process what that change means. Think about a time when a change occurred but you didn't know about it. You went on through your day happily unaware that there was anything wrong. But once you became aware of the event and processed the information through your brain, the stress level skyrocketed. Perhaps your employer had been struggling for many years trying to hold his company together but finally made the decision to shut the company down. If you were unaware of the financial instability of the company and the owners struggle to keep the company afloat, then you didn't feel the stress until you received the pink slip. If you did know about the financial struggles, you probably felt a constant stress for a long time.

Maybe there was an earthquake or a tornado in an area where most of your family live, but you were busy at work or cleaning the house and taking care of kids all day and didn't have the television or radio on to hear the news. Your stress didn't start when the event occurred. Your stress started when you were made aware of the event and processed it through your brain.

After a changing event occurs (stage 1), the information regarding the event comes into our brains through our senses—sight, sound, touch, smell, and taste. That information gets processed through our brains and quickly mixes with our thoughts and past experiences to lead to a perception of whether or not the new information is a threat or a danger to our safety.

In chapter three, we discussed the amygdala, that small almond-shaped section of our brain that scans incoming information to detect any threats to our safety. Other sections of our brain instantaneously retrieve knowledge, memories about past experiences, things we have been taught, and even our values, morals and principles, to rapidly form our perception. This extremely fast process helps us respond immediately to danger. It helps us quickly dart into the street to catch a toddler who has bolted out in front of an oncoming car, or quickly hide or leave a public place when we hear people yelling or sounds of gunfire.

Some of our stress is instantaneous. We need to respond quickly to avoid further damage. But some of our stress is *not* instantaneous. Some of our stress comes from changes in events that don't require immediate action even though we still perceive the change to be a threat or danger. Since many of the changes in events don't require our quick reflex reaction, we have time to think through what the change means and what we can do about it. Having time to think it through is a good thing. We can consider all the pros and cons and options before we make decisions on what to do next. Unfortunately, many of us shift this "gift of time" to think things through into a nightmare of negative thinking, stewing, fretting, worrying, agonizing, brooding, and over thinking.

We have all witnessed two people respond totally differently to the exact same situation. Why? The event is the same! Shouldn't the reaction be the same? If it is a stressful event, then shouldn't it be equally as stressful to both people? Not at all. Both people see the event, the options, and the pros and cons differently.

For some people, the stressful event combined with their perception propels them into a thoughtful evaluation of the situation, decision-making principles, and problem-solving skills. And, even though they feel some physiological changes from the fight-or-flight response, they handle the situation with a fairly clear head. Other people, faced with the exact same event, have thoughts and perceptions that send them into an enormous storm of excessive stress and a quandary of thought. Two different people respond in opposite ways to the exact same event. One person sees the change in events as a challenge to be resolved or an opportunity to make positive changes while the other person responds by crumbling into tears, negativism, and depression. Our thoughts and perceptions truly have the greatest influence on our overall stress.

WHERE DOES PERCEPTION COME FROM, AND HOW IS IT FORMED?

Perception is your explanation of what is happening. It is your view, your definition, your narrative of an event or situation. It is the way you see the world and is a reflection of your relationship with the universe. Your perception comes from the thoughts and experiences in your brain. Listen to different people describe the same event or activities and see how dramatically their perceptions differ. Just ask each family member to tell you about a recent family reunion. From their descriptions, one might think that they all attended *different* family reunions. When the event is more challenging, dangerous, or threatening than a family reunion, variations of perceptions seem to grow exponentially.

Why are all of our perceptions so different? The quick, simple answer is because we all have different information, thoughts, and experiences in our brains.

The brain is a very complex organ. If we were to dissect a brain in a laboratory, we would see that it has two half sections, cells, blood vessels, nerve connections, a brain stem, etc. What we would *not* see are the thoughts that go through that brain. There is no digital recording anywhere of the thoughts that are processed through the brain. (However, there is a new experimental brain-mapping process that may be able to detect the subject of our thoughts.) There is no evidence in the lab dissection that thoughts even exist, but we know they do. We think all day long.

To understand the process a little better, let's go back to the beginning of a person's life. In the beginning, our brain has limited information or experience. Our brain is much like a brand-new operating system in a brand-new computer. The newly formed brain and the new computer both have the capacity to receive and process information, but there are no documents stored there yet. There are no documents saved in the computer, and there is nothing yet stored in the frontal cortex (decision-making center) nor in the memory section of your brain. As you gather information and gain experience in life, your brain starts making connections between behaviors and consequences, so that we can use that information to make better decisions in the future.

H. Burke Peterson explains in a talk titled "Purify Your Thoughts":

When we were born on the earth, our minds and thoughts were clean and sweet and pure, unpolluted by the harmful impurities that come to us as a part of the experiences of this life. In our infancy, our minds are free from unrighteous and unwholesome thoughts. We are innocent and untouched by the harmful effects and influences of Satan. Our minds, which are like tremendous reservoirs themselves, are capable of taking in whatever they may be fed, good and bad, trash and garbage as well as righteous thoughts and experiences. As we go through life we may be exposed to stories, pictures, books, jokes, and language that are filthy and vulgar or to televisions shows, videos, or movies that are not right for us to see or hear. Our minds will take it all in. They have the capacity to store whatever we will give them. Unfortunately, what our minds take in they keep, sometimes forever.[29]

Your brain registers and stores whatever comes in through the senses of sight, sound, taste, touch, smell, and experience. We learn by watching what happens around us. We learn by what we experience. That is how we learn to walk and talk. We watch, we mimic, we try, we try again, we learn. That process occurs in everything we do in life, like how to behave in relationships, how to cope with challenges and disappointments, how to behave in socially acceptable ways, how to communicate kindly, how to handle money and follow a budget, how to treat others, and how to use grammar correctly. Whether we like it or not, we tend to do things the way our parents did them, since they are generally the ones with whom we spent the majority of the formative and developmental years of our lives.

We also learn from the controls that we are subjected to or not subjected to. If you got your mouth washed out with soap for saying mean things or inappropriate words, you learned not to use those words anymore. However, if you were allowed to swear and say mean things without any consequence, you continue to engage in that behavior. If you were repeatedly and consistently scolded for hitting

---

29. H. Burke Peterson, "Purify your Thoughts," BYU Speeches, Devotional, October 25, 1983.

your brother or for running around during dinner instead of sitting in your chair, you learned to not hit your brother and to stay in your chair during dinner. If you were not scolded or corrected in any way, you continued to run around during dinner and smack your brother whenever you wanted.

What we were taught or not taught, what behaviors were permitted or not permitted, and what we observe and experience are all stored in our brains. *Everything is stored*, whether the information is correct or incorrect, true or not true, important or not important.

The information, controls, observations, and experiences that come into our brains are not anywhere close to consistent and congruous. Parents aren't always consistent; sometimes they are happy, kind, sensitive, and loving but sometimes they are tired, cranky, overwhelmed, or stressed. Besides our parents, we also have a variety of grandparents, siblings, aunts, uncles, cousins, teachers, neighbors, baby sitters, and friends who also contribute to the plethora of information, experiences, adventures, distortions, inconsistencies, and "corrupt files" that end up in our brains. Perhaps you had an abusive parent who yelled at you even when you didn't do anything wrong. Maybe your parent told you to lie to your teacher, telling her that you missed school because you were sick but it was really because your parent was too high to drive you to school. However, if you told a lie to that same parent, you would get punished for it, causing you to be confused about whether lying was acceptable or not. Maybe you watched your parents constantly fighting so you never learned how to have a good relationship; you learned only to yell, scream, and fight when you didn't get your way. That information is stored in your brain along with every other experience and lesson learned—good or bad. Obviously, with tons of conflicting information to draw from, it can become very confusing to decide what information to use when you need it.

The amount of information in our brain is massive and comes from many different sources and situations. The information in *your* brain is significantly different than the information in *my* brain, thus leading us to have different perceptions of the same event.

The information and experiences stored in our brains tend to act as filters to all the new information that comes in. We might filter all new relationships through the wounds of past relationships. We automatically process all information coming in and reaction going out through the filters in our brains. We are usually unaware of these filters, but they influence all our thoughts and perceptions.

Since a large portion of our stress comes from our perceptions, it is critical to become aware of the information and filters stored in our brain. As we become aware of the filters that we unconsciously use to form our perceptions, we can begin to make necessary, even critical, changes to some of the faulty filters in order to decrease our stress.

Filters

The information that is stored in your brain begins to act as a filter to all the new incoming information, experiences, and observations. Like filters on a camera, our brain filters can change the nature of what we see. If we put a colored filter on a camera lens, the finished product reflects the change in hue of the filter. A blue filter makes a yellow shirt appear green. If we put a hazy filter on the camera lens, the finished picture of a sunny day looks like a storm is brewing. The point is those filters impose their characteristics onto reality and change the final perception. As we use our own filters on a situation, unbeknown to us, our filters change or distort the reality, thereby changing how we respond. Our filters can change a normal nonstressful situation into a stressful situation in a split second, just because we had a distorted filter.

There are many common filters. Some are stronger, some are weaker. The stronger the filter, the more influence it has on our perceptions. Filters gain strength in our brains if they come from information or events that are recent, painful, repetitive, important, high priority, attached to our values, emotionally charged, or delivered by someone important to us.

Some of our filters are good, positive, and healthy. Some of our filters are negative, detrimental, distorted, irrational, or simply untrue.

The easiest filters for us to see are the filters that come from the information, experiences, and observations we gather along our journey in life so we will take a look at those first. These filters come in many forms: definitions, past experiences, past wounds, lack of self-esteem, current situations, resources, etc.

There are thousands of pieces of information that act as filters. We cannot possibly discuss them all but in order to understand how filters impact our perceptions, let's take just a moment to look at a few of the more common filters and define them.

Filter: Definitions

We learn definitions all through life. Some from the context of the situation—or how words are used in sentences—some from school, some from asking grandma, "What does that mean?," some when we were learning to spell, and some from a dictionary. The challenge is that even if we learned the correct definition of all words and terms, some words have many different definitions, and some definitions change just by the tone we use when we say them. Also, some words have changed in meaning through the years. To complicate the definition filter, many people use words incorrectly because they learned an incorrect definition. Most of us don't know when we define words incorrectly; we automatically assume our definitions are correct.

Let's review a very easy example. As you see the upcoming word in capital letters, fix in your mind what picture you see *first*: MOVE.

What picture do you see in your brain for the word *move*? Did you see moving day with a lot of boxes, packing, a moving van, cleaning, chaos, and trying to find places to put things as you unpack in your new place? Or did *move* present a picture of a new adventure, going to a different residence, exploring a new neighborhood, and meeting new friends? Or did *move* evoke something entirely different? Did you hear dad yelling "Move!" as a command because you were sitting in his favorite chair? Or did you hear an army drill sergeant shouting, "Move, move, move, move!"? Or was the picture in your mind a picture of physical movement—the ability to run, dance, or hike? Maybe you saw *move* as a great blessing that you have the ability to move your body, no paralysis, no amputated limbs, no pain on every movement. The word *move* means all of those things. But when we must make a quick decision, we tend to draw on the definition that is most prominent in our brain. If we are not required to make a quick decision, it is helpful to be aware that there are many definitions besides the one you have in mind at the moment.

Each definition probably carries with it some different emotion as well. When I hear the word *move*, I shift through many of those definitions. Having moved residences many times, I cringe at the thought of having to pack, clean, move, and get settled again. Sometimes, I think of new experiences and have a twinge of excitement. Sometimes, I hear my dad, long passed away, yelling at me to get out of his favorite chair. That thought brings conflicting emotions—an unpleasant memory of being yelled at to get out of the comfortable chair and one of missing my dad. Sometimes, I am transported back to a difficult time when a very strange brain injury paralyzed my right side for a while, and the inability to move half my body became terrifying. Then I find myself engulfed in gratitude that the feeling and movement in my right side returned. Just *one word* has many different definitions, many different pictures, many different emotions, and many different perceptions.

Filter: Past Experiences

Past experiences we have had in life, along with the emotion we felt at the time, are stored in our brains as memories. All of our experiences are stored: experiences in childhood, school, vacations, summer activities, Christmases, family dinners, family squabbles, new cars or broken-down cars, the house you lived in, where you slept, when you were sick, the kids in the neighborhood, sports played in school, first jobs, lost jobs, dating, breakups, marriage, children, births and deaths, excitements and heartaches, and successes and failures. All of those past experiences are tucked away in your brain. All of the emotions, good or bad, that go with those experiences are tucked away as well. Experiences that are the most difficult, the most painful, or most profound tend to create a stronger memory and therefore a stronger filter through which we process future similar experiences.

Our past experiences help us process new events more quickly. When you walk into a movie theater, you find a seat in a section that you like and sit down. Past experiences taught you that, in a movie theater, you need to sit down as quickly as possible and other past experiences help you know where you like to sit: in the middle, on the side, in the back, on the end of a row, etc. So, that is what you look for quickly.

Past experience helps you filter through all the activities and rides in Disneyland so you can enjoy your favorite attractions in the two days you have in the park. Past experiences provide you with information about the things you like or don't like, things you are good at or not so good at, things you like to eat or don't like to eat. Sometimes the past experience isn't your own, but it is an experience that you watched. How often have people avoided getting married because they watched their parents fight constantly and end up getting a divorce? All of our past experiences have some degree of influence on our perceptions.

Filter: *Wounds*

It is likely that throughout our past experiences we lived through some painful situations that led to some deep wounds. These past wounds become incredibly strong filters to help protect us from going through another similar painful experience. Strong filters can be very helpful in preventing us from wandering into dangerous and threatening situations again. If you have a deep wound from living with an alcoholic parent, that wound might protect you from indulging in excessive alcohol consumption or provide you with red flags as you are developing a relationship with someone who seems to drink excessively. Conversely, you may have learned to cope with difficulties in the same way your parent did—by using alcohol.

However, sometimes these strong filters prevent us from moving forward or making good decisions or can even cause deep stress just from constantly remembering the wound. Perhaps a past wound came from the death of a beloved animal. This filter could prevent us from ever owning an animal again as our way to protect ourselves from having to endure grief again. Instead, we could choose to focus on the filter of the great joy we experienced from having the pet rather than on the wound of losing them.

Past wounds can protect us or they can prevent us from moving forward. When the wound is caused from a poor choice we made, the strength of the filter can serve to protect us from making another poor choice. However, as we scan some of those painful past experiences, we may find that many of them were caused by other people or by random events. If we choose to hold on tightly to these past wounds, they can become obstacles and barriers for us. At the very least, we use those wounds as filters, sometimes to protect us and sometimes to our distinct detriment.

Filter: Self-Esteem

Often, a very large filter is our self-esteem or lack of it. Self-esteem means realistically knowing your strengths *and* weaknesses, recognizing that your value is as much (not more, not less) than every other human being, understanding your divine nature, and treating yourself and others with equal respect.

Damaged self-esteem generally comes from a frequent lack of respect from others, especially those we love. That means you have been subjected to frequent attacks (or perceived attacks) to your value, worth, intelligence, talents, and/or behaviors from parents, siblings, teachers, friends, authorities, or community, which you then internalize to mean you have no value. This internalized lack of self-esteem then becomes a filter through which all your stress triggers pass, making your stress much more intense. Each new stressor then damages self-esteem even further. This one becomes cyclical.

I generally hesitate to use the term *self-esteem* because for many people it evokes the connotation of self-centeredness, self-indulgence, conceit, arrogance, and even cockiness. The self-esteem I am talking about has *nothing* to do with those connotations.

So, let's be clear on the definition we are using: *Self-esteem* means how much respect and value *you* place on *yourself.* It is *not* how much value someone else places on you. That is *other-esteem*, not self-esteem. Neither is self-esteem valuing or respecting yourself above another. That is arrogance, conceit, or self-indulgent entitlement.

How did you get low self-esteem? Generally, from lack of respect from others that you internalized, becoming your own low self-esteem. It is yours now. It needs to be fixed. As a matter of fact, this is one filter that needs concentrated attention to get it fixed *quickly*. It is not only a huge filter that negatively distorts your perceptions, but going through life without an understanding of your value attracts more people who will continue to disrespect you. You are of greater value than that.

Sadly, some people hold tightly to their lack of self-esteem, using it as an excuse to continue to play a victim role, to excuse their behavior, to justify a failure, to feel sorry for themselves, or to try to evoke sympathy for their lack of self-esteem. Self-esteem is *self*-esteem, not other-esteem. If your self-esteem is low, you may need to work with a counselor to help you fix previous damage that was done. Sometimes, self-esteem is low because there are unresolved mistakes or sins that need to be corrected.

Filter: Current Situation

Any change in events tends to affect or even disrupt our current situation and future plans. And conversely, our current situation can alter how we perceive a change in events. Therefore, it makes sense that one of the filters that leads to our perception is a quick review of our current situation and how this new change could affect what we are currently doing.

An example could be having your car break down. You find out that the engine is completely shot. If you were planning to purchase a new car anyway and had been searching for the car you wanted, you may just focus on gratitude that your car did not break down until you were ready to purchase your new car. Perhaps you are financially strapped. You have no ability to purchase a vehicle, not even an old beat-up clunker. The blown engine of your old car is the same. Your current situation is drastically different, therefore the current situation becomes a major filter in your perception of whether this is stressful or not.

Crisis is never convenient. Most of the stressful changes in events directly impact what we are doing at the time and maybe even cause us to change something in our future. The filter of current situation is generally one of the biggest contributors to our perception of stress because the event almost always impacts what you are doing now.

Filter: Resources

As new events occur, one of the filters that we automatically use is a quick review of our current resources. Resources can come in the form of money, assets, access to help, social support, access to knowledge, etc. Whatever the event is, it becomes more stressful if resources are minimal or less stressful when resources are plentiful.

If the event is an auto accident, part of the perception regarding how stressful the accident is, comes from an instantaneous review of what kind of resources you have available to solve the problem. Do you have health insurance to cover any medical attention you might need? What will the injuries do to your ability to maintain necessary responsibilities? Were there injuries that could prevent you from being able to work and bring home a paycheck? Do you have access to other transportation? Do you need a specific type of automobile large enough to transport children around? Do you have adequate insurance? Do you have money for the insurance deductible? Do you have the time to deal with the insurance and car repairs? Do you have car rental coverage on your insurance? Was the accident your fault, meaning it could lead to a lawsuit? Availability of resources is a significantly large filter in the perception of stress for the majority of people, especially for those with extremely limited resources.

Filter: Values, Morals, and Beliefs

We all have our own unique set of values, morals, and beliefs. We have beliefs in just about every aspect of our lives: political, environmental, religious, health, financial, emotional, communication, lifestyle, accountability, responsibility, legal, etc.

Each time we are presented with changes in events, we channel our options through our unique blend of values, morals, and beliefs. Those values, morals, and beliefs may be very strong in some areas and almost nonexistent in other areas. We often recognize what we value when there is a chance that we will lose it. There is no question that our values, morals, and beliefs can act as strong filters to a change in events if that change in events conflicts in any way with deeply held values, morals, and beliefs.

Filter: Culture/Geography

Another one of those unconscious filters comes from where and how we were raised. We learn cultural or geographical beliefs and norms while growing up and seeing them all around us. Many people have no idea that they have cultural/geographical influences in their daily thoughts and behaviors until they visit another part of the country or a different country in the world.

Food preferences are an obvious filter in our thoughts. If you were raised in a culture that believes that pigs are vile and filthy creatures and should not be eaten, you may be offended or insulted if someone innocently served you ham and eggs for breakfast or a bacon cheeseburger for lunch.

Cultural or geographical differences come in many forms. One culture may believe clothing should cover all parts of the body except hands and faces, while other cultures are comfortable with very revealing attire. One culture may honor and respect nature, while another is oblivious to how their behaviors impact the environment. Beliefs about health, illness, healing, and medical care differ widely depending on your race, ethnicity, culture, geography, etc.

With this wide range in cultural and geographical beliefs, it makes sense that our personal beliefs act as filters when we are confronted with differing beliefs and behaviors. For many, this filter is an adventure as we learn about different cultures and lifestyles. But for many others, facing differences in cultural beliefs is extremely stressful.

Filter: Coping Styles

Another filter that we learned by watching our parents, family, or caregivers is how to cope with things that we don't like. We watched how our parents coped when they had a disagreement and they didn't end up getting their way. If Dad's coping style is to yell, we unconsciously learn that yelling is what we do when we have to cope with something we don't like. Perhaps, Mom's coping style is to get very quiet, or cry, or mope around, so that's what we learn. If our parents or role models have good coping techniques, we learn good ways to cope with difficulties and challenges. If those people teaching us have very poor coping techniques, those are, unfortunately, the ones that we will learn.

Hopefully, we learn better coping styles as we get older. However, during times of stress, we tend to revert back to the coping style that is strongest and most familiar. It is well worth working hard to learn better coping styles, so we can make them the strongest and most familiar, because poor coping styles not only do not help us cope well with stress, they often make the stress more intense.

Filter: Mood

This one is definitely a filter that influences how you perceive stress. We all have examples of times when we responded well to the very same event that on another occasion caused us great stress because we happened to be in a bad mood. Sometimes that bad mood even caused the stressful event to occur to begin with. When we are in a bad mood, we don't want to believe that we are causing the stressful situation or that our negative attitude is distorting how we perceive a situation. And yet, it is impossible for our current mood or attitude to have no influence at all on whether or not we perceive something as stressful.

The Second Type of Filter: Unconscious Negative or Distorted Thought Processes

For some of you, this section may be one of the most critical stress-reduction sections in the entire book. Each of our stress-triggering events pass through all the filters we just discussed. In addition to those, we also have some *totally unconscious* thought processes that act as huge filters for everything we process. That means that these different thought processes influence *all* of our thinking, not just our perceptions regarding possible stressful triggers.

This section discusses many thought distortions that can turn nonstressful events into major stressors. Distorted thoughts cause perceptions of reality to be irrational, illogical, distorted, exaggerated, negative, or completely untrue. When you let a little poison into your thoughts, it poisons the whole stream and takes on a life of its own. However, according to Buddha, "When the mind is pure, joy follows like a shadow that never leaves."

We could liken these distorted thought processes to a computer virus. We could type in very accurate information into our document, but the virus, which is deep inside the computer, completely rearranges what comes out on the page._

Many psychiatrists, psychologists, counselors, social workers, and communication experts have identified several types of distorted thought processes and/or negative thinking. These negative thoughts and/or distorted thought processes filter *everything* we think about.

Dr. Daniel Amen, a well-known psychiatrist, suggests that these negative thoughts are different ways that your thoughts lie to you to make situations out to be worse than they really are.[30]

Most people with thought distortions are completely unaware of these distorted/negative thoughts. They don't know that they have them and don't know that their thoughts are distorting reality. It is important to recognize and correct these distortions and negative thoughts for several reasons. The first reason is the most critical and encompassing: We compromise our *agency*. When our thoughts are distorted, negative, irrational, or illogical, we cannot make good, wise, well-thought-out choices.

Distorted/negative thoughts make life difficult for you and for those around you. When your thoughts distort reality, your relationships become more difficult and contentious. Distorted/negative thoughts make it difficult to make good decisions. Furthermore, distorted/negative thoughts can most definitely turn a nonstressful event into an *unnecessarily* stressful event. Thought distortions lead to increased anxiety, depression, and more frequent and intense stress.

Another reason for fixing distorted or negative thoughts is because of their chemical effect on our brains. When the brain swarms with negative thoughts, the body produces chemicals that deactivate the cerebellum section of the brain, which leads to increased confusion and decreased coordination. The chemicals also fire up the left temporal lobe, which leads to increased irritability, negativity, and violence as well as decreased memory, learning, and mood stability.

Obviously, none of the effects of these chemical changes are positive. As a matter of fact, the negative effects are quite disturbing. When you live with a brain that is constantly swimming in negative thoughts, it means constantly dealing with confusion, irritability, negativity, and violence as well as decreased coordination, memory, learning, and mood stability. If these negative/distorted thoughts have this much impact on our normal daily life, imagine how much worse our stress is when all of the *changing events* are filtered through negative/distorted thoughts.

---

30. Daniel G. Amen, MD, "ANT Therapy: How to Develop Your Own Internal Anteater to Eradicate Automatic Negative Thoughts," American Holistic Health Association, https://ahha.org/selfhelp-articles/ant-therapy/.

There are many types of negative/distorted thoughts. A quick search on the Internet for *distorted thinking, thought distortions,* or *negative thoughts,* will provide you with many different lists of these distortions. These websites provide explanations about what the distortions are and how to get rid of them. I will present just a few of the more common distortions/negative thoughts identified and presented by several well-known authors, including John M. Grohol, Psy.D., David D. Burns, MD and Daniel G. Amen, MD.

Dr. Amen refers to his list of nine negative thoughts as Automatic Negative Thoughts (ANT's) because we use these distortions automatically, and we are unaware that we even have these negative/distorted thoughts; they are so pervasive and prevalent that we just accept them as normal.[31]

As we review the many common distorted/negative thoughts, it would be wise to take an honest assessment of how many of these negative thought processes we have. You will need to have someone who loves you help you with this section. As stated earlier, most people don't know they have thought distortions. These negative thought processes dramatically increase our stress levels, so if we can honestly recognize the ones that we have, we can begin to fix them and thus begin to *decrease* our stress. Most of us have at least one of these distorted/negative thought processes to some degree. It is not unusual to have many thought distortions. Sadly, as a matter of fact, I have had many students admit to having them all.

Many of these thought distortions build upon another one or are closely related. However, each distortion has some subtle difference.

1. Polarized Thinking

This is also known as absolute thinking or always/never, all/nothing, black/white, right/wrong, yes/no, or good/bad thinking. Polarized thinking is the most frequently used distorted/negative thought process. It is also the foundational thought process for many other thought distortions. This thought process is the main cause of such problems as stress, anxiety, depression, unrealistic standards, self-criticism, feelings of being trapped, feeling like a

---

31. John M. Grohol, "15 Common Cognitive Distortions," PsychCentral, June 24, 2019, https://psychcentral.com/lib/15-common-cognitive-distortions/.

failure, needing to be perfect, relationship problems, and addiction problems.

In polarized/absolute thinking, one sees things only in extremes or absolutes. The individual sees things as either/or. An event or a comment is either black or it is white, right or wrong, yes or no, good or bad, everyone or no one, always or never. There are no thoughts in between these extremes. However, life doesn't present itself in absolutes. We live in a world of extensive variety, vibrant colors, maybes, middle ground, options, and sliding scales, but when we think only in absolutes, where does all the variety end up? The variety is lost. The middle ground that is reality ceases to exist when our thoughts file the information in one of the absolute extremes.

An example of an all-or-nothing thought process would be if you haven't done something "perfectly," then you perceive it as you have done nothing at all. For those who don't have this absolute thought process, doing something less than perfectly is still really good, and you are thrilled to have completed your task. However, for those with this thought distortion it is considered a failure/nothing because it wasn't *all*.

Most areas of life are not absolutes of *always/never* but a continuum of possibilities, like *rarely, infrequently, periodically, sometimes, half the time, often, frequently, generally, most of the time,* and *usually.* Likewise, there are many shades of gray in the continuum between black and white, which you find out when you attempt to match the gray paint on your walls. In addition to all the different colors of gray, we have thousands of other colors in the world besides black and white. We have vibrant reds, yellows, oranges, pinks, blues, greens, teals, purples, violets, and thousands of variations, all of which get lost when we think only in black/white absolutes.

Another way *absolute thinking* manifests is in *always/never thinking.* People with this thought distortion think if something happened once, it will *always* happen. Or if something has not happened yet, it will *never* happen. For example, if your partner gets irritable and shuts down, you might think to yourself, *She's always giving me the silent treatment,* even though she goes silent only once in a while. If you were to tally all the interactions and all the time she goes silent, the reality would be that she shuts down twelve times out of one hundred interactions. Certainly the twelve instances of the silent treatment is not good for any relationship, but the thought *She's **always** giving me the silent treatment* is just as unhealthy for the relationship. Perhaps you stop talking with her or listening to her at all because you think she is always in silent treatment mode. If you were to tell your partner, "You are always giving me the cold shoulder/silent treatment," she will think I *just had a very long quiet conversation with you* or *I only shut down when you aren't listening to me.* As soon as your partner finds even one exception to your comment, she can dismiss the entire statement as not being true. She isn't *always* shutting down—and the distortion fight begins.

On the other end of this polarized thought might be the belief that you will *never* find another job after having been laid off of a job you had for twenty years. You revise your resume. You send out applications. You contact your network of friends and associates. You have several interviews, but you have not been hired by anyone *yet.* However, you don't focus on the *yet* part of that sentence. You only think *I will never find another job.* This absolute thought most definitely increases your stress level and, in all likelihood, decreases your motivation to keep looking.

I often see absolute thinking when a student takes a test. Somewhere along their educational journey, the student did poorly on a test for which they studied a lot. The absolute thought process registered *I never do well on tests. I always fail them.* From then on, the student tells himself that it doesn't matter how much they study because they always fail tests. The truth might have been that the first test was poorly written or the student didn't study enough or the student studied the wrong material. There are many explanations for failing that *one* test, but turning that experience into an all-or-nothing thought process affects the student's ability to take tests after that. It is easy to see that the student's stress levels will increase dramatically each time there is a test.

Another example of absolute thinking occurred in a conversation about an upcoming dinner:

Jean: "What vegetable should we serve? Green beans?"

Diane: "Yeah, they're okay."

Jean: "What about carrots?"

Diane: "Yeah, those are okay too."

Jean: "What about peas?"

Diane: "They're not my favorite, but okay."

Years later, in another discussion about what to serve for a special dinner, someone suggested baby peas as the vegetable. Jean interjected quickly, "No, Diane hates peas." Diane doesn't hate peas. That is *not* what Diane said. She said "They're not my favorite, but okay." That means peas would be somewhere in the *middle* of the continuum between love and hate. But when you have a polarized thinking process, you can't deal with anything but love/hate, yes/no, or good/bad. When you hear peas aren't Diane's favorite then your thought process becomes: *Diane doesn't love peas so I can't file this information under* love, *therefore the only other choice is to file it under* hate. The truth is peas may be tenth on the list of twenty-five vegetable preferences for Diane. But Jean's polarized thought process doesn't file the truth, she files the distortion.

Thinking in absolutes means distorting reality so that you can file it into nice neat absolute packages. It also means that the truth is no longer what you will use in making future decisions. The distorted information becomes one of those filters through which you process all other incoming information. This thought process distortion frequently *causes* needless stress, even at the very least, this thought distortion, *increases* stress.

2. Filtering Out the Positive/Focusing on the Negative

This thought distortion is when a person sees only the bad in a situation and ignores anything that is good. This person picks out one negative detail and focuses only on that to the exclusion of all else, discounting, rejecting, and even ignoring any positive information. I recently asked my granddaughter and her friend about their day at school. The friend said it was a terrible day. She had gotten in trouble during morning recess, and she knew then that the rest of the day was going to be horrible. My granddaughter said she had a great day at school except one little thing. She had gotten in trouble during their morning recess too, but then she said, "That was just one recess; the rest of the day was great." The same event was the *only event* my granddaughter's friend focused on. The *whole day* was what my granddaughter focused on. She didn't discard the positive because of the negative. Neither did she ignore that there was a part of the day where she learned a lesson when she did something wrong.

The individual with this thought distortion focuses only on the negative detail to the point that the vision of reality is totally darkened. For this individual, life is mostly negative. Life is just one disappointment after another.

This distortion occurs often for people who are frequently being evaluated (teachers, athletes, performers, entertainers, etc.). For students, maybe they only see the worst grade on their report card, ignoring all the good grades. For an employee, their yearly performance evaluation at work is lost because of one needs improvement comment. Athletes, performers, and entertainers are evaluated and critiqued constantly. It would be extremely difficult for one of these individuals to continue to perform if they have this thought distortion. For a speaker, even if the majority of the evaluations are positive and complimentary, if there is even one comment out of five hundred, that is less than positive—or there is a suggestion for a way to improve or a comment that was even critical or mean—the speaker with this type of distorted thinking will give all of their focus and attention to the negative comment, completely dismissing the larger quantity of positive comments. The negative comment will consume all thoughts associated with the evaluation.

In addition to focusing on the one negative and discounting the ninety-nine positives, the extreme side of this distortion is when the individual goes a step further and turns the positives into negatives. That occurs when we give negative motivation to the ninety-nine positives. Perhaps we discount all the positives as lies or we assume that the positives were meant to mock us and thereby humiliate us. We say things like, "She was too nice to say what she was really thinking," or, "They only invited me as a charity invitation," or, "He must have asked me out because he lost a bet."

Sadly, in our culture, social media has given a platform for people to more freely vent their criticisms or even attack another individual without having to look at the face of the person they are criticizing. This situation has given rise to people being on the receiving end of many more negative comments than ever before. For those who have this particular thought distortion, the emotional pain and stress can be immobilizing. We have even witnessed an increase in suicide rates in teenagers and young adults who have this thought distortion and have been publicly criticized. Criticism is tough for anyone to hear. For those with a negativity filter, the stress and emotional trauma can be unbearable. This thought distortion creates stress when none should have existed.

3. Labeling

In this distorted thinking process, the individual attaches an unhealthy or derogatory label to someone or something based on only one event or experience. We label ourselves, others, groups, events, or situations based on very limited information. Some of the negative labels that people frequently use that are not too vile to write here are: stupid, idiot, jerk, loser, incompetent, irresponsible, ridiculous, mean, and arrogant. Social media is filled with more vile labels I cannot and would not write in this book.

Labeling is irrational and harmful because when you label someone (including yourself) based on one event, mistake, or situation, you negate all the qualities that make that person a unique human being and instead lump them in with all the other people you have labeled as arrogant or jerks. No one is just one characteristic. Everyone is their own unique blend of good and bad characteristics. Labels are just monikers that lead to frustration and low self-esteem.

Instead of saying, "I made a mistake," the person with this thought distortion might say, "I'm such a loser," or "I'm an idiot." Instead of saying, "He probably cut me off because he didn't see me," or "Wow, he is in a big hurry," the distortion might be, "What an arrogant, pompous, road-rage-filled jerk." In this situation, a person is labeled based on their fifteen-second driving record. Those fifteen seconds could be because the driver was racing a bleeding child to the hospital or because the driver just received some devastating news. Their entire value as a human being should not be summed up in one label from a fifteen-second encounter. Instead of seeing the whole character of an individual, we see only one attribute, which we have labeled as bad and therefore the whole person is "bad" and not worth our time, energy, or attention. This distortion is an excellent way to make ourselves and/or others feel bad, angry, defensive, hopeless, hostile, worthless, and *stressed*. Labeling is a particularly dangerous and harmful thought distortion.

4. Catastrophizing (or Magnifying or Minimizing)

Catastrophizing occurs when an unpleasant situation is reported as the worst possible situation. It also includes exaggerating or magnifying the importance of an insignificant event or something that didn't go the way you wanted it to. I often hear students using this thought distortion if they fail a test. They say they will fail the entire course or even flunk out of school completely. It also shows up in mothers who proclaim, in a panic, that if they do not get their child into a particular sixth grade class with a specific teacher it will negatively impact the child "for the rest of their lives." This is the distortion that is frequently labeled as "making a mountain out of a molehill" or "blowing it all out of proportion." In this distortion, we often use what-if questions to build the magnitude of the story (e.g., "What if I had been in that car when it caught fire?"/"What if I hadn't gone to the doctor when I first got sick?").

In this distortion, you may also exaggerate the importance of your problems and/or shortcomings or the urgency of the events. Perhaps when the raise you received wasn't as high as you wanted, you say, "My life is a total mess, I am so depressed. I'm sure I will end up filing for bankruptcy." If that is the thought process when you keep your job *and* get a raise, what distortion might we see if you actually lost your job?

The thought distortion of catastrophizing most certainly leads to dramatically increasing stress. Thinking that an impending catastrophe is always just around the corner keeps your body and mind in a constant state of fight or flight.

5. Personalization

This thought distortion is where a person erroneously believes that they are responsible for some external, negative event over which they had little or no control. It includes a person thinking that there is some personal meaning in an innocuous event. The person believes that everything others do or say is somehow a personal reaction to them.

This distortion causes the individual to indulge in self-blame or the belief that anything bad that occurs around them is somehow their fault or occurred because of them.

One of the indications that an individual is engaging in the personalization thought distortion is they will often proclaim that a negative event was all their fault when they had nothing to do with it. For instance, "It's all my fault that my sister was in that accident, if I had called her sooner, she wouldn't have been on the road at that time." This thought process doesn't account for the weather, the road conditions, your sisters driving skills, the other driver's skills, etc. Personalization is taking responsibility or blame for something that has very little, if anything, to do with you.

Personalization also assumes that anything other people do or say is all about you, it is personal only to you. An example of that thinking would be when someone around you is being uncharacteristically quiet, cranky, upset, or aloof, you assume it is *because of you*. You believe that the person must be mad at you, or they don't like you, or you have offended them, or you have hurt them without knowing it, etc. It does not occur to you that the person might have had a bad day, or maybe they received some difficult news earlier, or perhaps they are cranky because they are tired or hungry or had a fight with a coworker. Those thoughts don't occur to you. You are certain the manifested behavior is personally directed at you or is because of you.

The distorted thought process of personalization leads to self-blame, *stress*, and frustration as well as feelings of inadequacy, shame, and overwhelming guilt.

6. Blaming

Blame is a particularly dangerous thought distortion. Blaming is the exact opposite of personalization. In personalization, you believe everything is your fault. In the blaming distortion, everything that goes wrong in your life is someone else's fault. We blame other people for our problems, our circumstances, our pain, our difficulties. Nothing is our fault. We are not contributing anything at all to the problems we are experiencing. Everything is someone else's fault.

This blaming thought distortion can often get very inventive. "It is your fault I forgot to take my laptop today. If you had awakened me earlier, I wouldn't have been rushing out the door," or, "It's your fault I didn't get the promotion at work. If you were nicer to me at home, I would be happier at work and would have gotten that promotion."

Blaming may work for you for a while, but it tends to backfire over time. Other people begin to resent being blamed for your mistakes. They get tired of being your scapegoat. Soon they will either toss the blame right back to you or just quit playing the game by walking away from you.

The other serious problem with this thought distortion is that when you blame someone else for all of your problems and take no accountability for what you contribute to those problems, you become powerless to stop the problems from occurring. Remember, one of the biggest contributors to *stress* is having *no* control over the stressful events that plague you. In the case of the blaming distortion, the truth is that you *do* have a great deal of control over the events but because you blame others, you do not think you have any control. If you don't think you have any control over the events because your thought distortions have blamed others, then you become incapable of changing anything. You become powerless to progress and move forward because you don't see anything that you need to fix or change in your life. This is the epitome of unnecessary stress.

7. Should and Guilt Beatings

Thoughts that include words like *should, shouldn't, ought to, ought not,* and *have to* are generally distorted thoughts. These words are used to try to motivate yourself or others. You have in mind the way things should be or how you hope or expect them to be. This type of thought distortion tends to lead to feelings of guilt or shame if the *should* is directed at yourself, or it could cause feelings of anger and frustration if the *should* is directed at others.

We hear these thought distortions often in phrases like, "I shouldn't eat this cheesecake," or, "I ought to get the house cleaned up," or, "She should have given me more notice if she needed help," or, "He ought to help around the house more."

Unfortunately, this thought distortion usually doesn't work in the way you might intend. When we use *should* on ourselves, we tend to feel increased stress until we accomplish what we think we should.

Sometimes, we even rebel. When we tell ourselves that we *should* do something, we will likely feel a bit defiant and refuse to do it, or worse—do the exact opposite.

When we use *should* on others, we are shifting our set of rules about how everyone *should* act and behave onto them. When others break our *should* rules, it increases our stress level as we feel angry and frustrated with the other person. In addition, the other people become angry, bitter, resentful, and stressed about the fact that they are expected to meet someone else's unrealistic expectations of them.

When we use this thought distortion of thinking about our life and the lives of others in terms of *should* and *shouldn't*, we subject ourselves to an abundance of stress, guilt feelings, frustrations, resentments, and anger.

8. Mind Reading or Jumping to Conclusions

In this thought distortion, we may think we know what another person is thinking/feeling without any evidence to verify it. We think we know why someone is acting in a certain way. We may conclude that someone has negative feelings toward us and then we act as though it is an established fact, even though the person has not given any indication that they have negative feelings toward us at all. Those thoughts were only in your head, not the other persons.

When we use this thought distortion, trying to read someone else's mind or jumping to conclusions about what they must be thinking, we attribute our distorted thoughts to the other person, and we are generally wrong.

An example of this thought distortion is when you start to act defensively and annoyed with someone because of personal thoughts springing up in your head like, *I know you are thinking I am an idiot.* Or you make up lies and stories about when you were leaving for and returning from work because you think things like, *I knew you would be mad that I changed my hours.* Or you get very depressed, sulky, and whiney and even disengage from a relationship because you think things like, *I am sure you have given up on me because I am such a screw-up.*

Obviously, this thought distortion increases stress as we jump to a negative conclusion and then react to that perceived negativity. This thought distortion is also a very common cause of conflict, contention, and difficult interactions between people because one person believes that they incorrectly know what the other person is thinking. The other person likely hasn't ever had any thoughts that the mind-reader thinks they have. This thought distortion dramatically increases stress for both parties. When one individual believes that they incorrectly know what the other person is thinking, productive communication becomes *very* difficult.

9. Fortune Telling or Predicting the Future

Right on the heels of mind reading and jumping to conclusions is the thought distortion of fortune telling and predicting the future. This thought distortion is where you arbitrarily predict the future and usually believe that things will turn out badly, even predicting the worst possible outcome to an event or situation. Sadly, these negative predictions often turn into self-fulfilling prophecies as individuals begin to change their behavior and react negatively in preparation for the poor outcome that they believe will occur thus *causing* it to occur.

An example of this distortion is thinking, *This is flu season, there is no way I will get through it without getting sick.* If we think we *know* the future and it is inevitable that we will get sick, we no longer take precautions to avoid getting sick; you think it is inevitable, a done deal, so why bother to exercise, eat right, wash your hands, and avoid people who are sick? *I am going to be sick, and there is nothing I can do about it, so why should I spend time and energy to prevent it?*

Another example might be thinking, *It is going to snow through May, so I am not going to plant my garden until June.* Not even the weather forecaster knows when it will snow. But since you believe you can predict the future, you delay planting, thereby shortening your growing season, which may end up with snow falling before it is time to harvest.

The thought distortions of mind reading, jumping to conclusions, fortune-telling or predicting the future are extremely damaging thought distortions in regards to stress. Those who use these thought distortions project negative outcomes that do not exist in reality, but because they believe the distortion to be true, they create stress where it doesn't exist. We have more than enough stress in our lives without letting our distorted thoughts create more stress for us.

There are many more types of thought distortion that you can find through online research. In addition to finding other types of thought distortion, you can also find a number of ways to fix those thought distortions or can work with a counselor to identify your unique thought distortions and ways to fix them.

It is important to note that most of us have been totally unaware that our thoughts were anything other than automatic functions over which we have no control. We have had thoughts for as long as we can remember, so we tend to assume that we were just born with the thoughts in our head, and therefore they must be correct. We are unaware that we learned to think from the same people who taught us to walk and talk, say please and thank you, and pretty much everything else we learned to do to function as human beings. We learned to think by listening to what other people said, watching what other people did, and by processing the things we experienced.

Most of us are not aware that the nature of our thoughts dictates our behaviors, our health, and our stress levels. We are seldom aware of our own thought distortions, though we sometimes recognize the thought distortions in others.

While we learn about which thought distortions we have and get assistance in fixing them, there is something that we can do to prevent more distortions from taking hold in our brains. We can begin to monitor everything that comes in to our brains: the music we listen to, the television programs we watch, the events we participate in, the conversations we are involved in, the articles/books we read. We can avoid negativity and distortions by being vigilant in not allowing the negative, vile, judgmental thoughts to enter our brains. President Ezra Taft Benson counseled, "Do not make your mind a dumping ground for other people's garbage. It is harder to purge the mind of rotten reading than to purge the body of rotten food, and it is more damaging to the soul."[32]

Dr. Caroline Leaf suggests, "No thought is harmless; no attitude can be hidden. If the brain gets worse when we constantly focus on

---

32. Ezra Taft Benson, "In His Steps," Brigham Young University Devotional, March 4, 1979.

the problem; then the brain will get better when we constantly focus on the solution."[33] We need to be vigilant in guarding our thoughts. We tend to believe that we can think whatever we want and no one will know. But our thoughts dictate our attitude, and our attitude affects our behavior. To sum it up, Ziad K. Abdelnour stated simply, "A negative mind will never give you a positive life."

As a child, I learned a beautiful little song in church: "I Have a Garden" written by Mary Hale Woolsey and arranged by Frances G. Bennett from an old French melody. The second verse, though not frequently sung, stuck in my mind as the most important part of the song because it held great wisdom regarding our thoughts:

> I have a garden, a secret garden,
> Where thot's, like flowers, grow day by day;
> 'Tis I must choose them and tend and use them,
> And cast all wrong ones, like weeds, away.
> Goodness and love are seeds that I sow;
> God up above will help me I know,
> To keep my garden, my heart's own garden,
> A place where beauty will always grow.

Many wise men and women through the centuries have added their counsel to keeping control over our thoughts. Following the garden theme, Brian Tracy added, "Whatever you think about the most will grow." Norman Vincent Peal added, "Change your thoughts and you change your world." President Gordon B. Hinckley counseled, "Be clean in mind, and then you will have greater control over your bodies. It was said of old, 'As [a man] thinketh in his heart, so is he' (Prov. 23:7). Unclean thoughts lead to unclean acts."[34]

You have the power to change the filters in your brain and choose which thoughts and perceptions you will focus on—and thereby decrease your stress levels.

Our thoughts shape our perceptions. Our thoughts and perceptions become the filters through which we process all of the new information that we receive. And since our thoughts and perceptions are

---

33. Caroline Leaf, Blog for Dr. Leaf, Episode 13, July 30, 2014.
34. Gordon B. Hinckley, "Be Ye Clean," *Ensign*, May 1996.

the second stage in the stress process, our thoughts and perceptions have the ability to filter information in many directions. Our thoughts can make events stressful when they really aren't, turn mildly stressful information into a mountain of stress, *or* turn potentially stressful events into an interesting learning experience rather than into crushing levels of stress. It is up to us. When you change your thoughts, you change your stress. We can choose our thoughts. When we choose our thoughts, we choose what realities will follow. Choose to be positive and you will have less stress in your life. John Locke said, "I have always thought the actions of men the best interpreters of their thoughts." That is certainly true in regards to stress.

Our thoughts can turn events that appear to be highly stressful into events that create feelings of motivations, challenge, or even a desire to be competitive. When you think *I can* like the little train that thought it could climb the mountain, you activate your motivation, confidence, and commitment to succeed.

Conversely, our perceptions can also change nonstressful events into crushing levels of extreme stress. Just because there is an event that might be stressful to someone, it doesn't mean you have to pick it up and own it for yourself as well. Even potentially stressful events do not have to cause stress. Instead of letting the fears and worries drag you into overwhelming stress, you can dissipate some of the fear by changing how you view the situation

John F. Kennedy reminds us that "when written in Chinese, the word *crisis* is composed of two characters. One represents danger and the other represents opportunity." We can choose where we focus. When we learn to choose to focus on the opportunity in a crisis rather than the danger, we will vastly decrease our stress levels without changing any of the events in our lives.

We must never underestimate how much power our thoughts have over our stress. We cannot dismiss the equation that A (the event) plus B (our thoughts/perceptions) and C (our physiological response) equals D (our stress). Our thoughts are a major component of our stress levels.

The Lord has proclaimed that "as a man thinketh in his heart, so is he" (Prov. 23:7). Our thoughts show in our attitudes and behaviors. His counsel to "let virtue garnish thy thoughts unceasingly" (D&C

121:45), is critical to our entire lives. But His counsel to "look unto me in every thought: doubt not, fear not" (D&C 6:36) is counsel specific to our stress levels. Stress comes from our doubts, our worries, our anxieties, and our fears. He is very clear that we should not doubt, we should not fear, but we should look to Him in *every* thought. The counsel can't be clearer than that.

CHAPTER 6

Breaking the Physiological Response

Stage 3 of the stress process is the physiological response. We discussed the physiological response in detail in chapter three as part of our discussion about bodies by design.

Change/Event + Perception (Thoughts) + Physiological Response =

STRESS

We also learned in chapter three, that when we perceive danger, threat or fear, our brain automatically and immediately sends out over 1,400 chemical messages to our entire body to prepare the body for the fight or flight stress response.

In addition, we learned that our body was designed to automatically return to its normal functioning level when our stress dissipates. However, when we experience constant, chronic stress, the physiological stress response does not resolve. Our body does not get the chance to return to its normal functioning state because our perceptions continue to register a constant danger, threat, or fear. Thus, our body continues to pour stress chemicals into our system, keeping us in a chronically stressed state.

There are many physical and mental indications that our body is stuck in the stressed state. Some of the more common physiological effects of chronic stress include muscle tension/strain, increased headaches and other pain, increased depression, increased irritability, inability to function well, lack of focus, problems in relationships, increased anger/hostility, increased illness and inability to sleep.

When our stress becomes chronic, it compromises all facets of our life: physical, mental, emotional, social, financial, and spiritual. When this happens, it becomes imperative for us to step in and intentionally break the physiological response, which is what we will learn how to do in this chapter.

Perhaps the best analogy of the difference between stress that resolves and chronic stress can be found in the story circulated around social media by Jimmy Harmon:

> A psychologist walked around a room while teaching stress management to an audience. As she raised a glass of water, everyone expected they'd be asked the half-empty or half-full question. Instead, with a smile on her face, she inquired: 'How heavy is this glass of water?' Answers called out ranged from 8 ounces to 20 ounces. She replied, 'The absolute weight doesn't matter. It depends on how long I hold it. If I hold it for a minute, it's not a problem. If I hold it for an hour, I'll have an ache in my arm. If I hold it for a day, my arm will feel numb and paralyzed. In each case, the weight of the glass doesn't change, but the longer I hold it, the heavier it becomes.' She continued, 'The stresses and worries in life are like that glass of water. Think about them for a while and nothing happens. Think about them a bit longer and they begin to hurt. And if you think about them all day long, you will feel paralyzed— incapable of doing anything. Remember to put the glass down.'[35]

So, how do we put down our glass of stress and break the physiological response?

First, solve what you can solve. Yes, I know this is the obvious thing to do and, in all likelihood, you have already fixed whatever you can fix and solved what you can solve. It probably goes without saying

---

35. Jimmy Harmon, "Mindful Schools," Facebook post, July 31, 2013, https://www.facebook.com/mindfulschools/photoo/a.203073253066340.49931.165948186778847/598713920168936/.

that if there are any components about our current stress that we can fix or solve, we should do that as quickly as we can. But sometimes, we just don't have a clue how to fix or solve a situation. So, let's review a few possibilities.

Like the water glass, we could simply put down the glass of stress for a while, even if we need to pick it up again soon. When we need to pick up the glass again, at least our arm will have had some critical rest from carrying the weight of the glass. Obviously, most of the types of chronic stress aren't solved by putting a glass of stress down. However, there are things that we can learn from this simple example that may help. Perhaps we can stop thinking about the stress for a short time to give our bodies a break from the stress hormones. That means, we take a mental break from the stress—get some sleep, watch a movie, go ice skating, do anything that gives your mind a little break. Perhaps we can solve some pieces of the stress and thereby lighten our load. Perhaps we can enlist some help in carrying the load at least for a while. Or perhaps we can change our perception of the situation by turning it into a choice rather than seeing the stressful situation as completely out of our control.

Let's take a look at some examples of how we might solve what we can solve. If your stress comes from your current employment, it may not be easy to just put the glass down and leave that employment, but you could put the glass down temporarily by taking a vacation. It is the equivalent of stopping to "sharpen our saw." Just like a good farmer knows that a field needs to be rested periodically in order to renew itself, we need to take a break and rest ourselves periodically. Often, when we return from a fun, relaxing vacation, we find we have been rejuvenated and have the strength to keep going at our job for a while longer.

Sometimes, taking a vacation isn't possible. In that case, we could take mini breaks while at work. Take a few minutes every hour to go for a walk around the office and clear your brain for a moment. You will find that you have given yourself a stress break as well as a little boost in productivity. This is just like putting the glass of water down every hour for five minutes, enough time to rest your arm, work out the tightened muscles, and pick up the glass again.

The Lord gave us a very good example about resting from our labors and our stresses as He instructed us about the Sabbath day. No matter how difficult our employment situation may be, make sure to keep the Sabbath day holy, resting from any employment responsibilities.

If taking a vacation or having hourly breaks does not help with the employment stress, perhaps we can try to solve some pieces. Are there components of your work that can be delegated to other employees? Are there individuals with whom you work who are unreasonable or abusive? If so, perhaps you could talk with their supervisor about their behavior. Is your work schedule or the hours you are required to work constantly conflicting with your responsibilities to your family? Perhaps you could talk with a supervisor or scheduler to change just a few parameters. If there is just too much work to do, perhaps you could request some short-term assistance to help catch up. There is usually some small piece of the whole that can be altered or fixed that will give you a little break.

If the employment issues aren't solvable and finding a new job in your field is not a viable option, or even if you have a good position with a good salary or excellent benefits and don't wish to leave, perhaps you can just change your thoughts to I am choosing to stay here rather than I have to stay and put up with this, I have no other choice. As you recall from chapter one, a contributing cause of our stress is lack of control over the situation. Take a moment to evaluate what is causing the stress, identify the components that you can control and which ones you cannot control. Do the benefits of your current job outweigh the stresses? Sometimes when we evaluate the job stresses and weigh the pros and cons, we realize that the pros outweigh the cons. The mere process of evaluating and then making a totally informed choice helps some of the stress to dissipate, because we just took control of our situation by making it a choice rather than feeling stuck. Sometimes just making the decision to start looking for a new job will provide you with a feeling of peace that you are actively doing something to reduce your stress. The sooner the stressful events are resolved, the sooner your body can automatically resolve on its own.

STOP THINKING ABOUT IT/DIVERT YOUR FOCUS

When you have solved what you can solve and the constant stress continues to plague your every waking hour, you have to try other options to break the physical cycle. We have learned that the physiological stress response actually comes from our perception, not from the event itself. Events don't cause our heart to race, our breathing rate to increase and our stomach to get queasy. The events are processed by our brain. Our brain provides our perception, and that perception kicks out the physiological blueprint that changes our bodily functions.

Dr. Margaret Kemeny, University of California San Francisco's director of the health psychology and behavioral neuroscience, said, "The body is responding to what is going on in the brain, not to what's going on in the environment."[36] Our stress is a result of our thoughts. Naomi Judd added this piece of wisdom: "Your body hears everything your mind says."

Our thoughts produce a chemical reaction in the body. As a matter of fact, every thought produces a chemical reaction in the body. Read that again: Every thought produces a chemical reaction in the body. Good thoughts or bad thoughts. All thoughts produce a chemical reaction. Some of those thoughts are calm and peaceful or loving and kind. Those thoughts produce calm chemical reactions. Some thoughts are about worry, anxiety, fear, or danger. Those thoughts produce a stress response.

Have you ever experienced a time when you were calm and then suddenly remembered something very important that you had forgotten to do? As you became conscious of that forgotten commitment, perhaps you began to experience the stress response. Your calm state changed in a few moments to a stressed state. There wasn't a stressful event that occurred. What occurred was a change in your thoughts— a thought that caused you to feel danger, a threat, or fear. It was the thought that caused the chemical reaction.

Whether it is a thought or a new stressful event, our body responds to it putting us in the fight-or-flight mode. Then we keep

---

36. Tori DeAngelis, "A Bright Future of PNI," *American Psychological Association* 33, no. 6 (June 2002), 47.

thinking about it and the physical response continues. Then we tell people about the stressful thing, and our thoughts continue to send out more stress chemicals. Pretty soon, the stressful situation consumes all of our thoughts. We just can't seem to shut those thoughts down. We stew about the situation and worry about how to solve the problem; with each thought, our body continues to spill out the stress chemicals.

Take a moment to think back about times in your life when you experienced something that you perceived as stressful. Did the stress stay with you only for a few moments after the event occurred, or did it stay with you for hours or even days? We have learned that every time you repeat a thought, you cause the same physiological reaction again and again and again and again. The physical response does not always come with the exact same intensity, but repeated thoughts of the same stressful events cause the same chemical changes in the body to occur.

Research shows us that our brain doesn't differentiate between reality and a thought of reality when it registers a threat. That means that when we experience a stressful event and then have repeated thoughts about that event, we are causing our body to stay in the stressed state. So, the first thing that we can do to help break the physiological response to stress is stop thinking about it. If you can stop the repeated thoughts about the event, you can help stop the constant chemical changes in your body and thereby help your body to return to a relaxed state.

Just this week, I attended the funeral of a friend from my youth. I am sharing this story with the expressed permission of his daughter, Joyce Woolf. Major Anthony DeVoe Woolf, a veteran of World War II, died at the tender age of 102. Yes, 102! He was a very calm, kind, strong, even-tempered man who was rarely angered. He said he remembered being angry only five times. He served an LDS mission in Germany, then was inducted into the U.S. Army during World War II, graduated from college, married the love of his life, secured employment that would support his family, and raised a wonderful family of seven children. He experienced the same disappointments, challenges, trials, and ups and downs of life that the rest of us do. After raising all of his seven children and sending them through college, he and his wife were able to retire and move to a home in the mountains of California. Sometime later, in their advancing years of life, the Woolf's home burned to the ground. They lost everything they owned. Tony Woolf quietly proclaimed as he walked away that he "came into the world with nothing and would go out of the world with nothing." Then he calmly moved on. How did he do it?

In one of the funeral addresses, his daughter Joyce, who acted as the caregiver for her parents the last years of their life, shared the answer. The reason Tony survived so long, in a relatively healthy state for his advanced age and with such a calm countenance and even temper, was because "he didn't absorb stress; he just didn't think about stressful things." His life was not without stress. It is not possible to live 102 years, serve a mission, fight in a world war, raise seven children, have your house burn to the ground, and have your spouse precede you in death without a hefty amount of stress. But this man encompassed the whole essence of this principle; he stopped thinking about it. He did not dwell on difficult things. He did not constantly think about challenging issues, absorbing the stress that accompanies those thoughts. He solved what needed to be solved and moved forward without stewing about the challenges. His health and demeanor attested to the effectiveness of the principle. Once you have solved what you can solve, fixed what you can fix, and made the necessary decisions, commit to stop thinking about it. Thank you, Tony Woolf, for being a great example of this principle.

Most of us have not learned this lesson to the degree that Tony Woolf learned it. When you have been through a traumatic, scary, stressful event, it feels difficult, if not impossible, to stop thinking about it. Yes, changing your thoughts seems difficult, but it is totally possible and even necessary.

Stressful thoughts tend to creep in without an invitation. It happens to all of us. Actually, many of us learned to absorb stress, dwell on the thoughts, and even embrace the turmoil. Clearly, thoughts about highly stressful events will continue to invade your thoughts and memories. That is normal and to be expected. However, it is not necessary to hold on to the thoughts and replay the memories of the stressful events over and over and over in your mind. You can just acknowledge that the thought has returned and once again push the thought out of your mind. It is your choice which thoughts you keep in your brain. You can choose to keep thinking the invasive stressful thoughts, dwell on them, and even embrace them, or you can choose to push stressful thoughts out of your mind. You choose!

Once you have pushed the invasive thought out of your brain, you need to divert your attention or the invasive thought will return. It is much like having a cavity in a tooth. The dentist drills the decayed material out of your tooth. Then he fills the hole with a filling. If the drilled hole in the tooth is not immediately filled with an appropriate decay-resistant substance, food, saliva, and bacteria will find its way into the hole and intensify the cavity and decay. The same thing occurs with our thoughts. If we find ourselves with a thought cavity (negative, stressful thoughts), and we choose to push the thought out (drill out the decay), then we need to fill the vacated thought-space with some other appropriate substance or the stressful thoughts will return and intensify.

How do we divert attention to stop the thought process? Make your brain think about something else: read a book, help someone in need, watch an interesting movie, work, do jigsaw puzzles, cook, engage in a hobby, build something, balance a checkbook, play a game with children, organize a closet, clean the house, learn something new, play the piano, or volunteer at a school or homeless shelter. A dear friend always cleans her house when she is stressed to divert her focus and dissipate her stress. She has the cleanest house of anyone I know. Another friend diverts attention by running. A family member loses herself in a good book.

When I find myself plagued with stressful thoughts, I sit down and play the piano or the harp. It is very cathartic to release emotion through playing an instrument. Through the piano, I have been able to release sadness, stress, anger, frustration, and confusion. It is very hard to keep thinking stressful thoughts in my head when I am concentrating on reading the music, making my fingers find the right keys, having my foot use the pedals, and singing the tune in my head.

It is helpful to start making a list of the things that work for you. Not all of the activities in these suggestions will work for every person. When you need to divert your attention, you can readily go to one of the things on your personal list. Some of you already inherently know which things work or don't work for you to divert your focus. Many of you automatically engage in your diversion activity when stressed. This is good; keep doing that.

Breaking the repetitive thoughts breaks the physiological response. Just like the example of putting down the glass of water that you may need to pick up again later, diverting your attention gives your mind a break from the stressful thoughts that in turn gives your body a break from the constant, intense stress chemicals.

Do Something Physical

Another way to break the physiological response is to do something physical. The fight-or-flight chemicals prepare your body to run or fight off the stressor. So, by doing some physical activity, you are burning off and clearing some of the chemicals from your system. In essence, you are doing exactly what your body was preparing to do—physical activity. Do whatever physical activity you feel like doing: run, walk, dance, play basketball, ride a bike, play catch with your kids, clean the house, garden, ride a horse, organize the garage, roller blade, play fetch with your dog, or play jump rope. Anything physically active will help decrease the chemicals in your system. In addition, physical activity also helps to divert your mental focus while changing the physiological chemicals.

Even though your brain sends out stress chemicals when it perceives stress, your body can send messages back to your brain. This is a critical principle. Just as the body's stress response follows the mind's perception, your mind's response will follow your body's direction. That means that when you do something physical, you trick your mind into thinking you are no longer stressed and everything is safe.

Make Yourself Laugh

Another way to trick your body into thinking you are no longer stressed is to make yourself laugh. If making yourself laugh is way too difficult to do in the midst of your overwhelming level of stress, just make yourself smile. You have complete control over your smile muscles to force out a smile. Smiles and laughter trick your mind into changing your perception to something more positive, then the feel-good chemicals start to replace the stress chemicals.

This may not be easy to do at first. I was lucky enough to have a husband who was skilled at looking for the humor in even the most difficult situations. I recall many times when we were feeling overwhelming stress, and out of the blue, he would say something that caused me to laugh hysterically. When I laughed, then he laughed. Though the stressful event didn't go away, the laughter dissipated the stress chemicals to a point where we could think and function more clearly. In addition, the laughter helped reshape the perception of the event enough that I could begin to see there were other ways to look at it. And for the extremely difficult situations, the laughter was at least a wonderful reprieve. Laughter is a chance to put the stress glass down, even if just for a few moments.

TAKE TIME OUT TO BREATHE

When you are stressed, your breathing automatically becomes more rapid and shallow. Chronic stress breathing limits the movement of the diaphragm and does not allow the lower lobes of the lungs to fully oxygenate. Focusing on your breathing helps you begin to correct the stress breathing by helping you to breathe slower, breathe more deeply, expand your lungs fully, and get more oxygen to your brain and vital organs. Breathing exercises distract your thoughts, divert your attention, lessen stressful sensations, and trick your body into thinking that if you are breathing slower and deeper, the stress must be going away. Breathing exercises are easy to learn. Breathing exercises can be done whenever you want, wherever you want, with or without additional relaxation techniques. There are no expenses for special equipment, tools, or spa memberships. You do not need another person to assist you. In addition to those benefits, focusing on your breathing is the first step of many of the relaxation techniques we will discuss later, so this is a great technique to learn first.

There are several different types of breathing exercises, each has a different specific benefit. You can find a variety of different breathing exercises on the Internet. However, to get you started, let's try a basic, deep-breathing exercise that you can do wherever you are, without disrupting what you are doing. If you are in a stressful work meeting, you can take a few moments to focus on your breathing and help it to be slower and deeper. This is also a good exercise to do to help you fall asleep when stress is keeping you awake.

Begin by focusing on your breathing. Be aware of how rapid or shallow your breathing is. Try to slow your breathing down and take deeper breaths. This will be hard to do at first. Remember you have stress chemicals pouring into your system that are increasing your breathing rate. You are consciously trying to stop and reverse that process. By forcing yourself to take slow deep breaths, you begin to trick your body into thinking you are no longer stressed and pretty soon, your body will stop sending out the stress alerts.

In this exercise, your breathing goal will be to inhale to the count of five and exhale to the count of five. When you begin this exercise in your stressed state, you may be lucky to do a fast count of two for each inhalation, but keep focusing on your breathing and keep trying to take progressively slower and deeper breaths. It will likely take several minutes to get to your goal. Once you get to the five-count goal, continue this slow, deep breathing for several more minutes. When you feel that you are breathing comfortably with the slow, deep breaths, you can go about your daily activities. However, if you find that your stressful thoughts return and your breathing becomes rapid again, just return to your breathing exercise.

LEARN RELAXATION TECHNIQUES

Relaxation is critical to breaking the physiological response. Stress makes us tense. It prepares all of our muscles to fight and run. Learning how to relax once again tricks our body and then our brain into thinking that the stress is gone and we can go back to normal. At the beginning of the chapter, we saw on the top of the list of physical manifestations of chronic stress muscle tension and aches and pains. We need to break the process that causes that pain.

When our brain continues to send stress chemicals to our body to fight or run, it keeps our muscles, including our heart, in a tense status. After several hours or days of tensed muscles, as we learned in the teacher's analogy of holding a glass of water, our muscles begin to ache. They may even cramp or spasm. Ironically, soon the body's aches and pains send their own messages of threat to our brains, which increases our stress and therefore intensifies the pain.

Relaxation techniques help relax our muscles as well as provide peace of mind. While we are in the midst of intense stress, relaxation techniques can help you cope better as well as decrease the other stress related health problems, like heart disease, stroke, memory loss, and pain.

Relaxation, as part of a daily routine, can have many health benefits, such as slowing breathing rate and heart rate, lowering blood pressure, reducing stress hormones, improving quality of sleep, improving digestion, increasing blood flow, reducing muscle tension, reducing anger, improving mood, improving focus, and improving concentration.

There are many types of relaxation techniques from which to choose, including guided imagery, visualization, progressive muscle relaxation, mindfulness, meditation, biofeedback, autogenic, tai chi, aromatherapy, yoga, music therapy, hydrotherapy, art therapy, massage therapy, and many others. Most of these relaxation techniques can be done alone without any outside assistance. Other techniques require a practitioner to assist or guide you through the process. As you consider which ones to try or need help to learn how to do them, you can obtain guidance by contacting your doctor or other health professionals, such as massage therapists, hypnotherapists, psychotherapists, meditation practitioners, yoga instructors, etc. Detailed information and considerations regarding each of these relaxation techniques can easily be found on the Internet. I will provide a short summary of several of them so you can see if any of them resonate with you.

Please bear in mind that not all techniques work the same for each individual. You may not respond well to art therapy or aromatherapy, but you may feel total relaxation after a massage or thirty minutes of meditation. Others respond well to aromatherapy but cannot stand the idea of another person touching them during a massage, which would increase their stress rather than induce relaxation.

If you have specific health concerns, please contact your physician before trying any of these techniques. The relaxation exercises covered here are progressive muscle relaxation, guided imagery, visualization, mindfulness, and meditation. For each of these techniques, you should prepare as follows:

- Wear comfortable, loose-fitting clothing. Remove your shoes and any constricting apparel.

- Find a comfortable, quiet place to sit or lie down. A comfortable supportive chair, a recliner, a sofa or a bed all work well.

- Lights can be left on or dimmed.

- Close your eyes and begin to let your body go limp.

- Begin with a breathing exercise of your choice.

Relaxation Exercises

The review of these techniques is intended to be an informative summary but not instructional. That means that there are a variety of different ways that each of these activities can be performed. In addition, you should do further research on whatever topics interests you to make sure there are no contraindications that may be specific to you and your unique health issues.

Progressive Muscle Relaxation

This relaxation exercise is one of the most commonly used exercises to induce muscle relaxation. This exercise helps you learn to distinguish between muscle tension and relaxed muscles. The goal in this exercise is to tightly tense separate muscles or muscle groups and then fully relax the tensed muscles. Tense your muscle for about five seconds and then relax that same muscle for fifteen to thirty seconds before moving to the next muscle or muscle group.

Some methods focus on muscle groups (legs, arms, torso, head/neck, etc.) while other methods try to isolate smaller groups of muscles (toes, foot, ankle, lower leg, knee, upper leg, buttocks, etc.). At the beginning, it will be hard to isolate muscles without tensing surrounding muscles as well, but with practice isolating muscle groups gets easier. Some methods start at the toes and work up while others start at the head and work down. Remember to continue your breathing exercises while you progressively relax your muscles.

For some people, it might be helpful to have someone guide you through the steps, at least at first. There are apps available that you can download to your phone or you can locate a script that you like and record your own. When I talk people through this exercise, I prefer to start at the head and work down. I suggest that as the participants relax each muscle; they should try to visualize the relaxing muscle as melting its stress away. When the muscle relaxes, the stress melts and slowly starts flowing down to the ground, where it will dissolve into the earth.

When you have become familiar with the tense-and-relax process and have practiced it many times, you can try a quicker version. Your muscles have been learning what it feels like to tense and relax so you can go through the process more quickly. In the shortened version, you can tense and relax larger groups of muscles at the same time, for example: head/neck, arms/shoulders, chest/back/abdomen, and lower limbs.

It is also helpful in this relaxation exercise to think of a word or phrase that you repeat to yourself each time you relax and exhale (such as peace, light, relax, melt, calm, or let go). The great part about using a word or phrase is that your muscles begin to associate the word with a relaxed muscle. As you become more practiced in this technique, you can just say the word to yourself and your body will begin to relax. When you become a real pro, you can delete the tense part and just tell your muscle groups to relax.

Visualization

The goal of this exercise is to help your brain learn to create mental images that are peaceful, relaxing, and calming rather than dwelling on the disturbing, stressful images that flood your brain. As you become more skilled at visualization, it allows you to stay focused on whatever image you create and not let stressful thoughts take center stage.

Visualization engages the right hemisphere of the brain to help you see clear mental images. This exercise will train your brain to focus on images that you create for yourself rather than being at the mercy of the images that pop into your brain uninvited. You can create images of peace, serenity, calmness, happiness, and whatever else calms you or motivates you. Perhaps you will choose to create images of places that bring you peace and happiness, like a beach, a mountain retreat, a quiet sailboat on a lake, watching a river in the mountains, or a beautiful sunset. By creating these images in your mind, you can switch the images in your brain when you feel stressed, frightened, frustrated, or chaotic to images of peace and tranquility.

As you try to learn the skill of visualization, it will help to start with the breathing exercise, then the progressive muscle relaxation exercise so you will be in a calm, relaxed state. Then begin learning visualization, try to imagine something simple and familiar to you; geometric shapes, your pet, an apple, a fence, a car, your favorite trinket or the sweet innocent face of a new baby or someone that makes you feel loved. Try to visualize the shape of the object, visualize all the sides, and observe the texture, the detail, the indentations, the curves, the color, and all of the tiny details.

As you continue to visualize your selected object, add in your other senses. Does your object have a taste that you can bring to your mind? What does the object or the environment smell like? Is there a texture that you can feel? Are there sounds that are associated with your object? The more senses you can involve in your visualization, the more you can distract your thoughts from stressful memories and images.

This exercise takes practice. It is likely that as you are learning this technique your mind will wander at some point. The more you practice, the longer you can stay with the visualization without having distracting, unwanted thoughts intrude. Like the muscle relaxation exercise, after practicing this technique for a while, you can quickly transport your brain to a favorite visualization place for a while until the stressful thoughts cease.

Meditation

In Psalms 46:10 and D&C 101:16, the Lord counsels us to "be still and know that I am God." Learning the practice of meditation is a very effective way to "be still." Meditation is one of the most effective ways to learn to decrease stress and quiet your mind from all the turmoil and chaos that seems to swirl around us. Meditation is another exercise that can be done anytime, anywhere, if you have a few minutes of undisturbed privacy and quiet.

The word meditation has many different meanings and contexts. It is the process of contemplating, thinking, reflecting, and pondering. The goal of meditation is to overcome negative thoughts and cultivate positive, peaceful, constructive thoughts.

In meditation exercises, you learn to train your mind to recognize thoughts without dwelling on them, or worse—incorporating them into your whole being. We talked extensively about our thoughts in chapter six. In meditation, you learn to focus on one word, mantra, phrase, etc. When other thoughts invade your mind, you learn to just see the thoughts, acknowledge them, and dismiss them.

When our mind learns to be calm and peaceful, we become free of unnecessary worries, stresses, and mental confusion. When our mind is not calm and peaceful, it becomes a playground for all sorts of negative, stressful, agitating, and frustrating thoughts.

It is important to note that neuroscientists tell us that mediation actually reshapes our brain as we continue to practice it. So far, 163 different studies suggest that mindfulness meditation has an overall positive effect on anxiety and stress. Our brain reshapes to activate the restful part of our brain/nervous system, which helps decrease our stress.

The practice of meditation can be summed up in a few sentences. However, as simple as it is to explain, it can be a challenge to learn. Your mind is not used to this process, especially for those who find themselves in constant anxiety and stress. To become proficient at meditation, you may want to consider attending a meditation class, finding a meditation app, downloading a guided meditation recording, or purchasing an audio recording to walk you through the process.

The simple instructions are as follows:

- Follow the process for preparing for relaxation on page 114.

- Begin with a breathing exercise.

- Proceed through your preferred muscle relaxation exercise.

- Concentrate your focus on a single point: staring at a candle flame; listening to a rhythmic gong, drum, or bell; or repeating to yourself a word, a phrase, or a mantra. You may find it helpful to repeat your chosen word, phrase, or mantra on each inhalation or exhalation of your breath.

- Each time you notice your mind starting to wander or intrusive thoughts coming in, just bring your focus back to your chosen focal point and simply let go of the invasive thoughts.

Mindfulness

Mindfulness is defined as the basic human ability to be fully present and aware of where we are and what we're doing rather than being overly reactive or overwhelmed by what's going on around us or what might happen in the future. The more we learn to live life mindfully, the less stress we absorb.

As a relaxation technique in stress management, mindfulness means achieving a mental state of focusing one's awareness on the present moment, while calmly acknowledging and accepting one's feelings, thoughts, and bodily sensations.

You can practice mindful meditation by following the steps for meditation (page 117). In mindful meditation, you learn to observe your wandering thoughts as they drift through your mind. The goal is to not get involved with the thoughts and not make judgments about the thoughts, but just make a mental note that the thought came in.

As you watch your thoughts as they wander in, you will start to notice some patterns in your thoughts, feelings, and judgments. By building an awareness of thought patterns, you start to notice how some of your negative, distorted thought patterns came to be. As you continue to practice mindful meditation, you will develop some balance for those thought distortions.

SUMMARY

Breaking the physiological response to chronic stress is a critical step in trying to survive in a world of ever-increasing stress. Remember we learned in chapter one, as we get deeper and farther into the last days, our stress levels will probably continue to increase. Learning and practicing these skills every day will be the determining factor between remaining sane and healthy or succumbing to the physical, mental, emotional, and social damage of chronic stress. It does us no good at all to know what the exercises and techniques are if we don't make them part of our normal practice when stress starts to climb.

The goal of these techniques is to break the physiological stress response when it does not spontaneously resolve itself. In addition, these techniques, when practiced daily, can help prevent stress from developing to a point that stress feels pervasive and overwhelming. We can look at these techniques as a way to give ourselves a break from the muscle tension and pain that develops because of the stress.

CHAPTER 7

Coping Techniques

We would be hard pressed to walk through a check-out counter in the grocery store without seeing a magazine with a blazing headline on "Ways to Cope with your Stress." The lists of how to manage stress or cope with stress or survive the stressful holidays or deal with the post-election feelings of stress are everywhere. These lists are readily available with just one simple click on the Internet.

We have already discussed what we can do to prevent the preventable stressful events, (chapter four), change our perceptions, which will dramatically reduce our stress (chapter five), and break the physiological response to stress (chapter six) so that our bodies can return to a normal functioning state. Working on the techniques in those three chapters will do a great deal to reduce or minimize the bulk of our avoidable and preventable stress.

However, recall from chapters one and two that we have stress in our lives by design. Stress teaches us, refines us, humbles us, and helps us to progress and grow. We will never be stress free while we live on this planet. There will definitely still be stress that we cannot prevent, we cannot quickly solve, we cannot change by changing our perceptions, and from which we cannot get our bodies to relax.

The majority of wise suggestions on the vast number of lists of coping strategies have already been addressed in previous chapters or will be covered in chapters eight and nine. This chapter is merely a quick and easy list of options for those who have skipped the other chapters or for those who just need a quick suggestion on how to cope right now.

Many of the items on this list come straight from the other chapters, while other suggestions are merely distractions that potentially give you a momentary break from your stress. Pick and choose whichever suggestion you think will help you most at the time. At the end of this list of suggestions is another list of things not to do to cope with stress. That list identifies things that people frequently do in response to stress that are harmful or will complicate your ability to handle stress productively.

Positive

- Breathe—focus on taking long, slow, deep breaths.

- Pray.

- Focus on solutions, not problems. Some cultures say they do not believe in problems because problems do not have solutions. Instead, they refer to them as situations because situations can be solved.

- Focus on good times—thinking positive thoughts may help you to see a situation in a better light.

- Surround yourself with uplifting, positive people. Avoid negative, cynical people—if people are complaining, don't join in.

- Think things through and make a plan before you start doing something.

- Count to ten slowly to help you calm down—or count to twenty-five or to fifty, if it takes that long.

- Think of the good in the world. Don't let yourself believe the world is against you—chances are you'll have good times ahead, even if you are going through a rough time now.

- Address the stressful situation a little bit at a time.

- "Many things which cannot be overcome when they are together, yield themselves up when taken little by little."— Plutarch

- Laugh, or just force yourself to smile.

- Listen to children laugh.

- Mentally wrap up bad feelings (anger, self-doubt, desire to get even, resentment, bitterness, jealousy, etc.), and choose to throw those feelings into the trash.

- Make goals achievable—don't set completely unrealistic goals for yourself that may lead to frustration, disappointment, or feelings of failure.

- Learn from your pet: Live in the moment. Take a nap. Be grateful for getting small treats. Enjoy the outdoors. Go on a long walk. Greet visitors with joy.

- Volunteer—service helps put your stress in perspective. There are lists of where volunteers are needed in the community (sometimes posted in the newspaper), or you can ask people for options in your church, school, hospital, sports, etc.

- Get constant distractions off your back. Turn off unnecessary alarms, ringers, and alerts. Let voice mail take care of any messages. Set specific, planned times to check email, instant messaging and, other media and stick to it.

- Take a technology break—at least short amounts of time every day. Consider taking longer technology breaks for even a week or an entire month.

- Take short, frequent breaks. Go get a drink, take a walk, or stand up and stretch.

- Eat a healthy meal.

- Shake or dance—exercise releases endorphins. We can't always go out and exercise, but you can stand up, shake your muscles and joints, and do a little joyful dancing movement.

- Sleep—take a nap or go to bed for a long night's sleep. Sleeping may be the best option, especially if you are sleep deprived or physical/emotionally exhausted.

- Meditate.

- Read scriptures.

- Practice some relaxation techniques.

- Be active. Do something that makes you get up and move.

- Quit comparing yourself to others. They don't have a stress-free life either.

- Review your priorities. Make sure you are giving the most time and energy to the things you value most.

- Talk to a friend, a confident, or a clergy member.

- Set boundaries. Boundaries are different than walls. Boundaries are the guidelines for what you will or will not accept from yourself or others. Walls shut people out. Boundaries just provide a safe place.

- Focus on gratitude.

- Be realistic. The world is not going to give you perfection 100 percent of the time.

- Take a break from the things that are causing you stress: work, children, spouse, the news proclaiming the problems in the world, etc.

- Write in a stress journal. What is causing you stress? Why? How do you feel? How did you respond? You can rip out the page, burn it, or ignore it. Let the paper worry about it for a while.

- Practice the four A's: **A**void unnecessary stress, **A**lter the situation, **A**dapt to the stressor, and **A**ccept the things you can't change.

- Simplify your life.

- Clean and organize your environment.

- Forgive.

- Get some fresh air.

- Take a hot bath.

- Look for the positive.

- Look for an acceptable compromise.

- Listen to your favorite playlist.

- Take the dog for a walk.

- Balance your schedule with time for work, play, family, solitude, and social activities.

- Get out of your head. Stop the negative thoughts (see chapter five).

- Build something.

- Go on a picnic.

- Look at the big picture. Will today's problem matter in a month?

- Do something with your hands: knit, crochet, saw, hammer, build, cook, clean, put together Legos, plant a garden, pull weeds, etc.

- Connect with your spiritual power.

- Take control of your time management.

- Learn to say, "No."

- Visualize calmness.

- Learn a new language to help distract yourself. Then make yourself tell yourself the story of what happened in the new language.

- Recall previous stressful situations that you solved and learned from.

- Unclutter your home.

- Ask for help.

- Plant a tree, a garden, a rose bush, or favorite plant.

- Feed the birds.

- Go to the zoo and make faces at the animals.

- Lay on the grass looking at the clouds, trees, or stars and find faces, animals, or objects in the configurations.

- Give a hug. Ask for a hug.

- Play fetch with a dog.

- Learn origami and fold paper into shapes that give you hope.

- Fly a kite with little children.

- Read a joke book.

- Go fishing.

- Blow bubbles in the back yard, and watch the children and dog chase the bubbles.

- Write in a journal. Writing is very cathartic.

- Reframe the problem. Try to think of a positive way to look at it.

- Find an exercise partner to add some social interaction to your exercise.

- Have a child teach you their favorite game.

- Call up an old friend that you haven't seen for a while and invite them to lunch.

- Write a letter.

- Check out the community class schedules and register for a fun class.

- Get a massage.

- Curl up and read your favorite book.

- Watch your favorite comedy movie or television show.

- Learn to play a new song on the piano or violin.

- Plan a menu for the week of healthy, well-balanced meals.

- Keep a positive attitude.

- Accept that you cannot control everything.

- Find ways to give back to your family, church, or community.

- Make a list of your top fifty blessings.

- Organize the junk drawer.

- Tie a quilt for a child who is sick or has a disability.

- Collect colorful rocks or collect plain rocks that you can paint.

- Learn a positive, upbeat song that you can hum in your head when you are tense.

- Make a friendship bracelet for someone who needs a friend.

- Go swimming.

- Make a short list of what things you will repent of and be grateful for the gift of the atonement.

- Make a new friend.

- Play in the rain and stomp in the puddles.

- Visit an elderly relative, take them to dinner, or to pick up their medications.

- Try a new aromatherapy scent to see if it works for you.

- Read the words of a soothing hymn.

- Go horseback riding.

- Take a bike ride.

- Relax in a hot tub.

- Record yourself reading a children's story that you can give to your children, grandchildren, nieces, nephews, or children at a children's hospital.

- Listen to sounds of nature: rain, waterfall, birds, animals, waves, the breeze through the trees, etc.

- Go to the temple.

- Focus on peace and hold on to it.

Do Not

- Take drugs or alcohol, caffeine, or nicotine. They may make you feel better for a short time, but in the long term they create additional problems and increase your stress.

- Take your stress out on others. It just heightens everyone's stress.

- Sleep constantly. That leads to depression.

- Isolate yourself from friends and family.

- Procrastinate.

- Indulge in addictive behaviors: gambling, shopping, pornography, video games, etc.

- Dwell on the negative.

- Drown yourself in food or eat away your sorrows.

- Numb yourself staring at a television, mobile phone, or computer screen for hours on end.

- Keep yourself so busy that you avoid solving the problem.

- Ignore the problem.

- Yell and scream at someone.

- Consider ending your life. That doesn't allow you the opportunity to solve any other problems or enjoy any other success.

- Get violent.

- Curl up in a little ball and become inactive.

- Complain constantly.

- Eat only junk food.

- Become abusive to children.

- Experiment with new drugs to see if they will numb the pain.

- Make big life-changing decisions in the depths of stress or depression.

- Hang out with negative, violent, abusive, or destructive people.

- Go on a spending spree to make yourself feel better.

- Break commandments.

- Blame God.

- Turn away from your faith.

Most importantly, remember that our job is to learn, grow, progress, and become stronger from the stress that is in our lives. We cannot accomplish the growth and humility that stress was created to develop in us if we are busy trying to cover up our stress with behaviors and attitudes that make it worse.

CHAPTER 8

Stop Creating
Your Own Stress

Recently, a very dear friend of mine, Jed Lyman, who also happened to be my bishop, was speaking to our sweet primary children. He told about his son's growing interest in nutrition. He said this young son was reading all the labels on food to check its nutritional value or lack thereof and using that information to make decisions about what he eats and what he shuns. It is incredible that this young man is paying such strict attention to taking care of his body and striving to nourish his body with nutrient-rich foods while avoiding the not-so-nutritious, harmful junk food. Then, in Jed's great wisdom, he said, "More importantly, I wish we could all look at the nutrition content labels of our activities." Such great wisdom in a single statement!

There are activities—like nutritious foods—that strengthen our character, build our stress capacity and enrich our souls. There are other activities—like some junk food—that have no stress-building capacity value at all, they just fill our time, like the junk food fills our stomach. There are even some activities, like some poisonous mushrooms, that are toxic and put us in great peril. These activities are the activities that damage our character, create stress rather than help us deal with stress, and lead us away from our eternal destination. Each activity we choose impacts our life. Each activity we choose impacts our stress level, our ability to manage stress, and our stress capacity.

Unfortunately, activities do not come with a nutrition label telling us how much stress-nutrition value they have or don't have, how good they are for us, or how dangerous and toxic they might be. However, in this chapter, we will look at a variety of traits, beliefs, attitudes, and emotions as they relate to stress. There is a wide variety of these activities that impact stress in some way. Some things decrease our stress capacity, some increase our stress capacity.

Perhaps you have heard the old phrase, "Accentuate the positive; eliminate the negative." This chapter is the one on eliminating the negative, including traits, behaviors, emotions, activities, and attitudes that tend to either create some of your own stress or at least make the normal stress worse. Some of these situations can't be avoided completely (grief, loneliness, financial debt, being overwhelmed, etc.). However, as we understand how these things can increase our stress or decrease our ability to deal with stress, it will help us decrease the behaviors that may create our own stress or makes our stress worse.

Addictions

There is no question that the warning in D&C 89:4 is being manifest: "In consequence of evils and designs which do and will exist in the hearts of conspiring men in the last days, I have warned you, and forewarn you, by giving unto you this word of wisdom by revelation." Addictions innocently begin when the challenges of the world cause you to look for something to help you get through. It seems fairly benign to take a drink of alcohol, smoke a cigarette, take drugs, go shopping, take a pill, set up your own chair in a gambling establishment, look at pornography, play a video game, or curl up in a little ball and watch television for three days straight to help you feel better or numb your pain. When the behavior helps, even a little bit, to allay your stress or pain, you may quickly turn to it again the next time you are feeling tense or sad. Most addictions start for those very reasons— the substance or behavior provides a way to escape or numb or cope with our stress and pain. Addictions are behaviors that you originally chose to do until you no longer have the ability to choose not to.

Unfortunately, addictions change the chemistry of the brain and in many cases, make it difficult or impossible to break the addiction without help. Samuel Johnson provided this wise caution: "The chains of habit are too weak to be felt until they are too strong to be broken."

Once habits become addictions, they are hard to break and very often require counseling or some type of intervention from professionals. Addictions drain your stress capacity and may also drain your bank account, damage relationships, and cause legal problems, which all increase stress. Avoid starting any behavior that could turn into an addiction. If you are already addicted to something, work to break the addiction as quickly as possible.

ANGER AND HOSTILITY

Ephesians 4:31 states, "Let all bitterness and wrath, and anger and clamour, and evil speaking, be put away from you." We are warned frequently in the scriptures to avoid anger and hostility. There must be great value in that counsel for the Lord to repeat it so many times and in so many ways. Anger and hostility are corrosive emotions. Anger is a strong feeling of annoyance, displeasure, rage, exasperation, irritability, indignation, fury, wrath, ire, or outrage. Anger is usually directed at a specific person in a specific situation. Hostility, on the other hand, incorporates the same feelings as anger but appears to be more like anger on steroids. Hostility is a constant, underlying feeling of ill will, unfriendliness, opposition, antagonism, malice, venom, hatred, loathing, resentment, and belligerence that explodes into emotionally charged aggressive behavior. Since hostility is an underlying, fairly constant feeling, it may erupt at any time, at any place, and at any person who just happens to trigger the explosion. Anger and hostility can lead to severe problems: at work, in relationships, and in the quality of your life. Uncontrolled anger and hostility can take a destructive toll on your health and your relationships. No one likes to be the recipient of another person's anger or hostility. If you have anger issues, get help and counsel from an anger management program. Work at finding the cause of your anger or hostility so that you can heal your soul and develop more positive attitudes.

DEBT

It is no surprise that financial challenges and debt are major causes of constant stress. Debt lingers for a very long time and causes a deep, underlying stress level. Financial challenges, financial priorities, and debt are also identified as one of the three leading causes for divorce. We have to pay for everything that we need in life: shelter, food, water, medical care, cars, beds, education, phones, etc. Our paychecks are never large enough, and our needs and wants seem never-ending.

We have certainly received a great deal of very clear, straight-forward counsel to avoid debt. And yet, we continue to get buried deeper and deeper in financial bondage. Some are victims of circumstances that financially alter their lives, like an unexpected loss of a job during a pandemic, a major medical complication that limits one's ability to work and leads to staggering medical bills, or even legal hassles brought on by predators trying to make money by suing whomever they can. Others slip into financial disaster because they are involved in uncontrolled spending, whether it be from constant shopping, purchasing everything they want, a need for constant travel and entertainment, or worse, from gambling, drugs, or other addictive behaviors.

Learning to be financially wise can help you avoid this stress trap. You are the driver of your financial situation, barring unexpected catastrophes. There are plenty of books, classes, financial consultants, and online resources to help you figure out the best budgeting practices that will work for you and your family. A budget should include necessary household expenses, as well as savings, tithes and offerings, savings for maintenance on homes and cars, and everything else. The "everything else" gets limited by the amount of income you bring in. The limit does not get moved for situations like, "But I deserve this vacation," or "I want it so I will just charge it." The counsel is clear. Avoid debt.

The reward for using financial wisdom is freedom from the stress of constant financial challenges and the burden of debt.

ENTITLEMENT

In recent years, the word entitlement has undergone a shift in its meaning/focus. Entitlement has become the belief that one is inherently deserving of privileges or special treatment and that privileges are no longer privileges, but instead they have become rights. A "sense of entitlement complex" means that a person arrogantly believes he deserves certain privileges. This belief is often linked with self-centeredness, narcissism, and borderline personality disorder. A sense of entitlement is often the result of failure to learn as a child that you are not the center of the universe and other people do not exist to serve your needs and wants. I recall one day when a mother called her twelve-year-old son over to see me. I had not seen him in several years. When he arrived, while looking at me she asked him, "Is there someone special over here?" He looked around and replied confidently, "Me!" Then as a bit of an embarrassed afterthought, Mom asked, "And is there anyone else over here that is special?" The young man looked around and without any hesitation said, "No, just me!" Not even his own mother was considered special to him.

The term culture of entitlement suggests that many people now have highly unreasonable expectations about what they are entitled to. Recently, I read the results of a survey where high school seniors and young adult ages eighteen to twenty-five were asked what, if anything, they thought they should be entitled to receive for free. The number one answer, selected by the majority of respondents, was a free college education provided by the government (aka the taxpayers), and in second place, a down payment on their first home—also provided by the government (the taxpayers). Other things chosen from the list included guaranteed job and salary, a thirty-hour work week with higher wages, free health care, interest-free loans for cars and homes, basic food needs, no income tax, no property tax, guaranteed income if they didn't work, a laptop, and a get out of jail free card for first offenses. That is entitlement.

Reading this survey reminded me of a conference talk given by Elder Dale G. Renlund. He referenced a comment made by Elder Wilford W. Andersen of the Seventy regarding helping saints who live in poverty. Elder Andersen said, "The greater the distance between the giver and the receiver, the more the receiver develops a sense of entitlement."[37] Is it any wonder that so many young adults felt like the distant "government" should provide them with so many privileges for free? Many of them had never been employed and of those who had been employed, most didn't make enough money to have to pay taxes. As a matter of fact, many had been the recipients of "earned income

---

37. Dale G. Renlund, "That I Might Draw All Men unto Me," *Ensign*, May 2016.

credit," so they ended up getting money they had not paid into the system. Obviously, not all young adults ages eighteen to twenty-five fit into the entitlement generation criteria. Many young adults are extremely dedicated to working hard and being very productive members of society, looking for ways to make their community and the world a much better place.

We all want things we can't afford. But some people feel they are entitled to whatever it is they want, and they deserve it all now at someone else's expense. How stressful is it to have so many unmet expectations? Entitlement can cause severe relationship problems, challenges in employment, a lot of disappointment, and extensive amounts of stress. Oddly, the attitude shows up from two different angles. Some people believe that they are better than everyone else and therefore they deserve special treatment. Others believe their life is worse than everyone else and therefore they deserve special treatment. Different roads that lead to the same entitlement. Having an attitude/belief that you are entitled to get things you have not earned can cause a great deal of stress throughout your life. Caution: This does not mean that we should not help those who are in need. The scriptures clearly tell us that we need to help the widows, fatherless, hungry, homeless, etc. The differences here are between want versus need and earned versus entitled to have at someone else's expense.

GRIEF

Grief is the complex negative mental, emotional, social, and physical effects that accompany loss, any loss. Many people believe that grief comes only from the loss of a loved one. This is not true. Symptoms of grief can occur in varying degrees for any loss. There are different intensities of grief, just as there are different intensities of loss and different intensities of stress. Grief is one of the most intense forms of stress. Remember stress comes as a reaction to fear, danger, or threat. So, grief comes when the fear of loss is being realized. When that happens, stress gets pushed to its extreme. And stress at its extreme means that the plethora of symptoms is also extreme.

First and foremost, most grief cannot be avoided. Grief can strike unexpectedly, without any warning, at any time; therefore, it is generally not preventable.

Grief is a multifaceted, natural response to losing someone or something that is important to you. Because grief is multifaceted, so is the stress that comes with grief. The symptoms show up physically, mentally, emotionally, socially, and spiritually. Each area has a multitude of symptoms. Since it can totally overwhelm us, most of our normal coping techniques are not as effective. However, it is critical to know that grief, like other stresses, can be coped with, worked through, and will subside over time. There are many resources, books, support groups, and professionals who can help you work through grief.

Jealousy, Covetousness, and Envy

"For the love of money is the root of all evil: which while some coveted after, they have erred from the faith, and pierced themselves through with many sorrows" (1 Tim. 6:10). Let's begin this discussion on jealousy, covetousness, and envy by defining what these words mean. Since their meanings are similar, we often use them interchangeably, but let's look at how they differ.

Jealousy is a feeling of unhappiness, uneasiness, anger, or resentment against someone because that person is a rival. Jealousy is mental anger or uneasiness from suspicion, belief, or fear of rivalry directed at someone or something you love and includes fear or suspicion of unfaithfulness from someone you love. Jealousy is the fear of losing something that you feel already belongs to you.

Envy and covet have meanings that are so similar that many definitions are exactly the same. These words are even listed as synonyms for each other. It is a feeling of wanting what someone else has, such as success, advantages, wealth, a job, or a spouse that you think you should have and the other person should not have. A slight difference in definitions suggested by some authors is that envy is the desire to have something that is not yours and you begrudge the person who actually possesses it. Covetousness is the desire to have something that is not yours, and it either lies outside your ability to get or is unattainable because it belongs to someone else. The main difference between envy/covetousness and jealousy is that envy/covetousness is an emotion of wanting what someone else has and resentment that the other person has it and you don't, while jealousy is the emotion of fear,

141

anger, or resentment that someone else is trying to take away from you what you already have.

Even though envy/covetousness and jealousy have different meanings, they all make you feel bad, sad, angry, resentful, fearful, inadequate, and stressed.

All of these words describe specific emotions of want or fear of loss of something. All of these emotions are dangerous because they include feelings of resentment, fearfulness, and anger. Yes, those emotions are all emotions that increase our stress. Remember, the emotion of fear is part of the definition of stress.

These emotions can be exacerbated by use of social media. People tend to post either the very best or the worst of their lives on social media. When we see pictures of all the trips people take, their new cars, the remodel of their kitchens and how many likes they get when they post a selfie, it is easy to become envious of what others have. Most people don't even recognize the feelings emerging in their emotions until the feelings become overwhelming.

Unfortunately, these feelings damage or destroy relationships, alter our priorities, change our focus from gratitude to greed, and shift our behaviors from love and service to self-indulgence and selfishness. Joseph B. Wirthlin cautioned us against having these emotions when he said, "Beware of covetousness. It is one of the great afflictions of these latter days. It creates greed and resentment. Often it leads to bondage, heartbreak, and crushing, grinding debt."[38] So true! These emotions do not lead to the best in us but rather lead us to more stress.

President Gordon B. Hinckley also gave very strong counsel regarding these emotions: "I wish to discuss a trap that can destroy any of us in our search for joy and happiness. It is that devious, sinister, evil influence that says, 'What I have is not enough. I must have more.' I have observed that there are many in our present generation who with careful design set out on a course to get rich while still young, to drive fancy automobiles, to wear the best of clothing, to have an apartment in the city and a house in the country—all of these, and more. This is the total end for which they live, and for some the means by which they get there is unimportant in terms of ethics

---

38. Joseph B. Wirthlin, "Earthly Debts, Heavenly Debts," *Ensign*, May 2004.

and morality. They covet that which others have, and selfishness and even greed are all a part of their process of acquisitiveness... Let not covetousness destroy our happiness. Let not greed for that which we do not need and cannot get with honesty and integrity bring us down to ruin and despair."[39]

There is no question that there are times when emotions of jealousy or covetousness sneak up on us. There will be times when someone else gets the very thing you wanted. There will be occasions when others get recognition, praise, jobs, winning lottery numbers, or great bonuses that you would love to have, or maybe even things that you really need to have. But please do not give in to feelings of envy, covetousness, or jealousy. In spite of needing some of the "advantages," we are not diminished when someone else receives them. We are only diminished when we let feelings of envy, covetousness, and jealousy run away with us. Once we recognize that we are feeling these emotions, we need to shift our focus to Christlike emotions of love, service, selflessness, and gratitude for what we already have.

JUDGMENT AND CRITICISM

"Judge not that ye be not judged" (Matt. 7:1). We have heard since we were young children that we shouldn't judge other people. And we were also taught to stay away from strangers, avoid people whose behavior was questionable, and not hang out with "the wrong kind of friends." How confusing. Indeed, we do have to make some judgments in life for our own safety. Given that we know that some judgments are necessary, let's focus on the judgments that are really just criticisms. We can find the criteria for that type of judgment in the scriptures: "For with what judgment ye judge, ye shall be judged: and with what measure ye mete, it shall be measured to you again. And why beholdest thou the mote that is in thy brother's eye, but considerest not the beam that is in thine own eye? Or how wilt thou say to thy brother, let me pull out the mote out of thine eye; and, behold, a beam is in thine own eye? Thou hypocrite, first cast out the beam out of thine own eye; and then shalt thou see clearly to cast out the mote

---

39. Gordon B. Hinckley, "Thou Shalt Not Covet," *Ensign*, March 1990.

out of thy brother's eye" (Matt. 7:2-5). This scripture counsels us that we need to be cautious about judging other people with a yardstick that we do not apply to ourselves.

In these latter days, our judgments have become more public, powerful, and harsh. Just take a short look at the comments on one of the many controversial issues on Facebook. I am appalled at how harsh peoples' judgments are. I am shocked at how many people feel entitled to tell other people how "stupid" they are (and that is the kindest word they use) just because they disagree. I am disgusted by the language that is used to verbally beat each other up because they have differing opinions and views in life. And I am completely disgusted at comments that say "go kill yourself" just because someone else doesn't like what you said.

If we continue reading the scriptures, we find additional clarity on what it means to judge. In John 7:24 we are taught to "judge not according to the appearance, but judge righteous judgment." We do need to make some judgments throughout life. We do need to judge others in regards to our safety in order to protect our family, our homes, and ourselves. We do need to judge if others are a major negative influence in our lives. We need to judge if our children are surrounded by friends who are pulling them into bad habits and attitudes.

So, what does judgment and criticism have to do with stress? It depends on which side of the judgment and criticism you are on. If you are the person being judged and criticized, your stress level is going to be overwhelming. You may constantly feel threatened, fearful, and in danger, never knowing when, where, or how the next attack will occur. Aggressive criticisms and judgments are called bullying. We have huge problems with bullying in our schools and on social media. This is not only a very scary social problem but a scary indicator of the character of the many people who indulge in this behavior. Many of our kids, and even many adults, are dealing with anxiety, depression, and suicidal thoughts because of the bullying that is rampant in schools, workplaces, and through social media. Being the target of judgments, criticism, and bullying is highly stressful. If you are being bullied, tell someone about it, even the police if need be, and then get professional help to deal with your feelings.

What about the other side of this judgment exchange? Is there stress in being the person who is judging, criticizing, or bullying? The answer is still yes, but not in the same way and certainly not even close to the same intensity. The person doing the judging, criticizing, and bullying often doesn't realize that they are creating their own stress. They believe their stress is caused by all the "idiots" whom they feel compelled to judge. They wouldn't have to spend so much time on the Internet challenging and correcting people if there weren't so many people who viewed life differently. I am reminded of a plaque that I have seen many times, "Don't judge me because I sin differently than you." Wouldn't it be great if everyone understood that principle and tried hard to be kinder?

The truth is that engaging in constant judgments and criticisms changes the focus of the brain to be negative and see only the negative in other people. This focus increases stress for everyone involved. Being judgmental and critical does not solve anything. It doesn't make people be more like you. It doesn't change anyone's opinions about controversial issues. It doesn't make you look better or smarter or "right." Instead, it creates dissention, conflict, anger, hatred, animosity, and war. It creates stress. President Ronald Reagan once said, "I've always believed that a lot of the trouble in the world would disappear if we were talking to each other instead of about each other." How true! I would add my plea to his and to the many I have seen on social media: "Can't we all just try to get along and quit criticizing each other?"

Ram Dass gave a good analogy that helps us understand judgments: "When you go out into the woods and you look at trees, you see all these different trees. And some of them are bent, and some of them are straight, and some of them are evergreens, and some of them are whatever. And you look at the tree and you allow it. You see why it is the way it is. You sort of understand that it didn't get enough light, and so it turned that way. And you don't get all emotional about it. You just allow it. You appreciate the tree. The minute you get near humans, you lose all that. And you are constantly saying 'You're too this, or I'm too this.' That judging mind comes in. And so, I practice turning people into trees. Which means appreciating them just the way they are."

When we look upon others, their appearance, or their behavior with a filter of negativity, criticism, or judgment, we will definitely find what we are looking for. If we look upon others, their appearance, or their behavior with a filter of love and acceptance, we will not only avoid a great deal of stress but we will build powerful Christlike relationships. At the end of the day, you need to honestly ask yourself what energy you bring to the world. Are you judgmental or accepting? Are your words poisonous or uplifting? Do you work toward peace or do you increase divisiveness? Are you the solution or the problem?

LONELINESS

Like grief, loneliness is a very intense form of stress. Loneliness is one of the most common types of stress people feel, without knowing that loneliness is causing their stress. One of the biggest challenges during the COVID-19 pandemic was people learning to deal with the loneliness that social distancing and shelter-in-place orders created. Loneliness strikes regardless of gender, income, ethnicity, or education. Loneliness is not the same as being alone. Being alone is a state of living or being by oneself. Loneliness is a feeling of unwanted isolation. You can feel lonely while in the midst of a group of people, in a marriage or in family, if you are not satisfied with the sense of connection you get from those people. On the other hand, you could be physically alone most of the time and not feel lonely if you get fulfillment from the relationships in your life.

Loneliness is caused by feeling disconnected from other people, feeling misunderstood, useless, unloved, or that you are different or defective in some way. Loneliness commonly accompanies grief. When you lose a loved one, you intensely miss the person that you loved. Feelings of loneliness are worse when the lonely person has low self-esteem or if they are surrounded by people who don't seem to be lonely. Feeling isolated is the most generic form of stress and one of the most intense as well. Even Mother Teresa commented on loneliness, saying, "The most terrible poverty is loneliness and the feeling of being unloved."

Loneliness, like other forms of intense stress, is a big risk factor for health problems and premature death. Loneliness is comparable to obesity, a sedentary lifestyle, and even smoking as a risk factor for chronic disease and death. It is linked to unhealthy behavior, major depression, and diminished immune function. When exposed to pathogens like bacteria and viruses, those who are lonely are more likely to get sick. Effects of loneliness can also increase the risks of developing cancer. Louise Bernikow cautions us by saying, "Loneliness can, indeed make you sick. Heart disease and hypertension are now generally thought of as loneliness diseases... Most addictions are also considered loneliness diseases." It is important to note here that these physiological effects affect those who are lonely, not those who are alone.

OFFENSE, BE NOT EASILY OFFENDED

Being easily offended is a totally unnecessary cause of your own stress. By learning to not be easily offended, you automatically reduce your stress levels.

What does it mean to not be easily offended? In simple terms, it means don't take other people's comments and behaviors personally. Don't get upset when someone is rude to you, acts offensively, or snubs you. The behavior and comments of others are a reflection of that other person's attitudes, thoughts, and character, not reflections of you. Remember the section on judgment and criticism? Social media is rampant with opportunities to be offended.

President Brigham Young counseled us to not be easily offended. He likened our positive or negative reaction when offensive comments are made to how we might also respond positively or negatively to a rattlesnake bite. "It is reported that President Brigham Young once said that he who takes offense when no offense was intended is a fool, and he who takes offense when offense was intended is usually a fool. It was then explained that there are two courses of action to follow when one is bitten by a rattlesnake. One may, in anger, fear, or vengefulness, pursue the creature and kill it. Or he may make full haste to get the venom out of his system. If we pursue the latter course we will likely survive, but if we attempt to follow the former, we may not be around long enough to finish it."[40] He tells us clearly that it is just plain foolish to be offended whether the other person intended to be rude or not.

---

40. Brigham Young, "Of You It Is Required to Forgive All Men," in Conference Report, October 1973, 15–16.

If someone offends you, let it go. If someone overlooks you or forgets to invite you to an event, let it go. It doesn't do you any good to hold on to the offense. Just like anger, lack of forgiveness, or any other emotion that causes stress, the person who feels the symptoms of offense is only you. Let it go. As you fret over what the other person did, why they did it, how hurt you are because of it, and what you should do about it, you are wasting a great deal of your energy trying to respond to the character of another person. To what avail? Will you be able to change their character? Probably not. Does feeling offended make you feel better? Definitely not. Let it go!

The way we respond when we feel offended could indeed have some serious consequences. What if the other person had no intention whatsoever to offend you or criticize you in any way, but you "felt criticized," so you respond by yelling and screaming and being even more offensive than you perceived the other person to be, just so you could make a point. Unfortunately, you just revealed in a huge, undeniable voice more about your own lack of character and your desire to inflict injury on purpose than about the other person. The other person had no intention at all to offend. Perhaps they were actually trying to be nice, maybe they were making a joke or just having a normal conversation, but your unwarranted and intentionally cruel response caused severe damage to your relationship and a great deal of stress for both of you. Whose character and intentions are questionable?

Elder Marion D. Hanks said that the way we handle situations in which we feel offended may have serious ramifications: "What is our response when we are offended, misunderstood, unfairly or unkindly treated, or sinned against, made an offender for a word, falsely accused, passed over, hurt by those we love, our offerings rejected? Do we feel resentful, become bitter, hold a grudge? Or do we resolve the problem if we can, forgive, and rid ourselves of the burden? The nature of our response to such situations may well determine the nature and quality of our lives, here and eternally."[41]

---

41. Marion D. Hanks, "Forgiveness: The Ultimate Form of Love," *Ensign*, January 1974.

What others say or do is a reflection of them, not of you. Elder David Bednar summed this principle up quite succinctly, saying, "You and I cannot control the intentions or behavior of other people. However, we do determine how we will act. Please remember that you and I are agents endowed with moral agency, and we can choose not to be offended."[42]

OVERWHELMED

"And see that all these things are done in wisdom and order: for it is not requisite that a man should run faster than he has strength…therefore, all things must be done in order" (Mosiah 4:27). "But Martha was cumbered about much serving, and came to him and said, Lord, dost thou not care that my sister hath left me to serve alone: bid her therefore that she help me. And Jesus answered and said unto her, Martha, Martha, thou art careful and troubled about many things: but one thing is needful: and Mary hath chosen that good part" (Luke 10:40–42).

In chapter one, we looked at a definition of stress suggested by Richard Lazarus: "Stress is a condition or feeling experienced when a person perceives that demands exceed the personal and social resources the individual is able to mobilize." Feeling overwhelmed is almost the definition of stress for most people.

In chapter four, we looked at the characteristics of a stressful event (nature, situation, frequency, controllability, and intensity). We looked at the Holmes and Rahe Stress Scale, which gave us some idea of how heavy each event could be. And we discussed how the frequency of having stressful events in rapid succession reduces our ability to cope with and adjust to each separate event. When too many stressful triggers occur too rapidly, it causes us to feel overwhelmed. When we are overwhelmed, we lose our capacity to deal with any of the events well.

Neal A. Maxwell counsels, "When in situations of stress we wonder if there is any more in us to give, we can be comforted to know that God, who knows our capacity perfectly, placed us here to succeed. No one was foreordained to fail or to be wicked. When

---

42. David A. Bednar, "And Nothing Shall Offend Them," *Ensign*, November 2006.

we have been weighed and found wanting, let us remember that we were measured before and we were found equal to our tasks and, therefore, let us continue, but with a more determined discipleship. When we feel overwhelmed, let us recall the assurance that God will not over program us: he will not press upon us more than we can bear (D&C 50:40)"[43] That is a great promise. The caveat to that is that though the Lord will not "over program" us, often we over program ourselves. We create our own stress.

There are two critical examples about how being overloaded and overwhelmed can teach us great lessons about stress:

Example #1: Handcart Pioneers

Through the years, I have had the opportunity of taking our Young Women and Young Men on trek several times. Trek is a recreation of the challenges experienced by the pioneers of The Church of Jesus Christ of Latter-Day Saints as they crossed the plains in covered wagons or pulling handcarts. These treks began at Martin's Cove in Wyoming, where each "family" picked up their handcarts. The youth are divided into "family" groups, headed by adult leaders who act as their "Ma and Pa."

Before we left on each of the treks, we instructed the youth to put their name on a five-gallon bucket, in which they would pack and store all of their personal clothing and hygiene supplies for the journey. The bucket also served as something to sit on. There was always a great deal of grumbling about how small the buckets were and how they needed more space to pack all their clothes and make-up and hair products and entertainment. The youth were not required to include in their buckets many of the necessities of life: sleeping bags, pillow, food, cooking supplies, tools, firewood, tents, etc. The buckets only held their personal items.

As we loaded the handcarts, the youth were told that many of the pioneer companies pulling handcart were permitted only seventeen pounds of gear per person. Also, in their handcarts were their tents, blankets, water, food, cast-iron cooking pans, tools, and many of their "treasured possessions." As the pioneers took their journey west, they began to feel the strain of all the weight in the handcarts.

---

43. Neal A Maxwell, "A More Determined Discipleship," *Ensign*, February 1979.

Handcarts that were heavily packed were much harder to pull. The heavier carts became stuck in the mud, sand, water, or ruts more frequently. Pulling heavy carts over rocks or up steep hills proved to be a very difficult task. In addition, heavier handcarts also experienced more broken wheels.

Soon, the pioneers, who were weary, fatigued, and starving, began to toss out some of those treasured items, even some necessities became too heavy to pull across the plains, through the rivers, and up over the mountains. They arrived in the Salt Lake Valley with much less than the minimal necessities for daily survival.

The pioneers learned that having a plethora of worldly possessions became too heavy and overwhelming to pull. "Things" became less important as their strength and energy waned.

Example #2: The Plimsoll Line

The following was taken from a talk "How Do I Love Thee?" from Jeffrey R. Holland:

As a youth in England, Samuel Plimsoll was fascinated with watching ships load and unload their cargos. He soon observed that, regardless of the cargo space available, each ship had its maximum capacity. If a ship exceeded its limit, it would likely sink at sea. In 1868, Plimsoll entered parliament and passed a merchant shipping act that, among other things, called for making calculations of how much a ship could carry. As a result, lines were drawn on the hull of each ship in England. As the cargo was loaded, the freighter would sink lower and lower into the water. When the water level on the side of the ship reached the Plimsoll mark, the ship was considered loaded to capacity, regardless of how much space remained. As a result, British deaths at sea were greatly reduced.[44]

Like the ships and the handcarts, we all have differing capacities in dealing with stress. Some people can carry the burden of large companies on their shoulders without much struggle while others feel greatly stressed by some of the small, unimportant tasks of daily

44. Jeffrey R. Holland, "How Do I Love Thee?" Brigham Young University Speeches, February 15, 2000.

living. We each have different skills and different capacities. Margaret Deland summed up this idea perfectly: "A pint can't hold a quart—if it holds a pint it is doing all that can be expected of it."

Sometimes, we optimistically think that we can handle significantly more changes and events than we realistically have the ability to manage. Often, though not always, we have the ability to prevent some of our own stress and keep ourselves from being overwhelmed by being wiser about how much we can realistically put in our handcarts.

I am often concerned when students come by my office the first week of the semester to tell me that they are getting married between midterms and finals or that a young female student is pregnant and the baby is due three months into the semester. A full-time university student who is carrying a full course load and working part time is usually stressed enough. Between midterms and finals, that stress level intensifies. To plan other stressful events to occur in an already stressful time frame is a classic example of filling the ship above the Plimsoll line, and it does not allow any room to deal with unanticipated events.

One of the challenges for us is that we see an event as only a one-time thing, one entry in our calendar, rather than a time-intensive process. We forget about all the planning, expense, time, problems, and adjustments that come with that one event. When we look at our calendar and see a free hour or afternoon, we don't always look at the days ahead to see what we need to be doing to prepare for other events. In other words, if the event fits on the calendar, we think it fits into our lives. That kind of thinking leads to overload. It leads to a heavily laden handcart getting stuck in the mud, or a ship whose Plimsoll line is five feet below the water as it sails off into an unseen violent storm. When our handcart or ship is already overloaded beyond its capacity, there is no room to deal with unexpected events that come into all of our lives. If we want to prevent stress or at least minimize it, we will spend some time in planning ahead. For each event that we add to our calendar, we also need to calendar in some realistic planning time.

It may be wise to do some whole-life spring cleaning. We can gain much better control of our stress levels by getting rid of some events, possessions, thoughts, responsibilities, or extracurricular activities. Dieter F. Uchtdorf counseled, "Let's be honest: it's rather easy to be busy. We all can think up a list of tasks that will overwhelm our schedules. Some might even think that their self-worth depends on the length of their to-do list. They flood the open spaces in their time with lists of meetings and minutia—even during times of stress and fatigue. Because they unnecessarily complicate their lives, they often feel increased frustration, diminished joy, and too little sense of meaning in their lives... Resist the temptation to get caught up in the frantic rush of everyday life... Focus on the things that matter most."[45]

When you can't do it all, do only what matters most. Not everything in life is an emergency and most things aren't important enough to put ourselves in high-stress overload. Try to remind yourself of times when the things that seemed so critical in the moment, became completely unimportant in your life as time went on. Think of a time when you were injured or seriously ill and you had no strength to do anything: What were the things that you discovered were not quite so important to do? Or think about a busy mother with four very young children, trying to take care of them all and get them all fed and clothed and calmed down; the list of things that she does for herself shrinks dramatically. Consider also those who are chronically ill or aged; their physical limitations quickly clarify their real priorities and necessities. I have the following quote by Johann Wolfgang von Goethe in my planner: "Things which matter most must never be at the mercy of things which matter least."

We don't need to "do it all." We need to do what is most important. Uchtdorf also wisely stated, "When stress levels rise, when distress appears, when tragedy strikes, too often we attempt to keep up the same frantic pace or even accelerate, thinking somehow that the more rushed our pace, the better off we will be... My dear brothers and sisters, we would do well to slow down a little, proceed at the optimum speed for our circumstances, focus on the significant, lift up our eyes, and truly see the things that matter most. Let us be mindful of the foundational precepts our Heavenly Father has given to

---

45. Dieter F. Uchtdorf, "Of Things That Matter Most," *Ensign*, November 2010.

His children that will establish the basis of a rich and fruitful mortal life with promises of eternal happiness. They will teach us to do 'all these things...in wisdom and order; for it is not requisite that [we] should run faster than [we have] strength. [But] it is expedient that [we] should be diligent, [and] thereby...win the prize.'"[46]

Trying to do it all is foolishly putting more stress on our own shoulders. There are definitely times when we do our best to clear away all the things on our plate but find ourselves still weighed down with too many demands and responsibilities.

The first step to keep us out of "overwhelmed" status is to use great wisdom on what things we say yes to and what things we put on our to-do list. We don't need to do it all. Ask the Lord, honestly, to help prioritize what is really important for you to do and which things can fall by the wayside and then follow His counsel.

During one particularly stressful time in my life, I became totally overwhelmed at the things on my to-do list. Everything on the list seemed to be of critical importance. I had already said no to many requests. I had dropped things off the list that could be done later. I delegated things on my list that could be delegated to others. I requested changes in due dates. I even stopped doing the daily chores of housekeeping, laundry, grocery shopping, and cooking so I could focus on the long, critical, overwhelming list of things that had to be done. I prioritized the list in hopes that something would fall off. Nothing did. I evaluated each item to see if there was an easier way to do it. Again, to no avail. In desperation, I found myself on my knees, reciting to the Lord all the things on the list. I asked for guidance on which things were most important and pleaded for the strength to do them all. I asked if there was anything on the list that I could drop off, totally expecting that nothing would fit that bill.

My prayer was answered. The most important things were identified. I received extra strength to do what I needed to do. And to my surprise, there were several things that I was told were not important to do right now—things that I had supposed were of critical importance. Following His counsel, I finished the things that needed to be

---

46. Dieter F. Uchtdorf, "Of Things That Matter Most," *Ensign*, November 2010.

done and gratefully discovered that the items that dropped off the list, never needed to be put back on the list.

It had been a very stressful time. It took all my strength to do what I needed to do. It took months to catch up on all the things that I had to sacrifice in order to accomplish that which truly was critical to do. I was comforted in knowing that the Lord will not press upon us more than we can bear. We usually do that to ourselves. Generally, when we are overwhelmed, it is not God's doing, it is our own.

PROCRASTINATION

Procrastination generally causes stress. The stress comes from having to hustle to race a deadline at work or speed through traffic to pick up little children from school on time. Procrastination causes increased stress as we realize we miscalculated how long things would take or how many more steps we needed to do to accomplish our task or that other things happen in the world, like traffic jams, flat tires, or dropping a glass bowl of spaghetti that was intended to be dinner.

Procrastination means to delay or postpone something. Generally, people procrastinate because the thing that needs to be done is something they don't want to do, or the task seems too big, or too vague, or too complicated, or they just don't know how to do it. Sometimes procrastination is due to having no sense of how long a task takes to get done and therefore doesn't need to be started yet, while others procrastinate due to sheer laziness. Jim Rohn observes, "If you want to do something, you find a way. If you don't want to do something, you find an excuse." Sometimes while procrastinating, we do something meaningless to fill our time, like spending hours watching television, making procrastination a big waste of time. Others feel less guilty for procrastinating if they do important things, just not the most important thing.

Recently, a friend told me she was scrubbing the kitchen floor because there was an important task that needed to be done, but she disliked doing it much more than she disliked scrubbing the floor. She figured she would feel less guilty about procrastinating if she was doing another distasteful task instead. Of course, others figure if they are going to procrastinate and not do the important task, they may as well do something they like instead.

When you find yourself delaying the completion of an important task, ask yourself why you are procrastinating. Is the task too difficult or too boring? Do you not know the best way to proceed so you just don't move at all? Are you afraid of the task? Does the task take more energy than you have? Are you too tired? When you figure out why you are procrastinating, you can do something about it. You can ask for help. You can revise your plan, scheduling the procrastinated task for a time you will have the appropriate amount of time, energy, or help. Procrastination is creating your own stress. You feel increased stress while you are procrastinating and you increase the "hurry sickness" when the thing that you procrastinated becomes due and you must hustle to get it done.

WORRY AND ANXIETY

"Take therefore no thought for the morrow: for the morrow shall take thought for the things of itself. Sufficient unto the day is the evil thereof" (Matthew 6:34; 3 Nephi 13:34). Throughout the scriptures, we are instructed not to worry about the cares of this life (see chapter one). We all know what worry means. It is allowing our mind to dwell on uncertainty of real or potential problems, difficulties, or troubles. It is sometimes referred to as concern, anxiety, brooding, fretting, or stewing about an issue. A little concern and worry are normal. Most of us worry at times, about an illness, an issue at work, a critical personal decision, a family member, loss of a job, etc.

Erin D. Maughan gave an example of this very issue in a Brigham Young University devotional: "About a year ago I was talking to a friend who turned to me and simply said, 'To worry is to lack faith.' This struck me quite hard. Think about it; it makes sense. If we worry and try to put it all on our own shoulders, we are not trusting that the Lord is in control or that He understands the situation. I cannot tell you the number of times this counsel has helped me and calmed me when I didn't understand why events occurred—and in the process, I think (at least hope) I have grown."[47]

---

47. Erin D. Maughan, "Be Still, and Know God," Brigham Young University Devotional, August 4, 2009.

Worry and anxiety are indications of a doubtful mind and little faith. Unfortunately, in these last days of increased stress, the emotions of worry and anxiety are no longer present in just normal or small portions. Sadly, worry and anxiety have become a major health issue.

Since Worry and anxiety come from repeated thoughts of concern, fretting, and stewing, we can learn to stop worrying by replacing those thoughts with thoughts of faith, trust, and belief. When we let ourselves slip into emotions of worry and anxiety, it shifts our thinking into irrational, illogical, distorted, or simply untrue thoughts (see chapter five). Worry is almost always future oriented so the focus is on the uncertainty of what might happen. These repetitious thoughts are generally combined with fear and doubt, which intensifies the magnitude of stress.

While you engage in the habit of worrying and being filled with anxiety, you are training your brain to think in terms of worry and anxiety. These are negative thoughts that bring about their own mental, emotional, and physical damage. The longer worry and anxiety go untreated and unaddressed, the more difficult they are to stop and reverse. Changing those thoughts becomes progressively harder and harder to do because the repetitive thoughts constantly reinforce the strength of the negative filters. Too much worry or worrying for too long takes a huge toll on us physically, mentally, and emotionally. Worry is a major cause of stress. One of my favorite quotes on worry comes from Corrie ten Boom. She said, "Worrying is carrying tomorrow's load with today's strength—carrying two days at once. It is moving into tomorrow ahead of time. Worrying doesn't empty tomorrow of its sorrow; it empties today of its strength."

If you find yourself constantly drowning in the emotions of worry and anxiety, you need to get help immediately. Actively treating worry and anxiety automatically helps to manage stress. There are medications that can help break the worry/anxiety cycle as counseling starts to work on changing the thoughts and filters. One filter you can start to work on now is repeating to yourself, Whatever happens, with the Lord's help, I will figure it out. You can also begin to work on building faith and trust in the Lord.

CHAPTER 9

Building Stress Capacity:
Accentuate the Positive

What does it mean to build stress capacity? We already know what stress means. So, let's add the definition of capacity to the phrase. Capacity means the amount that a container or vessel can hold or contain. Most physical containers can hold a specific maximum amount of a substance, for instance a one gallon plastic jug can only hold a maximum of one gallon of liquid. You can't force the one gallon jug to hold five gallons of liquid. It does not have the internal space and capacity to do that. We, as humans, have some limited capacities as well. We can only eat so much food in one sitting before we can hold no more and begin to regurgitate it. We can only function for a limited amount of time without any sleep before our brain no longer functions sanely. Our heart can only beat so fast before it no longer functions as a pump and shuts down. However, we as human vessels do have some unlimited capacity in many areas. For instance, how much you can love, how many different kinds of music humans can produce, how much wealth you can accumulate, and how much stress you can handle.

There are an overwhelming number of examples throughout the history of the world where we have witnessed human heroes' dealing with more stress than we can possibly imagine. How did they do it? Recall from earlier chapters, there are really only two major ways to deal with stress: We either decrease the amount of stress coming in to us (which we can do to a certain extent but cannot control all of it) and/or we increase our ability to deal with stress. In order to have the ability to deal with more stress, we need to build our stress capacity. This principle of building stress capacity is like the principle of building wealth. If you want to build wealth, you must decrease your expenses and/or increase your income. And so it is with building stress capacity. We must decrease as much stress as possible (see chapters four and eight) and then increase our ability to deal with stress by adding behaviors that are proven to build stress capacity.

Building stress capacity is based on the positive character traits, thoughts, beliefs, and behaviors we put into our stress capacity savings account. We already learned what things to decrease in the last chapter, which drain our stress account. Now, we need to review which things increase our stress account. As we build stress capacity, we find that the smaller daily stressors don't seem to be so stressful, and we are better able to deal with those events in stride. By doing so, we find we have plenty of capacity left to deal with the more difficult unforeseen crises that occur.

As you read through each of the activities in this chapter, pay attention to the principles that ring true for you. Those will be the best places to start in your attempt to manage stress and build your own personal stress capacity. The activities/beliefs are in alphabetical order to help you locate activities that you might be interested in.

Accountability and Choice

One attribute that makes the biggest impact on preventing, altering, minimizing, and managing stress is choice. Our life is a reflection of the choices we have made. If we want our life and our stress level to be different, we need to make some different choices. Making wise choices can prevent, alter, or minimize some of the events that cause us stress. Making wise choices is critical in managing stress. Choices occur before, during, and after stressful events.

Let's refer back to that War in Heaven, which was about one topic: agency, the right to make choices in life. Having agency to make choices was critical to our mortal experience. Our life is filled with opportunities to make choices. We learn from the choices we make. We learn from the consequences of choices, both good and bad. When we make poor choices, hopefully we learn that we don't want to suffer those consequences again and therefore make different choices in the future.

Our choices have a direct impact on our stress. Our choices can minimize our stress or intensify it. As we learn our way through life, we are going to make our fair share of good choices and poor choices. There is a difference between making choices that don't turn out the way we plan and making choices that were poor choices from the beginning. Sometimes we make every effort to make a wise decision but either we don't have adequate information or things change or there are unexpected complications that get in the way. Sometimes a good choice turns sour over time. Even when we have made every effort to make good decisions, things occur that we can't predict or avoid.

Sometimes, we make a poor choice right from the start. Those choices occur when we don't make any effort to study out the options, when we are aware of the consequences but ignore them, or when the only thing we care about is doing what we want to do when we want to do it. As much as we don't want to admit it, a great deal of our stress is the consequence of our own poor choices. We need to be vigilant in trying to avoid making poor choices. So, how do we make good decisions? Luckily, there are many classes and websites that teach in-depth decision-making principles. One quick search on the Internet will provide you with many different processes from which to choose.

One of the biggest causes of preventable stress is bearing the consequences of our choices. Those consequences can be small, frustrating annoyances, like having to pay a late charge for an overdue bill, or the consequence could be a large life-altering event like losing a job, going to jail, or premature death.

Accountability is taking responsibility for your choices, owning that you made the choice, and accepting the consequences that accompany your choice. It is not hard to take full credit and accountability when our choice turned out fabulously. Where we struggle with being accountable is when our choices brought consequences that we absolutely do not want to bear.

If we make poor decisions, we reap the stressful consequences. Most of us don't like to admit that the stressful event that we have to endure is the result of our own choices. So, many people will place the blame on someone else or deny that they had anything to do with it, or worse, they begin to make excuses to lie their way out of it, destroying trust in the process. Consequences are meant to teach us to make better decisions in the future.

Unfortunately, for all who shift blame to someone else, deny any responsibility, or make excuses and lie about what happened, they may feel like they got away with it. Instead, they merely impede their own progress and increase their own stress. If we don't feel accountable for the consequences of our own behavior, we will not learn to stop the behavior. We will just continue to do it and therefore continue to increase our own stress.

A few words of caution: Accountability does not mean beating yourself up for making a poor choice. It means taking responsibility for the choice you made, accepting the consequence, and learning the lesson so you can move forward. For each choice we make, we should automatically take a short look at it retrospectively, evaluate what can be learned from the experience, and use that knowledge to make better decisions in the future.

COMMUNICATIONS

All too often, people believe that since they know how to talk, they know how to communicate. That is so not true. Saying words certainly helps with communication, but it is not the complete communication package. Communication requires a clear message being sent and a clear message being received. Therefore, it is critical that we work hard to send clear messages and that we listen carefully to receive the accurate information. Both are critical components of communication

A very large cause of our stress is poor communication skills, either our own or from others. As a matter of fact, the top three reasons for divorce are listed as: infidelity, financial conflict, and communication problems. The order of these causes changes every year, but the causes do not. Even when people have developed very effective, polished communication skills, there are still some very difficult topics to discuss that make communication emotionally charged. When communication skills are poor, those difficult discussions often tend to explode into yelling, screaming, and volatile expressions of anger and frustration.

Unfortunately, among large numbers of people, communication skills are deteriorating rapidly for many reasons, including lack of mutual respect; increased anger, hostility, and stress; and increased use of abbreviated communication through email, text, and social media. In whatever way we choose to communicate, we will likely get our message across much more clearly and have it received much better if we communicate kindly and with a great deal of respect for the person with whom we are communicating. When we commit to let all of our communications be delivered with decency and respect, the process for communication will be much smoother.

Communication also depends on the receiver. Just as the sender needs to be kind to and respectful of the person with whom they are communicating, the receiver also needs to listen carefully, kindly, respectfully, and completely to what is being said not to what the receiver thinks might be said. The sender can communicate beautifully in very clear words and phrases with excellent communication skills, but if the receiver isn't listening, is busy planning a response before hearing the message, or is processing the information through a brain filled with distortions, the message will still not be received as intended.

Another obstacle to good communication is that people try to communicate while their emotions are running hot. They are angry, annoyed, frustrated, disinterested, or just don't care and don't want to be bothered. Communication is hard enough to get right. When we complicate it with a variety of intense emotions, the communication exchange spirals out of control fairly quickly. For instance, we know that the word finances is listed as one of the top three causes of divorce. Finances are not the cause of divorce. How you communicate about financial issues and priorities is the cause of divorce. Communication is the bigger problem, especially communication when emotions are running hot.

Good communication skills make life run much more smoothly and peacefully. After all, we communicate all day, every day. If we communicate well, we prevent a great deal of stress. On the other hand, poor communication skills can turn peace into volatility for no other reason than information was communicated in a very bad or incomplete way. You can receive the exact same information from a good communicator and feel just fine, but when it is delivered by someone with really bad communication skills, the result will be dramatically different. I had a boss once of whom it was said, "He is so kind and thoughtful that he could be firing you and you would want to thank him and give him a hug on your way out."

There are many classes, books, and online resources teaching good communication skills. Even for people who believe they have good communication skills (let's face it, very few people honestly believe that they are poor communicators), it would be advisable to review good communication skills periodically.

DECISION-MAKING/PROBLEM SOLVING

This section works hand in hand with choice and accountability. They are all part of agency. They are all part of the reason we are here on this earth: to learn how to make good choices, make wise decisions, and solve problems efficiently and effectively. We make many decisions every single day, many of those decisions are about solving problems. If you have children, you are solving problems constantly.

Unfortunately, many children are being raised without learning how to make decisions or solve problems, therefore they often end up making unwise or even foolish choices. Sometimes these children have neglectful parents, or conversely, they have parents who control everything they do. Therefore, the child doesn't have a chance to learn how to make decisions or solve problems for themselves. And still others make decisions and solve problems in very poor ways because they didn't learn to make good decisions or don't truly understand (or just don't wish to follow) the basic principles of these processes.

There are many different approaches to decision-making/problem-solving from which to choose, but they all have the same goal—identify the decision to be made or the problem to be solved and then evaluate all the options, evaluate the benefits and costs, determine the possible consequences or problems, and make a decision. If we want to reduce our stress, we can make a big impact on that goal by learning good decision-making/problem-solving skills. Whenever we ignore good decision-making principles/problem-solving techniques or the prayer that needs to accompany those techniques, we run the very real risk of making poor choices and increasing our own stress because of it. Even for those who feel like they make good decisions and solve problems well, it is helpful to review the steps for these processes. Often, we find that we routinely forget some of the steps.

Whether making decisions or solving problems, we should always add prayer to the process. Recently a young woman said she didn't pray about something that was bothering her a lot because "it's a no-brainer." Besides the fact that it apparently wasn't a no-brainer because she was constantly stewing about it, she forgot a very critical point: God knows things we do not know. Perhaps, based on what we know, a decision seems logical. But God knows information about the situation that we do not know. He knows things that may be looming in the future that would completely change our decision if we knew about it. He is omnipotent. Why wouldn't we humble ourselves in prayer to ask for His guidance?

DIET

Refer to D&C 89. In the Word of Wisdom, the Savior has been clear regarding what things we should eat and what things we should not eat. We have all heard the phrase, "You are what you eat." This phrase has been attributed to many different people, all of whom are attempting to say that our minds and bodies are a reflection of how well-nourished our bodies are. Food is the fuel that our body burns to provide us with strength, energy, cell repair, and growth. Just like a car that runs out of gas or runs low on oil or antifreeze, if we do not have fuel for our body, we shut down. We are reminded often that our body is a temple, it is not a garbage can, in spite of how many people fill it with garbage. When we change our thoughts about what our body really is, we will soon desire to treat our body like the temple that it is. If we do not take care of our body and give it appropriate nutrition, our body cannot function well to do all the things that are required of it. We feel sluggish or tired or weak. We end up with more risk of chronic diseases, which cause their own stress. And let's remember that the third phase of the stress cycle is the physiological response. Our body is part of the stress process. If we aren't nourished, the added burden of physically responding to stress may cause some long-term damage or injury.

DIVINE NATURE AND INDIVIDUAL WORTH

"Remember the worth of souls is great in the sight of God" (D&C 18:10). We often hear about or talk about self-esteem or lack of self-esteem. Many people do not like the term self-esteem because it focuses on self and for some people, that sounds self-absorbed or even conceited. In order to take the negative connotations of self-esteem out of the discussion, we will use the wiser and more accurate terms, taken from the Young Women program—divine nature and individual worth.

There is a great deal of stress that comes from not having a sure knowledge of our divine nature and our individual worth. We start having self-deprecating thoughts. We believe that we are inferior to others. We take everything that is said very personally when it was not personally intended. There is a great deal of damage to our soul when we believe the bullies, the critics, the judgers, and those who offend. When we truly know who we are, children of a loving Father in Heaven, and we know that we are of great worth to Him with unique talents and a divine mission to accomplish on this earth, it no longer matters what other people think. We do not need to seek other-esteem or be damaged when some of those others are rude or disrespectful. The behavior of others is a reflection of who they are and what their character is, not a reflection of you. Therefore, we have no need to internalize what they say. We always need to evaluate the comments of others to see if there is any truth or validity to what they say. Then we need to take accountability to change what we need to change. Then we can dismiss the rest and move forward in the sure knowledge that we are children of God, with an undeniable divine nature and individual worth.

ENVIRONMENT

There are several different environmental influences that have an impact on our stress levels. We will discuss cleanliness and organization of our environment, some influences that infiltrate our environment, interruptions in our environment, and the possessions we have surrounding us. Each of these components of our environment impact our stress in different ways.

Environment—Clean and Orderly

"Behold, mine house is a house of order, saith the Lord God, and not a house of confusion" (D&C 132:8). A very subtle—perhaps even unrecognized—yet pervasive cause of stress in our lives is having a disorganized, cluttered, messy home, car, or office. Living in an environment filled with clutter and disorganization often causes us to misplace things or lose them. Constant clutter leads to difficulty in keeping our homes/offices clean and free of filth. Having a disorganized and cluttered living/working space can cause us to have a constant underlying feeling of anxiety, irritability, and sense of being overwhelmed—all contributing to a constant increased stress level.

Our homes are supposed to be our refuge from the world, a place of peace where we can relax, replenish, and rejuvenate before we go back out to face the world. But if our homes are disorganized and filled with piles of laundry, dirty dishes, kid's toys, and ever-growing stacks of mail, magazines, articles to read, documents to file, and children's art to put in their scrapbooks, our stress levels will rise and stay elevated. Disorganization and clutter increase the chances that we will spend a great deal of time frantically looking for lost keys, the other shoe, the kids' permission slips, a credit card, a report for work, a clean plate to eat from or whatever else you desperately need.

A study done at Princeton University found that visual clutter can cause our minds and bodies to tire more quickly. When we see clutter, the clutter competes with your brain's ability to pay attention and therefore compromises your cognitive functions. Psychology professor Sabine Kastner explained the phenomenon in the Princeton Alumni Weekly: "The more objects in the visual field, the harder the brain has to work to filter them out, causing it to tire over time and reducing its ability to function."[48] That means that the bigger the mess in your environment, the more difficult it is for your brain to block it out, and it increases your stress level.

Throughout the scriptures, we are taught to be clean and orderly. A clean, organized, tidy home provides an environment that allows us to function smoothly. Our emotions can be more stable when we aren't living in constant frustration due to our physical environment. An organized, clean home gives our minds, emotions, and spirits a place to rejuvenate and flourish.

Environment—Infiltrating Influences

Another way that we increase or create our own stress is by the influences that we allow to infiltrate our homes. We can make the choice to create a nonstressful environment in which to live by evaluating what influences we allow, or even invite, into our homes through entertainment, music, art, substances, behaviors, people, etc.

If we do not want our environment to add to our underlying, constant stress levels, we can make very simple changes to the influences that we allow in our homes. I had some very dear family friends who decided to remove their telephone from their home. Though it was inconvenient for those of us who wanted to communicate with them, they made this choice because they received constant sales calls and work questions that came in at all hours of the day and night. These interruptions were very bothersome and stressful for this couple, so they removed the phone. They later brought in a cell phone so they could place calls due to some critical health issues, but they gave their number only to family members and did not give out the cell phone number to any businesses.

Another frequent negative influence that we invite into our homes is the television. Of course, we can opt to remove the television from our home or we can just evaluate which programs are allowed to be brought into the home. One night while my grandchildren were in my home, we accidently fell asleep with the television on. At about 3:00 a.m., my granddaughter awakened me shaking and scared. She said, "Gamma, there is a bad show on TV and it's scaring me." Yes, the

---

48. Michael Blanding, "Psychology: Your Attention Please," *Princeton Alumni Weekly,* June 3, 2015.

channel that had a good show on when we fell asleep was now airing a very violent show. My home was filled with a feeling of negativity, darkness, and evil. The contrast between the feelings we had while watching a cute movie, laughing, and eating popcorn and the evil influence that came through the television hours later was disturbing and palpable. The same can be said about the music that we choose to have permeate the walls of our homes or the sites that we choose to look at on our computers and cell phones.

Another influence that comes into our homes comes in with the people that walk through our doors. All who come into my home know that I have a few nonnegotiable rules: I do not allow yelling, screaming, fighting, vulgarity, nor using God's name in vain. The influence of those things is tangibly toxic, damaging, and highly stress-producing. Unless there is a fire or critical injury, there is no communication that cannot be accomplished in a calm, respectful, nonyelling voice. Yelling and fighting brings an atmosphere of anger, contention, divisiveness, and contempt to all in my home. All of those influences create a stress-filled environment that I will not allow to be part of my environment.

There are many avenues through which influences may enter your home, whether they come through electronics (television, computer, music, cell phones, and video games) or they come in through art and home décor or they come with the people who enter. We are all free to choose which influences we allow in our homes. We can bring in positive, peaceful, uplifting, cheerful, and stress-free influences or we can choose to let whatever shows up, come in, even if it is negative, angry, depressing, or evil. Choosing to make small adjustments to protect the environment of our homes will make much larger adjustments in our stress levels.

Environment—Interruptions

It is becoming increasingly more difficult to find time for peace and quiet, time to think, figure things out, balance a budget, pay bills, figure out taxes, read scriptures, ponder and pray, compose an email, have a critical conversation, or write this book. We have a culture of increasing avenues for interruption. In addition to the normal interruptions of raising a family, we have doorbells, telephones, cell phones, FaceTime, email, texts, Facebook, Instagram, personal messaging, and hundreds of other social media avenues for reaching us. Just in the last ten minutes of writing this paragraph, I received two phone calls, six text messages, a personal message alert, and someone at the door.

The challenge with interruptions is that they come in at someone else's convenience, not ours. The interruptions yank us away from what we are doing, whether that interruption is more important than our current task or not. Then it takes an average of twenty minutes to regain your focus and catch back up on the task that you were doing. Often, once we are interrupted, we end up staying with the interruption. For example, you get an alert to check out someone's response on Facebook and then stay on Facebook reading all the posts for another two hours, or while you are waiting for a specific email response, you open and answer all the other unimportant emails. And we certainly do not love pulling our hands out of cookie dough to answer a ringing phone only to hear—for the fiftieth time—a recorded sales pitch about a car warranty.

Many time management experts suggest turning off the things that interrupt us. They counsel us to not check email, texts, or phone messages each time we get an alert but rather turn off the alerts and designate certain times during the day when you will address all the incoming messages, especially those that are during the work day and are work related.

Obviously, we want to use wisdom in what things we turn off or limit access to. Children must be able to reach parents if they need us. Important messages must get through. You can let others in your family and those close to you know which avenues you leave open and which ones you don't. I have one friend who does not text but she checks email several times each day. Another friend doesn't answer her phone but does answer text messages. Another has set up some codes that alert her when a message or call is coming in from someone she knows and is important. My family knows that I don't answer a phone or texts while I am teaching or attending church or the temple, but if there is an emergency, they know the code that will get my attention and let me know I need to get back to them ASAP.

Environment—Possessions

Have you ever tried to make a list of all of your current possessions for an insurance company or an estate/will? A simple scan of our homes can be extremely revealing about the reality of how many possessions we have and how much space and time they take. Current research indicates that the more "stuff" we have surrounding us in our lives, the more underlying stress we feel. Why? There are several reasons: More possessions mean we have invested more of our financial resources into things. For most of us, financial considerations are a very real component of our stress level. Having more possessions means we have more things that we need to clean, dust, organize, maintain, repair, and store. That is no small task and certainly takes up a great deal of our time. More possessions mean more stuff occupying our living space. Whether the possessions are furniture, clothing, appliances, hobby supplies, toys, tools, or décor, they all take up space and tend to increase the likelihood of clutter and disorganization in our homes.

In a world filled with constant upgrades to everything we own and advertisements that tell us about the newest, latest, and greatest, it is extremely easy to be caught up in filling our homes with those newest, latest, and greatest possessions.

It might be helpful if we ask ourselves why we feel the need to fill our homes with so many possessions. Perhaps owning lots of possessions makes us feel more secure that we won't run out. Certainly, part of the lure is the fun of having the newest games, toys, electronics, and furnishings. And part of the lure is due to competition with our neighbors and friends. Remember the advertising that begins with "Be the first on your block to own..."? That advertisement is like waving a competitive flag in front of us that we just have to win.

Whatever our reason for collecting and/or keeping a house that groans with overflowing possessions, remember that all those possessions increase your stress. Recently, some of my dear friends who lost their home, cars, and business in one of the many California wildfires said that in addition to the intense sorrow of losing their home, business, and possessions, they also felt a sense of relief that they no longer had to take care of all those possessions. They decided that they would be wiser now in deciding which home to buy and the limited possessions they would choose to fill that home.

EXERCISE

Exercise is essential for the health and appropriate functioning of our body. Exercise helps our body to be healthy and strong. Exercise is also essential for our emotional stability and for the management of our stress. For some, exercise is a dirty word. Nevertheless, we cannot have a conversation about how to manage stress without talking about exercise. There is a great deal of research on the health effects of exercise, which include: reduces type 2 diabetes, promotes healthy weight, helps balance energy, increases musculoskeletal health, decreases risk of cancer, promotes good mental health, improves immune system functions, improves quality of sleep, improves stress management, improves overall mood, clears the brain, increases cognitive function, decreases your chance of depression and anxiety, and increases overall health.

Sadly, our lifestyles have changed to the point that we don't get the normal exercise from daily life that our ancestors did. Now, we have cars to drive wherever we wish to go, online shopping, computer-based work, and televisions that bring entertainment right into our home. Exercise needs to be a planned event. Not only does exercise help our bodies function better, stay healthy, and help us manage stress, exercise is also a good way to cope when we are feeling stressed. As you recall, the fight-or-flight response of stress prepares your body to run or fight; therefore, exercising as a way to cope with stress, helps to dissipate those stress chemicals. A good walk, run, basketball game, or game of tag with the kids can help break the stress response and ease you back into physiological recuperation.

FAITH AND HOPE

The Lord counsels us repeatedly to have Faith. When the disciples of Jesus Christ asked why they were unable to heal a child and cast out evil spirits, the Lord answered: "Because of your unbelief: for verily I say unto you, if ye have faith as a grain of mustard seed, ye shall say unto this mountain, remove hence to yonder place; and it shall remove; and nothing shall be impossible unto you" (Matt. 17:20).

Faith and fear cannot coexist. Remember the definition of stress in chapter one tells us that it is not the event that causes us stress but our perception that the event is a danger, a threat, or a fear. It is that fear of an event that causes our stress. Fear distorts our thinking. Fear spikes our stress levels. We should never take counsel from our fear. When we reduce fear, we reduce stress. Our faith can overcome our fears, and as it does, it minimizes the stress that is triggered by our fearful thoughts. Fear comes from relying only on yourself. Faith comes from relying and trusting in the Lord. During the COVID-19 pandemic, I noticed that many people were extremely stressed because their fear levels were so high. As the pandemic was becoming a more constant reality, and because I was considered high risk in several categories, I spent a great deal of time at the beginning of the pandemic fasting and praying for guidance and direction. I felt assured that as I followed the precautions, I would be protected from illness. From that point on, I did not feel fearful or stressed. I focused on faith in the Lord's assurance.

Elder M. Russell Ballard advised, "What I believe the Lord wants me to say is that we should replace fear with faith—faith in God and the power of the Atonement of the Lord Jesus Christ."[49] The Bible counsels and commands us over 365 times to "be not afraid" and "have no fear" but to "have faith" instead. To repeat this 365 times is clear indication that He means it.

Remember the story of Peter walking on water out to the Savior? As Peter saw the Savior, listened to Him, and stayed focused on Him, he walked on water. But when Peter's attention and focus were diverted to the storm, his fear took over and he sank. Faith and fear cannot coexist.

Some words of caution: Some people distort what faith really means. Our faith is supposed to be in God and His will. Faith does not mean that we get to pick a desired outcome to a specific situation and then proclaim that we will get what we want if we "just have faith." We often hear people say things like, "You will get that job; just have faith," or, "Everything will work out the way you want; just have Faith." Faith does indeed, move us to action, but faith does not give us everything we want just because we say we have the faith to get it. If that were the case, we would all have faith that we would win the

---

49. Russell M. Ballard, "Face the Future with Faith and Hope," *Ensign*, January 2014.

lottery. Our faith must be in line with God's will, not ours. Dieter F. Uchtdorf tells us, "The purpose of faith is not to change God's will but to empower us to act on God's will. Faith is trust—trust that God sees what we cannot and that He knows what we do not."[50] Another misconception is that if we have faith, things will be easy or even given to us. Faith is the power to get us through the things we cannot change.

In his concluding conference address in April 2009, President Thomas S. Monson assured us with this beautiful counsel: "My beloved brothers and sisters, fear not. Be of good cheer. The future is as bright as your faith."[51] When the prophet only has limited strength and a very short time to speak in conference, we would do well to follow every word of his counsel. "Fear not. Be of good cheer. The future is as bright as your faith."

As we strengthen our faith, our hope, and our trust in the Lord, our faith will automatically reduce our stress. We are assured, "For I do know that whosoever shall put their trust in God shall be supported in their trials, and their troubles, and their afflictions, and shall be lifted up at the last day" (Alma 36:3).

Focus, Avoid Distractions

Focus means to concentrate, to see clearly a sharply defined image. We focus our eyes so we can see an object more clearly. We focus our thoughts so we can see our goal, our path, our direction more clearly. We focus our attention so we can hear, understand, or perform in the way we intend to. We focus our driving so we can get where we are going while avoiding accidents. We focus when presented with a problem so we can effectively solve it. We focus on the target so we can hit it.

When we get distracted and lose our focus, obtaining the goal is at risk. Would you want someone shooting a gun at a target to get distracted by something that was happening next to you, shifting his body toward your direction? During the past several years, the number one cause of auto accidents and deaths has shifted from

50. Dieter F. Uchtdorf, "Fourth Floor, Last Door," *Ensign*, November 2016.
51. Thomas S. Monson, "Be of Good Cheer," *Ensign*, May 2009.

drinking and driving to distracted driving. Though drunk driving is still a large cause of preventable accidents and death, the distracted driver has moved into the number one position for causing injury and death. We have so many things vying for our attention while we drive: children, radios, commute traffic, people talking to us, road construction, crazy drivers. There are also the big issues: texting or talking on a cell phone.

A couple of years ago, I had an eighteen-year-old student who admitted that she had been in seven accidents and had even more traffic tickets in the two short years she had her driver's license. She said she was "easily distracted" so she would accidently hit parked cars, run red lights, inadvertently change lanes into another car, crash into a telephone pole, etc. I asked what was distracting her, to which she replied "generally texts." I ventured a plea; "Please don't text and drive," to which she quickly defended with very confident exuberance, "Oh that isn't a problem, I am really good at texting." Didn't she just say that the texts distracted her from driving? "Not the point," I answered. "It doesn't matter how good you are at texting; what matters is how good you are at driving. It is the vehicle that kills people, not your phone. So, not being distracted while you are driving is the critical piece of this story."

Keeping your eyes on the road heightens your chances of reaching your destination safely. Being distracted not only decreases your chances of a safe arrival, but dramatically decreases the chances of innocent people making it to their destination either. Staying focused helps prevent or reduce some of our stress while the effects of being distracted can create stress where it did not previously exist and did not need to need to be.

As the speed of change in the world increases, as discussed in chapter one, our ability to avoid distractions and stay focused becomes progressively more difficult. But focus is a skill that is required for us to avoid unnecessary stress. Think about how many times a lack of focus has caused you a problem: You forgot where you left your car keys, you got distracted at the store and forgot to pick up your kids from school, you didn't pay attention to the bill in the restaurant that you signed and discovered later that you were overcharged, you were distracted when the hospital gave you directions for where you needed to go for your surgery, you didn't pay attention to the dry clean only label on the new expensive jacket, you missed an important work meeting because you were distracted by email, the kids distracted you in the store and you ended up leaving the store without the one thing you went there to get, you were distracted in class and didn't hear that you were having a test tomorrow, or you promised the family to take them to an event today but got too distracted to get there in time so you promise to take them tomorrow without focusing on the fact that you were going today for the "closing event." The list of problems caused by being distracted is endless. Being distracted causes us a great deal of very preventable stress.

One caution here: Avoiding distractions does not mean that we become unaware of our surroundings, especially for parents raising small children. Children have unplanned needs and emergencies. We definitely should be distracted when a child suddenly screams or cries out in pain or wanders off. We just need to learn to filter out the unnecessary distractions that do not require us to shift our attention.

Dr. Daniel Goleman has written a book entitled *Focus: The Hidden Driver of Excellence.* He tells us this about focus: "Attention works much like a muscle: Use it poorly and it can wither; work it well and it grows… In an era of unstoppable distractions, now more than ever, we must learn to sharpen focus if we are to contend with, let alone thrive in, a complex world." The author has analyzed a great deal of research from education, business, the arts, and competitive sports on "paying attention" and concludes that those who are focused excel and are higher performers.

Many people have learned the art of focus. Our service men and women are trained to stay focused so they can survive in a war-ridden environment. Athletes are trained to focus on the ball, the performance, their surroundings, and their body's movements so they can compete at their best. A surgeon focuses on the surgical procedure he is performing in order to provide the patient with the best result. We wouldn't want our surgeon getting distracted while operating on us.

There is another caution, a caution about what we focus on: If we focus on the negative, the negative in our life will increase. If we focus on the distractions, we will not get anywhere. If we focus on being a victim, we will continue to be a victim. A great many authors, counselors, psychologists, and spiritual leaders have counseled us to be cautious of focusing on the wrong thing by warning, "What we focus on grows." Therefore, let's avoid focusing on problems, stress, negativity, criticism, judgments, and pain. Instead, let's focus on strength, wisdom, faith, hope, competence, success, and keeping our eyes single to the glory of God.

Follow the Prophet

One of the greatest blessings of the restoration of the gospel of Jesus Christ is that the Lord again called a prophet to be on the earth to lead His people. In these last days, we are incredibly blessed to have this divine guidance. Now, as much or more than ever before, we need a prophet who leads and directs Christ's church and provides the word of God to His children. Howard W. Hunter told us, "God has spoken anew and continues to provide guidance for all his children through a living prophet today. We declare that [God], as promised, is with his servants always and directs the affairs of his Church throughout the world."[52]

With the great blessing of having a living prophet on the earth to guide and direct us comes an accountability to listen to Him and follow His counsel. Elder David A. Bednar admonishes and promises, "May we hear and heed the eternal truths taught by the Lord's authorized representatives. As we do so, I promise our faith in Heavenly Father and Jesus Christ will be fortified, and we will receive spiritual guidance and protection for our specific circumstances and needs."[53]

In General Conference in October 2016 and again in April 2017, an aging prophet, President Thomas S. Monson, spoke for only five minutes. What did he say? If a prophet of God only has the strength to speak to us for five minutes, we can be absolutely certain that he will choose his messages very carefully and use his few minutes to give us the most important messages that we need to hear. It may be well to go back and reread his last words often.

---

52. Howard W. Hunter, "No Man Shall Add to or Take Away," *Ensign*, May 1981.
53. David A. Bednar, "Chosen to Bear Testimony of My Name," *Ensign*, November 2015.

In these days of increased commotion, change, stress, iniquity, and chaos, it is increasingly more critical that we listen to and follow the counsel and direction of our living prophet. He is the one appointed to guide us through these latter days. He is the one who has the authority, responsibility, and accountability to receive revelation for us. President Russel M. Nelson counseled us to build a gospel-centered home, take our vitamins, and get some rest, because we are in the last days. Much stress has been averted during the COVID-19 pandemic for those who followed his counsel.

The scriptures are filled with hundreds of examples of people who doubted and ignored the words of the prophets, drove them out of their lands, stoned them, and/or killed them. In all of those cases, the people who doubted, ignored, shunned, or killed the prophets paid the consequences of their iniquity. A prophet is here on the earth to give us the word of God, to guide us, lead us, and show us the way. In the final words of a popular primary song, "Follow the prophet. He knows the way."

FORGIVENESS

"I, the Lord, will forgive whom I will forgive, but of you it is required to forgive all men" (D&C 64:10). Forgiveness is often a difficult principle to understand and more difficult to do. In order to better understand what forgiveness is and what it is not, I have attempted to define it in easy terms: Forgiveness is the conscious, intentional, deliberate, and voluntary decision to release feelings of resentment and vengeance toward a person or group who has wronged you or caused you harm. Forgiveness is a process in which a victim attempts to change a feeling and attitude, releasing negative emotions toward the offender.

Understanding what forgiveness is, also requires an understanding of what forgiveness is not. I once heard a woman who was going through a painful divorce exclaim that she couldn't forgive her soon-to-be ex-husband. If she forgave him, she said, "He would get away with it." She said that if she let go of the anger and resentment, that he would be "off the hook." She is not alone in that thinking. To many people, forgiving someone who has caused you pain or offense seems like giving an undeserving person a gift. Forgiveness does not let the person get away with it or let them off the hook. They are still responsible for the consequences of their behavior. We are just releasing our own feelings of anger, contempt, or vengefulness.

Experts in the field of forgiveness have made it clear that when you forgive, you do not condone what happened, you do not pretend that you have not been injured, and you do not deny the seriousness or painfulness of the injury or offense against you. Forgiveness does not mean forgetting the wound nor does it obligate you to fix the damage, restore trust, release the offender from legal accountability, nor ignore that trust was broken. Forgiveness is not a release from consequences.

One of my favorite quotes regarding forgiveness is, "Holding onto anger (or not forgiving) is like drinking poison and expecting the other person to die." This quote has been credited to Buddha, Malachy McCourt, and many others. Understandably, many people want to make the same point: The toxins of anger and resentment are in you causing a chemical hurricane in your own body, not in the offender's. As a matter of fact, often the offender has walked away, totally unaware (or unconcerned) of the damage they have left in their wake, thereby leaving them physically, mentally, and emotionally unaffected.

Refusing to forgive subjects you to all of the negative health effects of stress, anger, guilt, fear, anxiety, blame, and frustration. Holding on to these toxic, negative emotions hinders your health, growth, and spiritual development. Lack of forgiving means that you will continue to release stress hormones into your own body, not someone else's. None of those stress hormones magically shift to the perpetrator and mess up their health. The act of forgiving releases you from those emotions, the stress, and the physiological response that accompanies it. Elder Hugh W. Pinnock taught, "Of course, heartache and pain can be spilled upon us by dishonest, manipulative, or unkind people. Accidents happen that can inflict terrible pain and sometimes lifetime disability. But to judge, blame, and not forgive always intensifies the problem. It pushes healing further into the future."[54] Forgiveness frees up the energy that we once used up by being resentful, holding grudges, and stewing in anger. It allows us to use that energy to move forward.

---

54. Hugh W. Pinnock, "Now Is the Time," *Ensign*, May 1989.

There is no question that it is difficult to forgive someone who has hurt you in some way. But here is the tricky part, there is no need to forgive someone who hasn't hurt you. Forgiveness is a principle directly related to living in a world where people make mistakes.

Forgiveness takes time, especially when the offense is significant and the loss is grievous to bear. But unless we stay committed to forgive and prepare our heart to be humble and open to forgive, it will not come.

While we are learning to forgive others, it is also important for us to learn to forgive ourselves. Not forgiving yourself has the same negative, toxic effects as not forgiving others. If you have done something that needs forgiveness, start with repentance and work through to forgiveness. Sadly, harboring anger, resentment, and bitterness corrode the container in which those emotions reside—you. We must forgive others and ourselves in order to move forward, decrease stress, and release the toxic chemicals from our body. It will help if we can truly and deeply trust that the Lord's judgments are both just and sufficient.

Another of my favorite quotes regarding forgiveness comes from Mark Twain who said, "Forgiveness is the fragrance that the violet sheds on the heel that has crushed it." Forgiveness is a choice. Forgiveness is great wisdom.

Gratitude

"And he who receiveth all things with thankfulness shall be made glorious: and the things of this earth shall be added unto him, even an hundred-fold, yea, more" (D&C 78:19).

Gratitude is a very powerful principle in learning to deal with stress. Remember the definition of stress is an event that "you perceive to be negative, dangerous, a threat or invoke fear." Gratitude does not prevent most events from occurring, but it does change how we perceive the event and recuperate from it. Remember from chapter five that your perception is part of the stress process.

As we learn to develop an attitude of gratitude, we train our brains to find the good in a situation and to focus on the things we can be grateful for in that event. The event may be extremely difficult and stressful. Gratitude doesn't negate the difficult event, but it does help ease the intensity. This shift in attitude helps to decrease what we perceive as stressful. For instance, the COVID-19 pandemic affected all of us. Many people spent a great deal of time airing their anger, frustrations, losses, and inconveniences on Facebook or Instagram. There were definitely many losses for which people needed to grieve: jobs, family members, graduations, funerals, weddings, income, etc. However, the posts expressing anger, frustrations, and inconveniences added to the stress of the writers and the readers. We all experienced frustrations and losses. And how grateful we have been for those who wisely posted humor, support, love, and gratitude. Each night we voiced gratitude for health, a paycheck or unemployment check, a year's supply of food, a prophet who told us to get that year's supply of food, a home-centered gospel learning program that started a year earlier, etc. Gratitude changed the little that we had into more than we needed.

Gratitude changes our attitude. Gratitude changes perception from what you lack, want, need, crave, etc. to being content with what you have. Gratitude helps us keep our focus on what we have rather than what we want. Gratitude allows us to see the good in the midst of a bad situation.

How often do we hear people who have been in an accident or have escaped a house fire or lost a home in a hurricane or tornado say, "I am just grateful that my family is safe," or, "I am so thankful the injuries weren't worse," or, "I am so glad I have family close by where I can stay for a while."? Yes, we still need to deal with the damage from the event, grieve the losses, figure out how to fix things, and survive in the process. But, focusing on gratitude automatically reduces the stress that comes with the event by changing our perception and focus.

President Thomas S. Monson admonished, "Sincerely giving thanks not only helps us recognize our blessings, but it also unlocks the doors of heaven and helps us feel God's love."[55] Unlocking the doors of heaven and feeling God's love through our trials most definitely reduces the stress of the situation we are in.

Through the years, research has been done measuring people's hormones and body chemistry as they thought "grateful thoughts."

---

55. Thomas S. Monson, "The Divine Gift of Gratitude," *Ensign*, November 2010.

Their stress hormones dropped. The research was repeated having the participants think grateful thoughts and verbalize those thoughts of gratitude to whomever provided them a service; the stress hormones dropped even more dramatically. In addition, they measured the stress hormones in the people who had provided the service and had been thanked for it. They too, had positive changes in their body chemistry and felt happier when someone expressed gratitude to them.

One day, my tiny angel granddaughter, Alexa, who was six years old at the time, was trying to figure out what she wanted to do next. She suddenly exclaimed she had "a great idea." Within a minute, this little angel said excitedly, "Thank you, brain, for giving me that great idea." Now, that is an attitude of gratitude. She is a very happy little girl. There is a strong relationship between gratitude and happiness. Gratitude helps us savor the positive things in our life, which in turn decreases the stress hormones and increases the feel-good hormones.

Gratitude is having a mindset of "abundance." Gratitude turns a little into enough. When you think abundantly, you begin to see how much you really have and how many blessings you enjoy. There are limitless opportunities and possibilities that open up for you. Gratitude helps you stop chasing each new-and-improved material possession or career advancement and instead find joy in what you already have, knowing that you have enough.

Sometimes in the midst of a great trial, when it feels like your world is falling apart, it is hard to find something for which to be grateful. During those times, I have found some peace in this suggestion from an unknown author: "If you haven't got all the things you want, be grateful for the things you don't have that you don't want." Be grateful that things aren't worse. During the COVID-19 shelter-in-place orders, I found myself being extremely grateful for listening to and following a prophet because I had food storage, disaster supplies, an established practice of gospel study, and strong faith.

Humility and Acceptance

"Whosoever therefore shall humble himself as this little child, the same is greatest in the kingdom of heaven" (Matt. 18:4). "Be thou humble; and the Lord thy God shall lead thee by the hand, and give thee answer to thy prayers" (D&C 112:10). The scriptures are filled with counsel regarding our need to be humble and to function in a state of humility. As you recall from chapter two, one of the big reasons we have stress in our life is so that we will be brought into humility, for without those trials, we often forget the Lord and cease to listen to him. If we can stay humble, perhaps we will not need quite so many stressful events to humble us.

So, what does it mean to be humble and why is it so important? Humility is the quality or state of not thinking you are better than other people, being humble and modest in your opinion or estimate of your own importance, rank, appearance, etc. To be truly humble is to have a realistic appreciation of your own strengths, while also being fully cognizant of your weaknesses. Humility is the ability to recognize your value and the value of others while looking to God as greater than us all.

We know that our world was designed from the very beginning to have trials, tribulations, afflictions, and challenges. These events are meant to teach us, humble us, and help us grow. Humility helps us realize and accept that in the whole spectrum of eternity, we are not in control. There is a higher power who has a plan for each one of us. When we fight to demand complete control of our lives and everything that happens to us, as we "kick against the pricks," we fight against God and His wisdom. This process comes from pride not from humility. Is there any slim chance that you are wiser than God? No. Not even close.

What exactly does it mean to kick against the pricks? The word pricks comes from the Greek word *kentron* meaning goads. A goad was a sharp, pointed stick used to urge some stubborn animals to move. Like many people, some animals would defiantly rebel and kick back at the pointed object, inflicting a stab wound upon itself.[56] Simply put, when we resist God's teachings, tests, tutoring, and afflictions, we are only hurting ourselves as we kick back against the creator who is trying to move us along the path. We inflict our own stress upon ourselves.

---

56. "What Is Meant by 'It Is Hard for Thee to Kick against the Pricks'?" Never Thirsty, https://www.neverthirsty.org/bible-qa/qa-archives/question /what-is-meant-by-it-is-hard-for-thee-to-kick-against-the-pricks/.

Humbly accepting God's plan for us helps us stop "kicking against the pricks." Throughout your lifetime, consider how much time, money, stress, and energy you may have expended while stubbornly resisting and fighting against the Lord's will or the challenges He gave to you? Accept that in the plan of exaltation, God is in control. Stop fighting against God's plan.

Humility and acceptance decrease the entire stress process by changing the filters in your brain. Once you have become humble enough to listen to the Lord and have progressed enough to accept that He is in charge and can guide you through, the stress response begins to decrease. Obviously, you will still have some stress regarding the event, but while you are in that humble state of acceptance, you can hear guidance, counsel, and even an assurance of the outcome. Ron Lee Davis suggests, "In this life, we will encounter hurts and trials that we will not be able to change: We are just going to have to allow them to change us."

Several years ago, I was blessed with having a dear friend invite me to join her on a church history tour. While in Nauvoo, Illinois, I walked down the Trail of Hope, also referred to as the Trail of Tears, which led from the city of Nauvoo down to the edge of the Missouri River. I was touched by the many stories of those who were being driven out of their homes in the winter and were living in camps on the shores of the Missouri River, which, at the time, was too icy to cross.

During their stay in the camp, many saints became very ill and died from the illness and extreme cold. I stopped by one plaque and read about Amy Sumner Porter. While Amy was living in this illness-ridden camp, her tiny infant son became ill. In spite of his mother's desperate attempt to keep her infant son safe and warm in this dire situation, this tiny infant lost his life. Of course, Amy was deeply grieved.

Later, our tour took us to Winter Quarters in Florence, Nebraska, where the saints had stopped for the winter. In the visitor's center there was a plaque with another short story about Amy Sumner Porter. The story told of how the headstones in the cemetery in that city were mostly destroyed, but they found a piece of one headstone—Amy Sumner Porter's. Since the pioneers kept detailed maps of their journey and clear cemetery plot maps, the historians were later able to reconstruct the cemetery. Next to Amy were the graves of her tiny newborn twins, who also perished. On the plaque was an excerpt from Amy's journal, which touched my heart deeply as I read: "I don't know why He requires such sacrifice, but my heart and all I have is His." Oh, that we could all have the humility and acceptance of Amy Sumner Porter, who, I am confident, was quickly reunited with her children and our Savior.

Amy's humility and acceptance did not free her from trials and stress. Clearly, her trials were intense and severe but her humility and acceptance helped her have the spiritual and emotional strength to go through these trials making her love for the Savior deeper and purer.

Humility and acceptance help us work through our trials by anchoring our hearts and minds on the Savior and trusting in his guidance and assurances. Recently one of my family members became critically ill. The entire family feared for the survival of our loved one. Sadly, there were many other trials and conflicts occurring at the same time, which scrambled my focus. As I could free myself from the other conflicts and return to humbly praying and listening to the Lord, I received a very calm assurance that all would be well and that our family member would be healed and returned to full health. Suddenly, a sense of calm took over where fear had prevailed. It was a very stark reminder to me that humility and acceptance are not just critical to our eternal salvation but can help us work our way through trials and stress.

INTEGRITY

"I, the Lord, love him because of the integrity of his heart, and because he loveth that which is right before me, saith the Lord" (D&C 124:15). "He that worketh deceit shall not dwell within my house: he that telleth lies shall not tarry in my sight" (Psalm 101:7). "Wo unto the liar, for he shall be thrust down to hell" (2 Nep 9:34). It is clear through the scriptures that honesty and integrity are important principles. The scriptures shared are only a few of the many scriptural references about integrity, honesty, and living without deceit in our lives. For a moment, consider how much of your stress might be caused by deceit, lies, and lack of integrity. I always wonder how stressful it must be to keep ones lies straight or remember what person was told which story. That stress in inconsequential in relation to the stress caused when trust is destroyed and relationships are damaged by deceit and lies.

Trying to define the word integrity is somewhat difficult. There are many misconceptions that integrity only refers to being honest, but honesty is only part of integrity. The word from which integrity comes means whole and complete. Integrity requires a whole and complete character filled with dedication and consistency to honesty, moral uprightness, principles, and character. It is knowing clearly what your values are and making the decision to be steadfast and immovable in living those values. Integrity requires completeness and consistency to live in accordance with your values, principles, thoughts, actions, and behaviors.

When you have integrity, you have it all the time: at work, at home, in business, with friends, with family, when life is difficult, when truth is hard to tell, and when you are in trouble. When you make the decision to have a life of complete integrity, you will likely eliminate some stressful events in your life that come from trying to hide lies, deceit, dishonesty, and immorality.

I had an administrator who told me that as a regional director, I had to learn to lie to my employees. Frequently in our leadership meetings, we were told of policy changes or upcoming challenges or future increased costs for our employees. On the heels of these announcements came the statement: "And this is what we want you to tell your staff about this issue." The words that followed were filled with deceit, twists, innuendos, and blatant lies. One day I finally mustered up the nerve to quietly ask this administrator why we intentionally destroy trust with our employees by telling them scripted lies. It was only a matter of time before the employees learned the truth anyway. The response was, "When the time comes, we will spin the situation so the employees won't know that we intentionally lied. By then we will be able to make it look like a good thing." This statement was followed with the same counsel again that, "If you want to be a good leader, you need to learn to lie to your employees." Of course, that was totally against my values and my commitment to integrity. I let the administrator know that I have a commitment to personal integrity.

The reply? "That is a good thing in your personal life, but this is business. You have to lie in business." Wrong. You choose to lie; it is not required.

Another lady told me that she tells people, especially family and friends "whatever they want to hear" when she is talking with them. It doesn't matter if it is true or not. Is lying, cheating, and lack of integrity really a trait you look for in a friend?

Integrity is a character trait that requires a complete dedication and 100 percent consistency. Both of these individuals later complained to me that "no one believes me. People act like they don't trust me anymore. I don't understand what happened. I haven't done anything differently. They just all of a sudden started to question my honesty. They have no right to question my honesty. They have no way to know it isn't true."

Yes, it may take people a little time to discover that you have lied to them, and perhaps more time to realize that the dishonesty is constant, but once trust is destroyed, it is very, very difficult, sometimes even impossible, to restore. Needless to say, they created their own stressful situations by their lack of integrity.

Think about a time in your life when you did not maintain integrity. Did it cause problems? Did it destroy trust? Did it hurt someone else? Did you feel unrelenting guilt? Did you go a little crazy trying to keep your lies straight and remember to whom you told which lie? Did it cause unnecessary stress in your life? Remember our choices have consequences. When we choose to compromise our integrity, consequences will follow.

Just think of how much stress we could all avoid if everyone was 100 percent committed to a life of full integrity. How many marriages would be saved if both individuals had integrity to their vows, promises, and commitments to each other? How stable would our country be if we were able to trust that our elected officials were honest and fair in how they represent us rather than themselves? Wouldn't it be great if we could trust what advertisers told us about their products so we could make wiser choices? How would it be to go into a car service department and have them tell you your car doesn't need that particular service right now? How much harder might we work for an employer if we knew that our employer was honest and fair in how they treated us? So much of the stress in this world would disappear if all of us were committed to integrity.

Laughter and Smiles

"A time to weep, and a time to laugh; a time to mourn, and a time to dance" (Eccl. 3:4). Like Brad Wilcox said, "Humor helps. Humor heals. In fact, many medical studies have linked laughter with better physical and mental health... If we can laugh at it, we can live with it."[57] Make time to laugh as frequently as possible. It is true, laughter is the best medicine. Humor helps change perceptions, which means humor decreases stress. Laughter reverses the stress chemicals, which means laughter reduces stress. Laughter tricks your body into thinking the stress is gone, which means the stress chemicals quit flooding your body. Laughter makes you feel better. And if you can't laugh, just smile instead. Force yourself to smile. The physical effect of a smile tricks your body into an immediate decrease of the stress hormones and increases the positive hormones, as we discussed in chapter six.

Smiling and laughing are critical to reduce the stress in our lives, and as an added benefit, it spreads stress-reducing feelings to those around us. As we change our perception to allow ourselves to smile and laugh, those around us get the benefit of the happier environment as well.

Smiling and laughing help in several ways. First, the ability to laugh when you are in a situation that could be stressful means that you have changed your thoughts to positive, less serious thoughts. Remember, the definition of stress is our perception of fear, danger, or threat when there is a change in events. Consider this: The average child laughs about four hundred times per day because they think everything is new and fun and hilarious. They don't have a filter that makes them see events as a threat to their ego. The average adult laughs only fifteen times per day. What happened to our perception that turned everything into stress?

Remember also that there are two operating systems in our brain, and we frequently use the wrong one in perceiving stress when danger truly does not exist. So, the first step to changing stress into laughter is changing the perception center in our brain to more accurately use the hot response only when it is a real danger or threat. There is no

---

57. Brad Wilcox, "If We Can Laugh at It, We Can Live with It," *Ensign*, March 2000.

question that it is difficult to smile, let alone laugh, when you are feeling stressed, but it is one of the best ways to reverse the stress response.

Norman Cousins, former editor-in-chief of the *Saturday Review*, learned a very powerful lesson while he was in the hospital with an extremely painful, sudden case of a crippling connective tissue disease and ankylosing spondylitis. Norman was in constant pain and was told that he had a 1 in 500 chance of recovery. He knew that stress caused many physical problems, disease, and long-term physical damage. He began to wonder if stress was that powerful in a negative way, could laughter be as powerful in a positive way? So, in addition to a very healthy diet, he prescribed for himself lots of laughter. He started watching the television show *Candid Camera* and Charlie Chaplin films. He discovered that ten minutes of genuine laughter would give him at least two hours of pain-free sleep. The pain pills only gave him about ten minutes of pain-free sleep.

Laughter has the ability to break the physiological effects of stress and even turn stress into non-stress. Therefore, it is a good idea to have things around you that can make you laugh when needed: a very funny friend, humorous movies, comics, joke books, funny songs or dances, goofy children or grandchildren who laugh freely, or anything that you can find that will make you smile or laugh.

LISTEN TO AND FOLLOW THE PROMPTINGS OF THE HOLY GHOST

A few months ago, I was traveling in a very large, unfamiliar city. I had a navigation app on my phone that gave me directions to each of the many locations we needed to get to. I had others traveling with me who tried to help with the navigation, since the city was complicated to navigate and the traffic was very heavy. On a couple of occasions, my navigation system gave some confusing instructions. We named the navigation app Crazy Daisy.

At one point, we were driving down the street to an activity when the GPS announced, "You have reached your final destination." We looked around; there was nothing around us but some empty fields and up ahead we saw an old rundown school building. This was not our destination. We were on the correct street, but there were no addresses on the empty fields, so we didn't know if we had missed our location or if we weren't there yet.

I turned around to head back to see if we missed our location and pulled over to reset the GPS. At the same time, another person in the car, looked up a different GPS app to see if it offered any additional insights. My GPS told me to turn around again and head back the direction I was originally going, which I did. Then the trouble started. My GPS was giving me the directions that landed me by the empty field again and her GPS told me to turn right and then make another turn that led directly away from the street we needed to be on. Suddenly there were many voices in the car shouting out different directions. How in the world are we supposed to know which one to follow? It was getting very frustrating and stressful. So, I started to pray to try to tap into the only true navigating system. I knew I was on the right street, so I continued several blocks past the open fields and finally found the correct destination. Even as we were parking the car at our correct destination, the other GPS app was relentless in telling me to turn around and go a different direction.

How many times have you had similar experiences in life? Everyone you talk to gives you different advice or counsel. Sometimes, many of the different voices are in your own head. You tell yourself you should go one direction and then you think maybe you should go a different direction but then you have a thought about a totally different option. And then you sit down and bemoan, "I just don't know which way to go. I wish someone could just tell me the right thing to do."

Is there a 100 percent accurate life-direction GPS? Yes, we all have the Light of Christ to help guide us through life. Even greater is when we have the gift of the Holy Ghost to guide us whenever we ask. The trouble is that many people aren't able to recognize and hear any promptings from the Holy Ghost in a sea of earthly differing voices. We know that the Lord is likely trying to answer our prayer, but we just don't have any idea which voice is His. That is usually the toughest part. What good does it do for us to have a life-direction GPS if we can't recognize which voice it is?

It would be incredibly wise for us to learn to recognize and follow the promptings of the spirit while we are not in crisis. We know that the voice of the spirit is a "still small voice," a voice that will likely be much harder to hear when the earthly voices are screaming at us. But if we will take the time to learn to recognize how the Spirit speaks to us and which voice is His, it will make our times of crisis and stress substantially easier. President Russell M. Nelson has counseled us to learn how to "Hear Him." A critical thing for us to learn to help us navigate these last days.

The next piece of this process is when we recognize and listen to the prompting of the Spirit, we must act on it. Unfortunately, we often dismiss that still, small voice as just a fleeting thought, or we tell ourselves that we will do it later or we think we aren't capable of doing what we were instructed to do or capable of doing it well. There are hundreds of reasons that we don't end up following the promptings. However, think this through: If we don't follow the counsel the Lord gives us, we may find ourselves not getting guidance when we need it the most. We are accountable to act on what we have been prompted to do. Make it a commitment to learn to recognize the Spirits promptings, listen to them, and then act on them.

LOVE, SERVICE, AND ALTRUISM

"A new commandment I give unto you, that ye love one another; as I have loved you, that ye also love one another" (John 13:34).

There is no shortage of scriptures that command us to love the Lord as the first commandment, and to love one another as the second commandment. Throughout the scriptures, there are many commandments about what we should do in this earthly existence, but loving the Lord and loving one another are the first and second priority. What is it about love that makes it more important than the commandments against stealing or lying? I might suggest that many of the other commandments and most of our laws would not need to exist if we truly loved the Lord and our fellowman. If we love others, we would not want to take from them that which is theirs. We would not want to lie to them and destroy trust. We would not want to judge them or be unkind to them. One commandment, if we would genuinely learn to love others, could automatically help us keep all the rest of the commandments.

On the flip side, most of the problems in the world are caused by lack of love: wars, murder, thefts, violence, domestic violence, bullying, adultery, lying as well as the poverty, neglect, starvation, and homelessness of thousands around the world. This means that the majority of our stress comes from living in a world lacking in love. Pierre-Augustin Caron de Beaumarchais observed, "Where love is concerned, too much is not even enough." So true.

Elder Dieter F. Uchtdorf also gives us wise counsel on the principle of love: "Love is the healing balm that repairs rifts in personal and family relationships. It is the bond that unites families, communities, and nations. Love is the power that initiates friendship, tolerance, civility, and respect. It is the source that overcomes divisiveness and hate. Love is the fire that warms our lives with unparalleled joy and divine hope. Love should be our walk and our talk."[58] What more needs to be said about the power of love? During the COVID-19 pandemic, California wildfires, earthquakes, hurricanes, and tornados, we have witnessed so many acts of love that people showed to one another. It was touching to see that love for mankind in action. Sadly, we also witnessed many acts of violence, rioting, fighting, looting, stealing, and disregard for each other. A total lack of love in action.

So how does love help reduce stress? Consider that we have often been taught that how we treat others is what we get in return. Try a simple experiment: The next time you go through a drive-through, when you pick up your order, take just two short seconds to look the cashier in the eye, smile at him, genuinely thank him for helping you, and wish him a very pleasant day. More often than not, you will get a smile and a bidding for you to have a pleasant day as well. We underestimate how much impact simple acts of love, service, and kindness can have on others. How often have we heard someone say, "Thanks, I really needed that today."? Or, "You have no idea how much you changed my life."? That which we send out into the world is what we receive reflected back to us. Send out love! It automatically reduces your stress.

---

58. Dieter F. Uchtdorf, "The Love of God," *Ensign*, November 2009.

Partnered tightly with love is the responsibility to serve and altruism. We should be encouraged and uplifted by witnessing how many people step forward to provide service in thousands of different ways: providing meals at a homeless shelter, taking groceries to the homebound, volunteering in hospitals, helping at schools, donating time and financial resources to charities and foundations as well as the massive outpouring of service during earthquakes, tornados, hurricanes, pandemics, and other disasters. We have witnessed very creative ways people have figured out how to serve others. It is so heartwarming to watch as total strangers figure out ways that they can help reduce the stress of others.

Giving service to others has an added benefit. As we lose ourselves in the service of others, somehow it lessens our own stress. We hear hundreds of stories of people that were greatly stressed or depressed, but they found a way to go out and serve others. Generally, the feelings of depression or stress lessen or completely resolve within the first ten minutes of their service experience. We do not serve others in order to lessen our stress. We serve others because we love mankind and we see a need that we can help fill. However, we also receive a great benefit. Serving others just naturally changes our mindset and our perception of the trials in our own life; it also changes the negative chemicals that our body releases when we are stressed to positive, feel-good chemicals that come from love and service.

Meditation and Mindfulness

"Be still and know that I am God" (Psalms 46:10; D&C 101:16). To meditate means to reflect upon, ponder, contemplate, have peace of mind, quiet the mind, balance life, and increase intuition. The goal of meditation is to quiet the mind to attain an inner state of awareness, intensify spiritual growth, and spend time in thought or relaxation. The practice of meditation is a process of learning how to operate or train the mind to be still and quiet, yet focused and alert. As you recall from chapter six, meditation begins with focusing on the breath and involves concentrated focus on a mantra, something such as a sound, a word, an image, or a feeling. Included in meditation is learning to be able to choose where to give your attention while blocking out other distractions.

Meditation not only helps to lessen depression, anxiety, and stress, but it helps to prevent those emotions from returning in abundance. It brings you clarity regarding your core values and helps you find solutions to your problems and challenges in life by allowing you to tap into your inner, wiser, spiritual mind. Being still in a meditative process helps you gain a better understanding of life's events and why things happen the way they do, or why things don't happen the way we wish they would happen. For many, meditation can enhance spiritual connectedness and provide a pathway to develop a deeper understanding of and trust in God.

In addition to helping focus your mind and thoughts, meditation has many health benefits. Research has confirmed that physiological and psychological changes take place in the body during meditation. Perhaps the most important physiological benefit to meditation is that it quiets the central nervous system, which has been revved up by stress. Specifically, meditation lowers catecholamines (stress hormones) and reverses the negative effects on the heart and blood vessels that high levels of epinephrine and norepinephrine (stress hormones) cause. It reverses several of the processes caused by mental stress and depression, including the following: decreases arterial plaque, spasms, and blood clots; stops vessel wall damage; decreases perspiration; slows the respiratory rate; lowers blood pressure; reduces pain and anxiety; bolsters the immune system; helps the body fight cancer and other illnesses; increases central nervous system serotonin; increases resilience, alertness, and focus; improves sleep; and helps alleviate insomnia. The effects of meditation are often much better than the chemical effects of anti-depressants. It calms the overresponsive nervous system, which tends to be a component of headaches, irritable bowel syndrome, anxiety, or chronic pain. Everything on this list helps to decrease our overall stress.

One of the great benefits of meditation is that it teaches you to stay in the present moment. When we worry about the future or have anxiety about what happened in the past, we are not living in the present. Learn to be more mindful and live in the present.

There are several meditative methods and many relaxation exercises that include meditation that can be found in specialized meditation classes, yoga classes, relaxation classes, or on the Internet.

Meditation is one of the best tools for preventing, minimizing, and breaking the physiological response of stress. Daily practice of meditation can make life much better, calmer, and more focused and alert and can allow us to function on a deeper mental, emotional, and spiritual level. It is the epitome of the scripture, "Be still and know that I am God" (Psalm 46:10).

MUSIC

"And David spake to the chief of the Levites to appoint their brethren to be the singers with instruments of music, psalteries and harps and cymbals, sounding, by lifting up the voice with joy" (1 Chronicles 15:16). "If thou are merry, praise the Lord with singing, with music, with dancing, and with a prayer of praise and thanksgiving" (D&C 136:28).

Music is very powerful. Throughout the scriptures, we see that music was used for a variety of reasons. Music's influence impacts the mind, the body, the heart, and the soul. It can heal. It can calm a troubled heart. It can be used as a positive tool to teach, celebrate, relax, reduce stress, or to praise the Lord. Music is so powerful that it is used as a separate therapy in hospitals to help patients relax before surgery, ease pain, promote healing, comfort the dying, and sooth the sorrows of grief. Sadly, the power of music can also be used negatively, to incite anger, hatred, immorality, or worse.

Music has the power to elicit emotions of every kind. Many people have different playlists of music to choose from for different moods or needs. If you need to get going through the day and need energy, you play the upbeat playlist. If you are sad and want to indulge in a good cry for a short time, you play the sad songs. Music can inspire patriotism; transport your heart to a beautiful, joyful, white Christmas; lull a child to sleep; or make you want to get up and dance.

For all the good that music can do, we need to be cautious to monitor the music we listen to and especially the music that our children listen to. Think about the last music you listened to. Did it make you happy or make you depressed? Did it lead you to the Savior, or did it lead you away from Him? Was the music uplifting, or did it plummet you into depression?

Since music has emotional power, it obviously can impact our stress levels, both positively or negatively. For instance, if we are being subjected to someone else's taste in music from which we cannot escape, it can be very stressful for us, especially if that music is extremely loud, raunchy, and incites anger or sin.

Music can definitely decrease stress. When hospitals began using music therapy for patients, they began with a box of cassette tapes of various types of music from which patients, awaiting surgery, could choose. The goal was to help the patients stay calm during those seemingly endless wait times. Even though the hospital's music selections were helpful, they soon realized that the highest potential impact for calming the patient's anxiety of the impending surgery could be attained if the patient brought in their own music selections from home. Patients were also encouraged to use their own music library during hospital stays to help reduce pain, induce relaxation, and encourage the healing process.

When my husband was dying from a massive brain tumor, frequently the anxiety, discomfort, and stress caused him severe insomnia. The last several weeks of his life, I received a nightly request somewhere between 2:00 a.m. and 3:00 a.m.: "Can you play the harp for me?" I had just started taking harp lessons and was barely able to play scales. My beginner's repertoire consisted of exercises, "Minuet for Water Bugs," and "Lullaby for a Young Squirrel." Every night, I reminded him of my limited ability and that I would be repeating the same short songs over and over. "I don't care," he answered, "when you play the harp for me, it soothes my soul." Sure enough, after I played the same simple tunes repeatedly for fifteen to twenty minutes, he would fall asleep. Music has power. Music heals. Music can indeed "soothe the soul."

It does not matter in what form the music comes: You can listen to music or you can create your own music through singing or playing a musical instrument. Many studies indicate that all forms of music have healing, stress-reducing power. However, creating music, especially through voice or playing string instruments like the piano, cello, viola, violin, base, and of course, the harp is more beneficial. Perhaps my husband's soul was truly soothed by the vibration of the harp strings.

NATURE

For centuries, man has known about the healing powers of nature. Right from the very beginning, the Lord told us that the earth and all things in and on the earth, were created for us. He created our planet to have cycles of light and darkness. He created plants, animals, fish, birds, and insects in perfect balance so that life could be maintained. Man was commanded to take care of the earth. The main source of our food supply is grown in and on the ground.

We began the process of learning about nature in elementary school. Perhaps you even did a science project about the life cycle of circulating water or made your own papier-mâché volcano. And the learning continued as we discovered how plants grow, taking nutrients from the earth and water and gaining life-sustaining energy from the sun. Plants and animals survive best in nature. Why would we think that nature doesn't have any benefits for us as well? There are many positive, healthy, and stress-reducing elements in nature.

There are many who recognize that nature has vast emotional and spiritual influence. John Muir, an environmentalist, once wrote, "Keep close to nature's heart…and break clear away once in a while, and climb a mountain or spend a week in the woods. Wash your spirit clean… I go to nature to be soothed and healed, and to have my senses put in tune once more." I grew up near one of his many pro-tected environments, the Muir Woods National Monument in Marin County, California. Many times in my childhood, I was privileged to visit that beautiful place. Walking through those gorgeous and serene woods—located so close to San Francisco and other sprawl-ing urban developments—absolutely soothed and healed my heart and soul. Studies indicate that spending time outdoors is a great way to reset your life, gain new insights and perspective, and clear the stressors from your mind. For some, the healing power of the earth comes from working in their gardens, digging in the soil, relaxing on a beach, watching the waves of the ocean, hiking in the woods, watching clouds float across the sky, or just walking barefoot in the grass. My grandmother found healing and stress-reducing power from taking long walks on the beach, just watching and listening to the waves come in. As a youth, I found healing power in the majestic Sierra Nevada Mountains. I remember how calm I felt as I heard the gentle wind rustling through the trees, hiking on quiet paths winding through the mountains, looking in awe at the giant trees, hearing the sounds of rivers and streams winding down the mountainside, and seeing the vastness of the crystal-clear night sky filled with stars that could not be seen in the city. A few days in those mountains recharged my battery, dissolved all stress, and soothed my soul.

We do not need to travel to some distant place to take advantage of the benefits of nature. We can just step outside our front door and take a quick walk around the neighborhood, appreciating the sunshine, feeling the gentle breeze on our face, and enjoying all the foliage that lines our streets and surrounds our homes.

Obedience—Commandments, Laws of the Land, and Rules

Obedience is not always a very popular word, and for many it is not a popular principle. Most children—and sadly many adults—see obedience as a principle to avoid. We live in a time when many people purport the idea of "doing whatever you want, whenever you want," ignoring the rules, laws, and commandments whenever they can get away with it. A prevailing thought in the world is that rules, laws, and commandments limit freedom, and they even act like bars in a jail cell. The goal, then becomes, walking a fine line between trying to stay out of serious trouble but ignoring whatever laws/rules get in your way.

Most parents know the challenges that exist in the world. They know the consequences of certain behaviors. Parents do their best to teach their children the things that will keep them safe, prevent them being hurt, and provide some protection from painful consequences. "Don't touch the hot stove so you won't get burned." "Look both ways before you step into the street so you won't get hit by a car." "Don't take candy from strangers so you won't be kidnapped or drugged." "Do your homework so you can get a good job when you become an adult." "Stay away from drugs so you won't become addicted." "Be home at curfew to prevent getting into trouble late at night."

As I got older, I learned that my parent's rules had good reason. They were for my own good. They were designed to prevent me from making mistakes that might bring consequences that would be hard for me to bear or consequences that could negatively alter the trajectory of my life and future. Sometimes I didn't follow the rules; I usually regretted it. I never liked the consequences—natural or parent-imposed.

As I gained understanding about my parent's rules, I also began to realize that the Lord's commandments have the same, though much wiser, goals in mind. He knows the pitfalls, the trials, the pain, and the consequences that follow certain behaviors. He counsels us not to smoke because He created our bodies and He knows what tobacco does to them. He knows the effect that tar and nicotine have on our lungs and heart. He knows which substances are good for our body and which are bad. He knows which substances are addictive. He knows which substances are harmful or even fatal. His commandments were not given to us to make our life miserable or prevent our fun. This concept is stated plainly in 1 John 5:3, we are told "his commandments are not grievous." And in Mosiah 2:22, we read: "And behold, all that he requires of you is to keep his commandments; and he has promised you that if ye would keep his commandments ye should prosper in the land; and he never doth vary from that which he hath said; therefore, if ye do keep his commandments he doth bless you and prosper you."

Elder Dallin H. Oaks sums up the need for us to make the personal choice to obey rules, laws, and commandments. "Our society is not held together primarily by law and its enforcement, but most importantly by those who voluntarily obey the unenforceable because of their internalized norms of righteous or correct behavior."[59]

---

59. Dallin H. Oaks, "Elder Oaks Encourages Members to Understand, Promote Religious Freedom," as reported by Marianne Homan Prescott, *Church News*, September 11, 2016.

Some may feel that commandments "restrict" our freedom or diminish life's adventures.

The Lord tells us that His commandments are for our good. "And the Lord commands to do all these statutes, to fear the Lord our God, for our good always" (Deut. 6:24). Commandments provide us with a God-given framework that protects our freedom from consequences that bind and ensnare us: "For the commandment is a lamp; and the law is light" (Prov. 6:23).

Many of the events that cause our stress are caused by our decisions to break the very commandments that are meant to protect us. For instance, we are commanded to be honest; when we break that commandment, we destroy trust. Consider the freedom to do drugs and the consequence of being so addicted to drugs that all freedom in life is lost. Or consider the commandment to not commit adultery and the consequences of breaking that commandment, divorce, broken trust, broken hearts, shattered families, and sexually transmitted infections.

Keeping the commandments protects our freedom by keeping us free from consequences. Paying the consequences of breaking the commandments restricts our freedom. In regards to keeping the commandments, President Thomas S. Monson warned, "The Commandments were God-given. Using our agency, we can set them aside. We cannot, however, change them, just as we cannot change the consequences which come from disobeying and breaking them."[60]

The consequences of *keeping* the commandments are positive and are clearly stated: "If ye walk in my statutes, and keep my commandments, and do them...I will give *peace* in the land, and ye shall lie down, and none shall make you afraid" (Leviticus 26:3, 6). "Inasmuch as ye will keep my commandments ye shall prosper in the land" (Jarom 1:9). "There is a law, irrevocably decreed in heaven before the foundations of this world, upon which all blessings are predicated—And when we obtain any blessing from God, it is by obedience to that law upon which it is predicated" (D&C 130:20–21).

We are truly blessed when we keep the commandments and we prevent many of the stress triggers that add to our already heavily

---

60. Thomas S. Monson, "Keep the Commandments," *Ensign*, November 2015.

stressed lives. Ezra Taft Benson counseled, "When obedience ceases to be an irritant and becomes our quest, in that moment God will endow us with power."[61]

President Thomas S. Monson promises, "When we keep the commandments, our lives will be happier, more fulfilling, and less complicated."[62] President Benson added, "You cannot do wrong and feel right!"[63]

But what about being obedient to the laws of the land? "Let no man break the laws of the land, for he that keepeth the laws of God hath no need to break the laws of the land" (D&C 58:21).

Though the laws of the land are written by men and not by an omnipotent God, the same principles of behavior and consequences apply here. The laws of the land are generally (though not always) enacted to minimize chaos and provide an environment of safety for its citizens. If you ignore the law to stop at a red light, the consequences could be a terrible accident, a totaled car, severe injuries, or even death to one or more of the occupants—followed by police reports, insurance claims, medical bills, medical injuries, fines, lack of transportation, potential jail time, and law suits. How much stress could have been prevented or minimized by obeying just one of the laws of the land?

The laws of the land have defined punishments attached. We have law enforcement personnel employed to enforce those laws. Those minor infractions could result in such consequences as a fine, a court-imposed drug treatment program, required defensive driving course, hours of community service, attendance at an anger management class, etc. Imagine how much you increase your own stress by breaking a significant law that might lead to a trial and jail time.

Besides the legal ramifications of breaking a law, there are other consequences to our lives from breaking the laws of the land, like relationship issues, financial problems, daily hassles, and family turmoil. All are "events" that can be prevented or minimized by following the laws of the land.

---

61. Ezra Taft Benson, In Conference Report, April 1998, 108.
62. Thomas S. Monson, "Keep the Commandments," *Ensign*, November 2015.
63. Ezra Taft Benson, "Seek the Spirit in All You Do," in *Teachings of the Presidents of the Church: Ezra Taft Benson* (Salt Lake City: Church of Jesus Christ of Latter-day Saints, 2014).

OPTIMISM/PESSIMISM

"And now, verily I say unto you, and what I say unto one I say unto all, be of good cheer, little children: for I am in your midst, and I have not forsaken you" (D&C 61:36). "A merry heart doeth good like a medicine" (Prov. 17:22). "Wherefore, be of good cheer and do not fear, for I the Lord am with you, and will stand by you" (D&C 68:6).

Much has been written about optimism, positive mental attitudes, and positive self-talk as well as the opposite of these attitudes: pessimism and negativity. It would be wise to start off the discussion about optimism and pessimism with some composite definitions of each. *Optimism* is an inclination or disposition of hopefulness, to look at events and actions in the most favorable way. It is a tendency to anticipate the best possible outcome. Pessimism is exactly the opposite. It is an inclination or disposition to look at events and actions in the worst way, a tendency to believe that the worst will happen. *Pessimism* is a lack of hope or confidence that outcomes will be anything but negative.

These attitudes are a function of our thoughts. And our thoughts are a matter of personal choice. We can choose to be optimistic or pessimistic. Viktor Frankl, a Holocaust survivor, learned this lesson during his horrendous ordeal in several Nazi prison camps. He reminds us, "Everything can be taken from a man but one thing: the last of human freedoms—to choose one's attitude in any given set of circumstances, to choose one's own way."[64]

The scriptures contain many references that encourage us to be of good cheer, have a merry heart, put on a positive countenance, and be hopeful. Why? What difference does it make whether our thoughts are optimistic or pessimistic? The outcome will be whatever the outcome will be, won't it? Not exactly. If we refer back to chapter five, we see that our thoughts have great power to impact our activities, our stress, our health, and our future. You will also see in that chapter some very specific things that negative thoughts cause, like a change in the chemistry of the left temporal lobe of our brain, which causes increased irritability, decreased coordination, and decreased focus.

---

64. Viktor Frankl, *Man's Search for Meaning* (New York: Washington Square Press, 1984).

Optimism and cheerfulness change the chemistry of the brain as well and shift where the brain focuses. Positive thoughts increase life expectancy, decrease depression, decrease distress, increase immune function and resistance to the common cold, decrease cardio vascular disease, and increase coping skills. When perceptions are more positive, stress is diminished. Remember: "A merry heart doeth good like a medicine" (Prov. 17:22). Pessimism, on the other hand, increases stress and damages your health. There is nothing medicinally positive in negativity.

From a very young age, if we seemed pessimistic, we were quickly reminded of the analogy of the glass of water. Do we see it as half full or half empty? I was delighted and amused to see the comments of speaker and author Simon Sinek regarding this analogy: "People who wonder if the glass is half empty or half full miss the point. The glass is refillable." Another analogy regarding optimism and pessimism comes from William Arthur Ward: "The pessimist complains about the wind; the optimist expects it to change; the realist adjusts the sails."

The bottom line is that our chosen attitude can directly impact our stress level. Negativity increases the chances that we will find fear, danger, or threat in any change in life events that we experience. Thus, pessimism and negativity directly affect what we perceive as stressful. When we perceive something as stressful, our body responds accordingly. We just created our own stress. I have a sign in my home that prevents any tendency to slip into pessimistic thinking It features a quote by Mandy Hale that reads, "Happiness is an inside job." We are responsible and accountable to harbor positive, optimistic, "be of good cheer" thoughts. I take great inspiration and hope from a comment by Thomas Edison,: "Results! Why man, I have gotten a lot of results. I know several thousand things that won't work." But he did not give up. He did not let negativity grab hold of him. He continued with his work and found just a few very critical things that did work—to the benefit of the whole world.

PATIENCE/ENDURE

"And now my beloved brethren, I would exhort you to have patience, and that ye bear with all manner of afflictions...with a hope that ye shall one day rest from all your afflictions" (Alma 34:40–41). "And again, be patient in tribulation until I come, and, behold, I come quickly, and my reward is with me, and they who have sought me early shall find rest to their souls" (D&C 54:10). President Henry B. Eyring said, "We can't insist on our timetable when the Lord has His own... Sometimes our insistence on acting according to our own timetable can obscure His will for us."[65] Notice in the scriptures above how many references there are to tribulation and afflictions in conjunction with the admonition to be patient. In 1994, Lili de Hoyos Anderson summed up the need to endure and be patient in the refining work of stress: "As we suffer the stress of refining ourselves, we may wonder what we are doing wrong. Like Joseph Smith, like Nephi, we may be living lives of obedience and service and yet still need to endure. Enduring is a refining process, teaching patience, increasing our eternal perspective, softening our hearts, strengthening our conviction, molding our will to the Father's... The Lord does not remove this kind of stress—indeed, for our sakes, cannot remove this stress of refining ourselves."[66]

As we learned in chapters one and two, we have stress in our lives by design. Stress teaches us, helps us grow, refines us, and humbles us. It is not fun. Remember the words for stress prior to 1932 were afflictions, adversity, trials, tribulation, troubles, challenges, problems, etc. These words imply a great deal of discomfort, even pain, while we work through the stress process.

While we work through and solve the events that have caused our stress and afflictions, patience is a necessary companion. However, for many, patience is nowhere to be found. We want trials to end immediately. We want stressful situations to be resolved and go away quickly.

As children, we learn that scraped knees heal in stages. It takes some time for a scab to form over the open wound to protect the delicate, traumatized skin underneath. And if we can avoid the temptation

65. Henry B. Eyring, "Where Is the Pavilion?," *Ensign*, November 2012.
66. Lili De Hoyos Anderson, "The Stress of Life," *Ensign*, February 1994.

to pick at that scab, the wound—depending on how big and how deep—will take another week, or two or three, to completely heal. When we look at physical injuries, we have no trouble understanding this healing process. However, when it comes to healing from trials and stress, we get a bit more impatient, perhaps because we cannot visibly see each stage of the process.

People often confuse being patient with waiting. The word *waiting* has a passive connotation, while patience is an active word. Patience is the capacity to accept, endure, bear, or tolerate unpleasant, annoying, even painful delays without complaint, provocation, anger, annoyance, or frustration. Elder Neal Maxwell, who endured painful cancer and cancer treatments, developed a wise understanding of patience. He said, "Patience is not indifference. Actually, it means caring very much but being willing, nevertheless, to submit to the Lord and to what the scriptures call the 'process of time'... Patience is a willingness, in a sense, to watch the unfolding purposes of God with a sense of wonder and awe, rather than pacing up and down within the cell of our circumstance. Put another way, too much anxious opening of the oven door and the cake falls instead of rising. So it is with us. If we are always selfishly taking our temperature to see if we are happy, we will not be... Patience is, therefore, clearly not fatalistic, shoulder-shrugging resignation... Patience stoutly resists pulling up the daisies to see how the roots are doing."[67] In the last televised interview with Maxwell, his body was frail and fading, but his spirit showed an incredible increase in Christlike attributes. Patience had refined him to near perfection.

PETS

Several years ago, while a close family member was recovering from a significant illness, his cardiologist strongly suggested that he get a cat. Not really a cat lover, he balked at the suggestion. But the doctor was persistent in his encouragement, telling him that the cat could help him to relax, perhaps lower his heart rate, and maybe even bring

---

67. Neal A. Maxwell, "Patience," Brigham Young University Speeches, November 27, 1979.

down his blood pressure. So, the search for a good cat began. Finally, they found Albert, a very quiet, mellow cat. As Albert became more comfortable with his new owners and his new home, a strong attachment between patient and cat developed. It was not unusual to see Albert sitting contentedly on his owner's lap or chest, purring away. It didn't take long for our patient to feel the effects of a little pet therapy. It was easier for him to relax and feel calmer. Our patient talked with Albert, being able to voice his frustrations about his illness to his furry companion without judgment. It was quite the loving relationship. Physical healing began. Even on the tough days of relapse, filled with pain, discomfort, and waning energy, Albert could be found curled up next to his best friend; they were each providing one another with much needed love, support, relaxation, comfort, stress relief, and healing powers. There is great power in the love of an animal.

The benefits of having a pet are numerous and well documented. Many pet therapy organizations have collected and shared extensive scientific research of the therapeutic effects of animals. These organizations pair different types of animals with different health issues for mental, emotional, and physical illnesses. You have probably already seen pets used in hospitals, nursing homes, rehab facilities, pediatric units, schools, and psychiatric facilities. Many children and teens with emotional wounds have been drawn to equine therapy. Children with developmental issues and special needs are often paired with dolphins. And of course, dogs lead the blind, help with PTSD, and provide companionship for adults with epilepsy, emotional disorders, and other special needs.

Animals are extremely helpful in reducing stress. They provide social contact, companionship, purpose, calming influence, and loyalty and improve overall physical, mental, and emotional health. In addition, many pet owners have gratefully experienced some degree of perceived pain relief, lowered heart rate, decreased respiratory rate, faster recovery from surgery or illness, mood stabilization, comfort, emotional support, increased happiness, decreased loneliness, stimulus for exercise, increased sense of safety, and a reduction in anxiety and stress.

More than half of the homes in America have at least one pet. It doesn't matter what type of pet you have, they all provide some stress relief, though for in-home pets, dogs and cats seem to provide the most benefit. Even though sometimes our pets add a little to our stress when they chew up a slipper, dump over the trash can, or need medical attention, the benefits that they bring to our lives far outweigh the challenges.

Plan Ahead, Be Prepared

"If ye are prepared, ye shall not fear" (D&C 38:30). "Organize yourselves: prepare every needful thing: and establish a house…even a house of order" (D&C 88:119, 109:8).

A significant part of stress is caused by procrastination, being overwhelmed, being taken off-guard by unpleasant, unexpected surprises, and lack of preparation to meet the challenges that we face. Think about something as simple as a flat tire on your car. If you have a spare tire, a car jack, and a tire iron to remove the tire, you have an unpleasant blip in your day but you deal with it and go on. But what happens if you do not have a spare tire, a car jack, or a tire iron? Suddenly that unpleasant blip in your day has gotten much more extensive. You may be stranded far away from home. It may take the entire day to resolve an issue that could have been resolved in a short time had you been prepared.

Benjamin Franklin warned, "By failing to prepare, you are preparing to fail." At the very least, if you fail to prepare, you set yourself up to deal with a lot of unnecessary stress.

We have been counseled by a prophet to plan ahead and prepare for unexpected challenges or disasters. We have been instructed to have at least a seventy-two-hour survival kit; a year's supply of food; necessary supplies for light, warmth, shelter, and fuel; and financial savings equal to six months of expenses. We never know when an earthquake will occur or a tornado or a hurricane or a flood or a pandemic. Frederick W. Lewis instructed, "Prepare. The time to win your battle is before it starts." And Henry Ford suggests, "Getting ready is the secret to success." If we procrastinate preparation and planning ahead, we will be caught lacking the ability to accomplish the things that need to be done, or worse the ability to provide for our essential needs. Recall that as the COVID-19 pandemic approached, there was a desperate run on supplies like water, toilet paper, food, batteries, sanitizers, etc. In other types of disasters, we may not have the option to run to a store to gather supplies.

Planning ahead also allows us to use the full capacity of our brain to figure out what needs to be done and how to do it during an expected event rather than using a stress-compromised brain in a time-crunch situation when we need it to function rapidly and clearly.

Think about the last time you did not prepare for something that you knew was coming up, or you procrastinated preparing a report, packing for a trip, or getting ready for a big party. How high was your stress level in the hours before the deadline? How clear were your thoughts while racing about to accomplish your task? How many things did you forget?

Another critical component to planning ahead and being prepared is the ability to project possible consequences of actions and anticipate potential challenges that may jump into our path. This is an ability that comes with experience, thought, humility, and wisdom. For many years, the disaster preparedness manager at our hospital reported to me. She spent many hours learning, preparing, and ordering supplies to cover the myriad potential disasters that could impact a hospital. We both attended national emergency management classes, simulations, and rigorous training events. She ran drills and trained employees. Her skill set was extremely valuable. Many of us could sleep much better at night knowing that she had prepared us all for the many challenges that we could potentially face.

Many people believe that they are invincible and therefore nothing will go wrong in their lives. With that attitude, they will not prepare for the unexpected. They do not believe that anything they do can go wrong, so they do not prepare for any potential unforeseen consequences. Imagine how much more stressful challenges and negative events can be for the person who doesn't plan ahead or prepare because they believe they shouldn't have to. Regret is one of the worst components of stress.

Even the Boy Scouts of America motto encourages us to "Be Prepared!" Good advice for all. Recently, during all the hurricanes and fires that were plaguing the United States, I received many texts and email from friends in danger zones who were being evacuated. They said things like, "What should we take?" and, "It looks like we are going to have to leave our home and we have no idea what we should do." Gratefully, a prophet of God has counseled us to have a seventy-two-hour kit ready, as well as money, legal documents, pictures, insurance policies, and even genealogy or other important irreplaceable items. Being prepared means planning ahead physically, mentally, emotionally, and spiritually.

Prayer

"Counsel with the Lord in all thy doings and he will direct thee for good" (Alma 37:37). "Verily, Verily, I say unto you, ye must watch and pray always, lest ye be tempted by the devil, and ye be led away captive by him" (3 Nephi 18:15).

Prayer, our communion with our Father in Heaven, affects every stage of the stress process. Let's refer to the Lord's promise and assurance if we turn to Him during times of tribulation and stress: "When thou art in tribulation, and all these things are come upon thee, even in the latter days, if thou turn to the Lord thy God, and shall be obedient unto his voice...he will not forsake thee, neither destroy thee, nor forget the covenant of thy fathers which he swear unto them" (Deut. 4:30–31).

President Thomas S. Monson reinforced the message of that scripture: "To those within the sound of my voice who are struggling with challenges and difficulties large and small, prayer is the provider of spiritual strength: it is the passport to peace. Prayer is the means by which we approach our Father in Heaven, who loves us. Speak to Him in prayer and then listen for the answers. Miracles are wrought through prayer."[68] When we are stressed, we absolutely need the promises in that prophetic quote: strength, peace, and miracles.

Earnest prayer is a process of becoming humble and talking honestly and openly with our Father in Heaven while pouring out our concerns, trials, and needs. When we engage in this focused process, we manifest faith in our Father in Heaven, which changes the area of the brain that we are using and decreases the amount of stress chemicals released into our body. Prayer also puts us in connection with the best "social support" we could ever need—our Creator. Prayer can also quiet the mind from all the outside noise as we focus

---

68. Thomas S. Monson, "Be Your Best Self," *Ensign*, May 2009.

on our genuine communication with the Lord and prepare to receive divine guidance.

That last sentence highlights another critical component of prayer, the need to listen for the answer. We were taught to pray using the Lord's Prayer as our example of how to pray. And we were taught the steps of prayer: to address our Father in Heaven, give thanks, ask for what we need, and close in the name of Jesus Christ. In the process of learning to pray, sometimes the last step—to listen—has been forgotten. Listening is critical. We are praying for guidance, yet all too often, we finish our prayer without taking the time to stay quiet and still for a while to listen for the Lord's counsel. During the course of working through challenges and trials, there are so many voices telling us what to do that they can drown out the promptings of the Holy Ghost. When we separate ourselves from the world and engage in quiet, heartfelt prayer, we prepare ourselves to be humble enough to hear the answers that He gives.

There is one more step in this process: Act on the answers we are given. Once we have prayed for help, guidance, and comfort, we are accountable to listen to the answers and then follow the promptings of the Holy Ghost. It makes no sense to spend time pleading for the Lord's guidance if we are not going to follow it.

The process of engaging in frequent prayer also has a positive side effect. "Research indicates that twelve minutes of daily focused prayer over an eight-week period can change the brain to such an extent it can be measured on a brain scan and that turning to God rather than rejecting God appears to boost your immune system and stave off disease nearly five times as effectively."[69] Prayer and meditation seem to have the same healthy, healing affect. Prayer provides the environment to study things out in your mind and then helps quiet the mind.

Prayer is our way to stay in constant company with our Father in Heaven and our Lord and Savior, Jesus Christ. Prayer is critical to our lives and to dealing with stress in every stage of the stress process. Next time you feel stressed, refer to the wisdom of Nephi to his

---

69. Andrew Newberg and Mark Robert Waldman, *How God Changes Your Brain: Breakthrough Findings from a Leading Neuroscientist* (New York: Ballantine Books, 2010), 26.

befuddled brothers in 1 Nephi 15:8: "And I said unto them: Have ye inquired of the Lord?" Hopefully your answer will be yes.

PRIORITIES

"But seek ye first the kingdom of God, and his righteousness; and all these things shall be added unto you" (Matt. 6:33; 2 Nephi 2:18; 3 Nephi 13:33). "And see that all these things are done in wisdom and order: for it is not requisite that a man should run faster than he has strength...therefore, all things must be done in order" (Mosiah 4:27).

The Lord has been clear that we need to set priorities and has even told us what some of those priorities should be. What does priority mean? A priority is a thing that is regarded as more important than another. Our priorities determine what we seek in life.

We often find ourselves racing, working faster and faster just to meet someone else's priorities and deadlines, leaving little or no time to meet our own needs, let alone our own priorities. We also might find ourselves believing that something is a priority for us because someone in the media told us it should be. Or perhaps we see a ton of tweets on Twitter about an issue, and we begin to internalize those messages turning them into our priorities because we want to belong. Steve Jobs advised, "Your time is limited, so don't waste it living someone else's life." When we let others set our priorities and use our time, we increase our stress substantially because we are no longer living within our own priorities and value system.

To live within our own priorities, we each have the responsibility to know what our own priorities are. No one else can tell you what is important to you. The things that are priorities to me are not the things that are priorities for you and vice versa. Sometimes we are so busy focusing on the priorities set by our boss or a spouse or a family member or the rest of the world that we never consciously recognize what our own priorities are. However, deep down, we know that the things we are doing don't give us satisfaction. Deep restlessness from our own unmet priorities leads to some pervasive underlying stress in our lives.

Sometimes we do know what our priorities are and still feel compelled to meet the priorities of others. For instance, in a job, you need to follow the priorities of the boss in order to keep the job. In a marriage, you might give up your priorities to keep the peace or save the marriage. As a parent, you shuffle your priorities because one of your biggest priorities is to be a good, attentive parent, and you feel like you need to be on demand for your children.

We have choices. If the priorities of your boss are at complete odds with yours, and that constant disparity is causing severe stress, you can look for a different job. If your priorities are at odds with your spouse, you can sit down and review both of your priorities and look for ways to meet them both, or at least come up with some type of compromise that doesn't sacrifice either of the priorities of each spouse.

When we are clear about what our priorities are and what things we might be willing to compromise on, working out the disparity of priorities with a boss or a spouse or anyone else becomes easier. We find that when we understand what things are of greatest importance to others, we can talk with each other more effectively. If you know that your boss's first and most important priority is something that you just can't live with, it makes your decision to look elsewhere for employment much easier. There is a massive amount of stress that finds its way into our lives by constantly living someone else's priorities.

Feeling like we need to give up our priorities for work or family or other people is just one issue under this topic. Another issue is how we set priorities for our own lives and if our behavior reflects those priorities. President Russel M. Nelson provided great counsel on this subject: "The word religion literally means…'to tie back' to God. The question we might ask ourselves is, are we securely tied to God so that our faith shows, or are we actually tied to something else… Many put other priorities ahead of God… God's laws must ever be our standard. In dealing with controversial issues, we should first search for God's guidance… The temptation to be popular may prioritize public opinion above the word of God… Even if 'everyone is doing it,' wrong is never right."[70]

Perhaps you know what your priorities are but for some reason, you don't make daily decisions based on them. Or you might make choices that are exactly contrary to your priorities. Maybe you know what things are most important to do today, but you spend the whole

---

70. Russel M. Nelson, "Let Your Faith Show," *Ensign*, May 2014.

day busily doing the unimportant things. Maybe you think you will do the important things later but right now you just want to watch TV, veg out, or play a video game, but then you run out of time to do the important things. Henry David Thoreau addressed this principle by saying, "It's not enough to be busy; so are the ants. The question is: What are we busy about?" How often do we sacrifice what we want most for what we want now?

There is an oft repeated analogy about priorities: Putting big rocks, little rocks, and sand in a jar and making them all fit. When you put the sand in the jar first, then the little rocks, you find there is no room for the big rocks. But when you put the big rocks in first, then the little rocks, then pour in the sand, the sand flows all around the rocks and everything fits. Such is life, when we spend our day doing the sand-sized activities; there is no room for the most important activities—the big rocks won't fit. But when we do the important activities (big rocks) first, then the little-rock activities, we can pour in as much sand as we wish. Everything will fit. All the tasks will get done.

Elder Dieter F. Uchtdorf offered this suggestion: "If life and its rushed pace and many stresses have made it difficult for you to feel like rejoicing, then perhaps now is a good time to refocus on what matters most."[71] Lili de Hoyos Anderson adds, "We can create unhealthy stress in our lives by knowingly or unintentionally striving for the wrong things."[72]

It is important to note that often the "sand" activities don't need to be done. Sometimes trying to fit the unimportant items into our lives just creates more stress. Benjamin Hardy said, "Most people's lives are filled to the brim with the nonessential and trivial."

Someone once said, "If we do not choose the kingdom of God first, it will make little difference in the long run what we have chosen instead of it." Jesus taught about priorities when He said, "Seek not the things of this world but seek ye first to build up the kingdom of God, and to establish his righteousness, and all these things shall be added unto you" (JST, Matt. 6:38; Matt. 6:33, footnote a).

---

71. Dieter F. Uchtdorf, "Of Things That Matter Most," *Ensign*, November 2010.
72. Lili De Hoyos Anderson, "The Stress of Life," *Ensign*, February 1994.

Repentance and the Atonement

"Therefore, repent ye, repent ye, lest by knowing these things and not doing them ye shall suffer yourselves to come under condemnation, and ye are brought down unto this second death" (Helaman 14:19).

There are hundreds of scriptures that command us to repent. The fourth article of faith declares that the second principle of the gospel is *repentance*. Repentance is a critical principle for us to understand since it directly affects our life and our eternal progression. Repentance means to turn from sin, and feel regret, remorse, or contrition. Repentance is not optional for salvation; it is a commandment of God.

When we have hurt someone or broken a commandment, it generally brings some degree of guilt to our hearts and minds. The weight of that guilt causes intense stress. That stress is totally unnecessary stress that we have brought upon ourselves through some type of sin or mistake. That guilt can feel unrelentingly heavy. Knowing that sin could cause us to become constantly stressed from guilt, sorrow, and depression to the point of giving up hope, the Savior provided the atonement so that we could repent of our sins and free our conscience.

The third article of faith states, "We believe that through the Atonement of Christ, all mankind may be saved, by obedience to the laws and ordinances of the Gospel." The Savior's atoning sacrifice opened the way for washing away our sins through the process of repentance. We can absolutely quit carrying around the weight of sin and the unrelenting stress. There is great joy and increased wisdom as we repent from our sins, allowing the cleansing power of the atonement to clear our heart, soul, and mind from the guilt. Alexander Pope advised, "A man should never be ashamed to own he has been in the wrong... In other words, that he is wiser today than he was yesterday."

Failure to repent attests to the fact that our hearts have not been turned to the Savior. Marilyn vos Savant humorously summed up this attitude in saying, "A fool is someone whose pencil wears out before its eraser does." We should consistently be trying to identify our errors and correct them. As we increase in our love for our Father in Heaven and for our Savior, Jesus Christ, we want to be more like them. We want to turn away from our mistakes and sins and purify our lives.

Repentance requires humility and a recognition and confession that we made a mistake. It requires a willingness to admit that we are not perfect and that we are willing and committed to turn away from sin and dedicate ourselves to serving the Lord. Repentance and the atonement of Christ are amongst the greatest gifts that we have been given. It is essential to both our earthly happiness and our eternal salvation.

SABBATH DAY—KEEP IT HOLY

"Remember the sabbath day, to keep it holy" (Mosiah 13:16). "For in six days the Lord made heaven and earth, the sea, and all that in them is, and rested the seventh day: wherefore the Lord blessed the sabbath day, and hallowed it" (Exodus 20:11).

The commandment to keep the Sabbath day holy has been repeated many times throughout the scriptures. It is a very clear commandment. When commanded to keep the Sabbath day holy, the Lord clarified what that meant in the next three verses: "Six days thou shalt labour, and do all they work: But the seventh day is the sabbath of the Lord thy God: in it thou shalt not do any work, thou, nor thy son, nor thy daughter, nor thy manservant, nor thine ox, nor thine ass, nor any of thy cattle, nor thy stranger that is within thy gates; that thy manservant and thy maidservant may rest as well as thou" (Deut. 5:12–14). We are clearly commanded not to do any work nor require work from any one around us. We are further commanded that we should use the Sabbath day as a day to rest from our labors and keep the day holy. How much clearer can a commandment be?

In chapter one we discussed why stress levels are increasing. One of the many reasons is that we no longer follow the commandment to take a rest break every seven days. The Lord knows what it takes for our body, mind, and spirit to function effectively. He has guided us in how to take care of our temporal body by giving us a health code to follow. He tells us to get adequate sleep every day. He tells us what substances to take into our body and what substances should not go into our body. Is it any wonder that He would tell us how frequently we need to shut down from working? We need time to reset our physical, mental, and spiritual reservoir.

There are many benefits to keeping the Sabbath day holy. Taking a break from work and changing our focus to thoughts of the Savior gives us the chance to let our mind shift away from the constant stressors that beset us. This day gives our body, mind, and spirit a weekly break to help dissipate some of the stress that builds up during the week. Keeping the Sabbath day holy is an automatic reset button to our hectic, stressful lives. As we stop working and instead focus on the Lord, we give our mind and our body the chance to stop the stress process. Diverting your focus changes your thoughts, stops or slows down the amygdala from sending stress hormones to your body, and thus slows down or stops the physiological response. In addition, keeping the Sabbath day holy allows our mind to be still, which opens it up to receiving revelation. For me, answers to prayers, solutions to problems, and greater insights come when my mind is calm, still, and focused on the Savior. In essence, keeping the Sabbath day holy gives us a break from the stressful storms in our life and gives us the chance to nourish our spirit.

SCRIPTURES

"They had waxed strong in the knowledge of the truth: for they were men of a sound understanding and they had searched the scriptures diligently, that they might know the word of God" (Alma 17:2).

The Holy Bible is one of the most widely read books in the world. It is the textual foundation of Christian religions. It is in such wide use that there are many different translations available of this sacred record. The messages in its pages are so universally needed and desired that it is quite common to find a bible in a hotel room so that a weary traveler can find peace, comfort, and answers in the sacred pages. The bible is widely accepted and acclaimed as the word of God.

There are other scriptures available for our guidance as well: the Book of Mormon, Doctrine and Covenants, the Pearl of Great Price, and the words of our living prophets. There are also other sacred writings that follow Buddha, Muhammad, etc. that provide wisdom and insights. The scriptures are given to us as a gift so we can know the words of God and receive the commandments, the direction, and comfort that He sends to us. But what good are all of the scriptures if we do not read them? An unknown author once said, "The man who doesn't read good books has no advantage over the man who can't read them." How lucky are we to have the scriptures available to all people in most languages and formats? We have no excuse for not reading/listening to them.

President Thomas S. Monson admonished, "Search the scriptures with diligence. The scriptures testify of God and contain the words of eternal life... We are encouraged, as well, to study the scriptures each day both individually and with our families." He did not suggest that we casually read through them once and then put them up on the shelf for reference later. He admonished that we "search the scriptures with diligence." The word diligence implies consistent work and effort on our part. That admonition suggests that we study the scriptures frequently and thoroughly, searching the pages for answers, insights, commandments, and a deeper understanding of the nature of God.

Elder Dieter F. Uchtdorf gave us great counsel concerning the scriptures, "The holy scriptures and the spoken word of the living prophets give emphasis to the fundamental principles and doctrines of the gospel. The reason we return to these foundational principles, to the pure doctrines, is because they are the gateway to truths of profound meaning. They are the door to experiences of sublime importance that would otherwise be beyond our capacity to comprehend. These simple, basic principles are the key to living in harmony with God and man. They are the keys to opening the windows of heaven. They lead us to the peace, joy, and understanding that Heavenly Father has promised to His children who hear and obey Him."[73]

We learned in chapter five that our reactions to incoming information, especially stressful information, goes through many filters in our brain. We learned that the strongest filters in our brain are those that are the most current; they are messages that are repetitive and information that is accompanied by strong emotions. Is it any wonder that we are encouraged to read the scriptures daily? There is great wisdom in making the strongest, most recent and repetitive filters in our brain filters that come from the principles and words of the scriptures. Daily scripture study helps us to learn the principles that teach

---

73. Dieter F. Uchtdorf, "Of Things That Matter Most," *Ensign*, November 2010.

us how to manage stress and keeps us grounded in the gospel. When we process all the incoming information in our lives through filters based on the counsel of the scriptures, we automatically decrease the number of things we perceive to be stressful. Daily scripture study helps decrease the thought distortions that frequently cause unnecessary stress. In addition, by having current and repeated knowledge of the scriptures, we have embedded into our brain correct information to help us know how to resolve challenges as they arise, ways to cope when we are in the depths of pain and sorrow, and receive comfort from the constant promises and assurances that the scriptures provide.

It is likely that you have seen the oft-circulated questions by an unknown author that offer us great food for thought: "What if we began to treat our Bibles the way we treat our cell phones? What if we carried it with us everywhere? What if we turned back to get it if we forgot it? What if we checked it for messages throughout the day? What if we used it in case of an emergency? What if we spent an hour or more using it every day?" Losing a cell phone would cause many people to be highly stressed. The answers to dealing with our stress are in the scriptures. Should we not be more diligent in reading those scriptures every day?

SIMPLIFY

"By simple things are great things brought to pass" (Alma 37:6). We can greatly decrease our stress in life by implementing this principle: simplify. Perhaps you have seen the picture on social media of the beautiful, tranquil cabin in the woods with a caption that reads: "Would you live here for a month?" An overwhelming number of responses are affirmative but have this one caveat: "Oh, how I wish I could, but I have so much to take care of at home." Go through the list of things in your life that cause you stress. Now focus on the things that could be considered to cause unnecessary stress. How many of those things on the unnecessary stress list are things that could be considered the complexities of life or the cares of this world? How much of our stress is perpetuated by the massive amount of possessions that we own, store, clean, maintain, and repair? How many non-life-sustaining activities do we engage in on a daily basis? Which things on our to-do lists are a direct result of living and functioning in a very complex world?

We have a lot of complexities that are part of life: the many forms that we wade through every April in order to calculate and pay taxes; the biggest, most complex, most complicated, and most expensive healthcare system in the world; an education system that is not standardized; and the very delicate balance between spending, borrowing, interest, investments, income, and debt that make up our national economy. Whatever happened to that old philosophy to KISS: Keep It Simple Stupid? It seems that we often go out of our way to make life more complicated than it needs to be.

Elder Dieter F. Uchtdorf counsels, "There is a beauty and clarity that comes from simplicity that we sometimes do not appreciate in our thirst for intricate solutions... If life and its rushed pace and many stresses have made it difficult for you to feel like rejoicing, then perhaps now is a good time to refocus on what matters most... Let us simplify our lives a little. Let us make the changes necessary to refocus our lives on the sublime beauty of the simple, humble path of Christian discipleship—the path that leads always toward a life of meaning, gladness, and peace."[74]

I am often amused at the gadgets and appliances that are constantly advertised in catalogues, on television, and on social media. People are inventing new things to sell and many people feel compelled to acquire these newest, creative inventions. The advertisements suggest that there is a special tool, pan, utensil, and new electronic equipment to meet every single specific need. Some of them are helpful. Some of them just wasted money and take up a ton of space in our homes.

Recently, I observed one friend who has thirty-seven different types and forms of cake pans. Each time she bakes, she has to hunt for just the right pan. Plus, she had to install several shelves in her garage to store all the cake pans, not including loaf pans, cookie sheets, pie pans, and many pans that were unrecognizable. From there, we went to another installed garage shelf for a huge variety of baskets in every size, shape, and style. In scanning the many shelving units and

---

74. Dieter F. Uchtdorf, "Of Things That Matter Most," *Ensign*, November 2010.

varieties of possessions in this home, garage, and three storage sheds, I found myself reflecting on the words of Elder L. Tom Perry: "In our search to obtain relief from the stresses of life, may we earnestly seek ways to simplify our lives."[75]

If you find yourself reviewing repeatedly the section on being over-whelmed, perhaps it would be wise to do an aggressive spring cleaning of possessions as well as a spring cleaning of life. Determine which activities are not necessary in your life and slowly extricate yourself from them. Downsize the possessions you find in all the cupboards, closets, and shelves in your home. Find simple ways to do necessary things. Practice simplicity in your home and in your character. If you have been so entrenched in complexity for too long, pray for wisdom and insights into ways to simplify your life. It automatically decreases your stress.

SLEEP

Sleep is a normal, natural, daily component of life. It is a necessary process that allows your body to repair itself, grow, rest, and even appropriately file daily events in your brain. Sleep is essential. It is critical for good physical health as well as mental and emotional stability. Getting adequate sleep consistently is also essential in dealing with stress. When we do not get enough sleep, it is much easier for us to perceive things as stressful when they are not. There are many health effects of getting appropriate amounts of sleep, such as increased memory, longer life, decreased inflammation, increased creativity, increased attention and focus, lower stress, decreased dependence on stimulants like caffeine, decreased risk of getting into accidents, and decreased risk of depression.

Unfortunately, many Americans are sleep deprived. Sleep depri-vation can increase all stages of the stress process. Several different studies indicate that anywhere from 20 to 60 percent of Americans are sleep deprived. Sleep deprivation has become a national epidemic. Sleeplessness is related to health issues such as reduced stress toler-ance, lack of energy, increased irritability, short temper, aggressive

---

75. L. Tom Perry, "Let Him Do It with Simplicity," *Ensign*, November 2008.

behavior, increased anxiety, weakened short-term memory, changes in the nervous system, changes in appetite, attention deficit, problems with processing information, sensory problems, decreased problem solving, decreased hand-eye coordination, decreased reaction time, decreased performance and motivation, hormonal changes, weight gain, decreased immune system function, increased chance of illness, fatigue/tiredness, blurred vision, decreased concentration, physical and mental exhaustion, depression, lethargy, forgetfulness, increased inflammation, decreased awareness, weakness, impaired judgment, increased moodiness, increased accidents, decreased alertness, increased social problems, increased impulsive behavior, decreased quality of life, increased incidence of heart attacks, high blood pressure, congestive heart failure, diabetes, stroke, obesity, mental impairment, uncontrolled blood glucose, and decreased mental focus. Now that is a very long list of detrimental effects just because we don't get adequate sleep.

The most important point here is that sleep helps reset the chemicals in our body. That is critical for stress management. But if one looks at the list of detrimental results from sleep deprivation, you will discover that the very long list are all stress-inducing triggers. I have heard tons of excuses for not getting sleep: "I will sleep when I am dead," "We are on vacation, I am not wasting vacation time on sleep," "I have too much to do to sleep," "I don't want to miss things," etc. To that list of excuses for not getting enough sleep, we should add "and I love being completely stressed" because that is what you are doing to yourself. Sleep is wisdom.

Social Support, Marriage, and Family

The scriptures are filled with references that encourage us, even command us, to cling to our family, love one another, give service to our fellow man, be a friend to others, and meet in fellowship with each other. In recent years, we received even more encouragement to protect marriage and family in the family proclamation.

It is clear that we all need each other to function well in this world. Families are eternal units. The structure of family units was implemented right from the organization of the world. There must be massive value in the relationships among family members if the Lord designed the entire world to be structured in family units and has proclaimed that families should be supported and protected as eternal relationships.

There is a great deal of research available that suggests that we are hardwired to connect with other human beings so much that we feel intense loneliness when we do not have meaningful relationships. Most of the research regarding the benefits of social support is readily available to anyone who is interested in gaining a more in-depth review than can be adequately discussed in this short section. I would highly recommend examining that research.

Amy Banks, a medical doctor and researcher in social connections, tells us that "neuroscience is confirming that our nervous systems want us to connect with other human beings... Being pushed out of social relationships and into isolation has health ramifications." She suggests that when we are excluded from a group, we register that social pain in the same area of the brain that we feel physical pain.[76] Watching people who suffer from social rejection or loneliness verifies the truthfulness of her research. The pandemic has been a vivid manifestation of how social connectedness has caused great loneliness, isolation, pain, and stress.

Marriage, family, and close social support groups can protect us from stressful situations and help reduce stress. Unfortunately, the opposite is also true. Severe challenges in marriage and family relationships or lack of strong social support can increase stress and reduce our ability to deal with stress.

From a logistic point of view, it is obvious that family, friends, and other social support groups can provide physical assistance, like assistance in changing a flat tire, moving furniture, repairing a broken fence, or resolving plumbing issues. Family and friends can also provide moral support, emotional understanding, a shoulder to cry on, someone to bounce ideas off of and wise counsel. In addition, social support helps build and sustain a healthy body, protect us from infection, lower our risk of heart disease, and reduce the chances of developing dementia in

---

76. Amy Banks, "Humans Are Hardwired for Connection? Neurobiology 101 for Parents, Educators, Practitioners, and the General Public," Wellesley Centers for Women, September 15, 2010.

old age. The wisdom of the Dalai Lama adds, "Without love we could not survive. Human beings are social creatures, and a concern for each other is the very basis of our life together."

All of the benefits of marriage, family, and social support systems help reduce our stress as well as help us to cope with stress when needed. Once again, we turn to the wisdom of the Dalai Lama to summarize the necessity and benefits of social support, "We humans are social beings. We come into the world as the result of others' actions. We survive here in dependence on others. Whether we like it or not, there is hardly a moment of our lives in which we do not benefit from others' activities. For this reason, it is hardly surprising that most of our happiness arises in the context of our relationships with others. Nor is it so remarkable that our greatest joy should come when we are motivated by concern for others. But that is not all. We find that not only do altruistic actions bring about happiness, they also lessen our experience of suffering. Here I am not suggesting that the individual whose actions are motivated by the wish to bring others happiness necessarily meets with less misfortune than the one who does not. Sickness, old age, or mishaps of one sort or another are the same for us all. But the sufferings which undermine our internal peace—anxiety, doubt, disappointment—these are definitely less."

TEMPLE ATTENDANCE

"And I say unto you, let this house be built unto my name, that I may reveal mine ordinances therein unto my people: For I deign to reveal unto my church things which have been kept hid from before the foundation of the world, things that pertain to the dispensation of the fulness of times" (D&C 124: 40–41).

Anyone who has walked through the doors of the temple knows there is a different atmosphere in this holy edifice. It is a place of peace, quiet, reverence, comfort, and solitude. It is a place we can more fully commune with the Savior; to plead for comfort, insights, and answers to our prayers; and learn eternal lessons. As we walk into the temple, we leave the world and its problems behind. I often feel like stepping into the temple is taking a step into heaven. I know of no better place to go when the challenges, stresses, and trials of the world weigh heavily on our shoulders.

How blessed we are to live in the last days where temples dot the world. Most people no longer need to travel many thousands of miles to attend the temple and receive the blessings of the temple ordinances. Many people are fortunate enough to have a temple within easy travel range and are able to attend the temple frequently. There is great wisdom in availing ourselves of this opportunity. As the temples closed during the COVID-19 pandemic, many people quickly felt the effects of not being able to go to the temple frequently.

There are many great blessings that come from temple attendance. President Thomas S. Monson described just one of those blessings and promises: "The world can be a challenging and difficult place in which to live. We are often surrounded by that which would drag us down. As you and I go to the holy houses of God, as we remember the covenants we make within, we will be more able to bear every trial and to overcome each temptation. In this sacred sanctuary, we will find peace; we will be renewed and fortified."[77] This is exactly the blessing we need when we find ourselves deeply stressed from the challenges of life: The blessing of peace. President Gordon B. Hinckley also affirmed this blessing: "Every man or woman who goes to the temple comes out of that building a better man or woman than he or she was when entering into it… Do you have problems and concerns and worries? Do you want for peace in your heart and an opportunity to commune with the Lord and meditate upon His way? Go to the house of the Lord and there feel of His Spirit and commune with Him and you will know a peace that you will find nowhere else."[78] Having our stress and turmoil from living in the world replaced with peace and comfort is a precious and powerful blessing.

President Thomas S. Monson assured us in saying, "As we enter through the doors of the temple, we leave behind us the distractions and confusion of the world… There is rest for our souls and a respite

---

77. Thomas S. Monson, "The Holy Temple—A Beacon to the World," *Ensign*, May 2011.
78. Gordon B. Hinckley, "Rejoice in the Blessings of the Temple," *Liahona*, December 2002, from a talk given in stake conference, Wadsworth, England, August 27, 1995.

from the cares of our lives. As we attend the temple, there can come to us a dimension of spirituality and a feeling of peace which will transcend any other feeling which could come into the human heart... Such peace can permeate any heart—hearts that are troubled, hearts that are burdened down with grief, hearts that feel confusion, hearts that plead for help... In our lives we will have temptations; we will have trials and challenges. As we go to the temple, as we remember the covenants, we make there, we will be better able to overcome those temptations and to bear our trials. In the temple we can find peace. The blessings of the temple are priceless."[79] We could ask for no greater blessings or more profound assurance from a prophet of God. The temple can do a great deal to relieve our stress.

Time Management

Our priorities in life are most visible in how we use our time. Once we know our priorities and how important each one is, we can then use our time more wisely. Christopher Rice counsels, "Every day is a bank account, and time is our currency. No one is rich, no one is poor, we've got twenty-four hours each."

Even though we each have the same number of hours in a day, how many times do you find yourselves saying, "I just don't have enough time," or "I don't have time to do the things I want to do?" Perhaps the wiser questions should be, "Am I using my time efficiently?" or, "Are there unimportant things I spend my time doing that take time away from the more important things I need to do?" We are constantly racing deadlines and cutting into our critical sleep time to find a few more hours every day to do a few more things that we think have to be done. The more demands we add to life, the higher our stress level goes.

We live in an era that seems to require that we do more and more, faster and faster in the quest to do all and be all. This attitude is so prevalent that it has its own name: the hurry sickness. Hurry sickness is a behavior pattern in which people are constantly in a hurry, feeling rushed, overwhelmed, pressed for time, and in a constant state

---

79. Thomas S. Monson, "Blessings of the Temple," *Ensign*, May 2015.

of urgency. Hurry sickness is a major contributor to our overall stress level. This drive to hurry through every activity is not just wearing us out but it is destroying our ability to find any joy or peace in what we are doing.

Time management is the process of finding a balance between utilizing our time efficiently and trying to accomplish the most important things on our to-do list. Time is a valuable commodity. Many notable quotes have been offered in reference to time. Hal Sparks offers, "It's better to waste money than it is to waste time. You can always get more money." Dallin H. Oaks explains, "Because of increased life expectancies and modern timesaving devices, most of us have far more discretionary time than our predecessors. We are accountable for how we use that time… We cannot recycle or save the time allotted to us each day. With time, we have only one opportunity for choice, and then it is gone forever."[80]

None of us know how much time we have on this earth. We don't even know how much productive time we will have today or this week. Perhaps there is a broken ankle coming our way as we walk out the door, which will rearrange our entire schedule for the day and for the next six to eight weeks. Perhaps there is a major illness that hits unexpectedly and takes five months of our life to recuperate. We never know what challenges await us or how much time we will have, therefore, it is incumbent on each of us to use our time wisely in order to prevent or minimize some of our stress.

Caution: Using time wisely does not mean that we must be busily accomplishing something every second of the day. It is wise to get needful amounts of sleep daily. It is wise to use the Sabbath day to "rest from our labors." It is wise to take time to play with our children. It is wise to spend quality time with family and friends. It is wise to take time to develop and share our talents. It is wise to take some time to unwind from the stresses of life by enjoying some entertainment.

Making wise use of our time means that we don't waste it doing things that aren't important. I frequently have students come into my office to tell me that they don't have time to get an assignment in on time. For some of them, that is true: they work full time, have a

---

80. Dallin H. Oaks, "Focus and Priorities," *Ensign*, May 2001.

family, and they are trying to go to school as well. Suddenly, they have critical demands at work or a sick spouse or child, and they really do not have the time to work on a school assignment. However, other students confess that they only work eight to ten hours per week (or not at all) and have a very light course load, but they spend eight to ten hours per day playing video games, watching television, participating in their favorite sport, or reading every post on social media. No wonder they have no time to do school work when they are wasting precious hours on unimportant stuff.

In order to use our time more wisely, it is helpful to learn time management skills and techniques. There are many available programs that teach these principles on the Internet, community classes, or even from publishers of time management systems. Most of us would benefit from a frequent review of those principles. Those materials teach us to use our time and attention for what matters most.

VALUES SYSTEM AND MORAL CODE

In several previous sections, especially the sections on priorities and integrity, there were many references to the fact that values and morals were the foundation of most of our behaviors. Values and morals, though different in their exact definitions, have the same core. Values are the things that we deem to have importance, usefulness, and worth. It is what one judges to be important in life. It includes the principles and standards of one's behaviors. Morals come from the same core. They are the principles and standards of one's behaviors. Morals have the additional component of what we believe to be behaviors that are right or wrong, good or bad, acceptable or unacceptable.

In order to practice our values and morals, we first need to know what ours are. In earlier generations, people's values, morals, and principles used to be clear and widely accepted. Those morals and values were the way for individuals to stay grounded. However, today we live in a world where values, morals, and principles are changing faster than the seasons' fashions. When we have values that change and become unstable, it is difficult to feel a foundation underneath us to support us through the tough times.

We need to understand that people change, cultures change, the values in society change but truth does not change. Our values should be based on truth. Once we know what we truly value, it will give us clarity, focus, a compass to guide our path, and an anchor to our soul.

As we all know, the purpose of an anchor is to keep a ship stable, stationary, safe, and secure in a desired location or to help the ship stay stable and controlled in a storm-tossed sea. The anchor must be strong, solid, weighted, and used properly in order for the anchor to secure the ship. An anchor made of flimsy, lightweight, floatable material will not accomplish any of the stabilizing goals. So it is with our values. They must be solid, strong, secure, and able to hold our lives in a secure, grounded position—especially during the storms of stress, crisis, turmoil, and disasters.

Have you ever acted in a way that was completely contrary to your own personal values or morals? How did that feel? For most people, doing something that goes against what they personally value and believe is moral causes a great deal of internal stress and dissonance. Living outside of your value system and moral code always causes at least some amount of stress. If we behave in ways that contradict what we say we value, we should probably reevaluate both our values and our behaviors, because the dissonance is increasing our stress level.

This section is not meant to be a discussion on what your personal values or personal moral code should or should not be but rather a discussion on how we create our own stress when we behave in ways that contradict our personal values/morals, whatever they may be.

We can tell what we or other people value by watching how we/ they spend their time, energy, and money. It is worth the time to do some honest introspection to assess how you spend your energy and your money to assess your values and morals. Some of us only get a clear understanding of what we value and believe when we get stung with regret and guilt for acting against those values and morals.

If you struggle with gaining clarity about what you value, just go to the Internet and type the words values and morals into your search engine. Such a search will provide you with many sites that have very comprehensive lists of potential values and morals. You can take those lists and rate each item to see what you value most and least. Then for the next week, be cognizant of your behavior. Watch how you spend your time, your energy, and your money. Does it match what you say you value? If someone else were watching how you spend your time, your energy, and your money, would they be able to figure out which things you rated as your highest priorities, values, and morals?

If the answer to either of those questions is no, then you have some deep thinking and introspection to do. This lack of connection and harmony between what you think and what you do is called cognitive dissonance. Cognitive dissonance is a major source of stress in life. To decrease your stress, you need to figure out if you honestly value what you say you value. If you really do value what you think you value, then you need to figure out why your behavior doesn't match so that you can fix the dissonance. Our actions should reflect our values.

That last sentence is not as easy to do as it may sound. Sometimes, we have two or more values/morals that conflict with each other. You may value the job that you do as a good way to serve others but do not agree with the values of the people running the company. You may value participating in sports but you also value keeping the Sabbath day holy. What do you do then about the sporting events scheduled on the Sabbath? As you are confronted with these conflicting values/morals, you will quickly learn which values and moral behaviors are more important to you by the stress you feel when you put one value above its counterpart.

Living outside our value system and our moral code causes stress. The stress may be deep, underlying, and pervasive. If the consequences of our behaviors affect others, as they usually do, our stress and guilt can compound exponentially. Make it a conscious choice to identify your personal values and morals and then commit to follow them.

Write/Keep a Journal

How grateful I am, especially during times of great tribulation and grief, that I can turn to the scriptures to find solace, comfort, counsel, and peace. I am further grateful to all of those who followed a commandment to keep a record of their life, the events transpiring in the world, and their spiritual insights and revelations, which have given us those scriptures. I am also grateful to a grandfather who kept a daily journal of his life. Reading his journal and subsequent autobiography gave me great insight into his life, a lot of entertainment from his great storytelling, and some spiritual wisdom regarding his departure from the gospel and his humble return to spend most of his retirement as a dedicated temple worker. All of those blessings are due to so many answering the call to write a record of remembrance.

I recall as a young woman, we were encouraged to keep a book of remembrance. Our books contained certificates, awards, and narratives of important events in our lives. Later, I heard the counsel to keep a daily journal. The journal I kept while I was serving a mission reminds me of the challenges, trials, precious relationships, and spiritual transformation I experienced during that time.

We are still encouraged to keep a daily journal to record our thoughts, feelings, lessons learned, and spiritual journey through life. President Spencer W. Kimball stated, "The Savior emphasized the importance of keeping records. And one of the most valuable records is the one you keep of your own life... Accordingly, we urge our young people to begin today to write and keep records of all the important things in their own lives and also the lives of their antecedents in the event that their parents should fail to record all the important incidents in their own lives. Your own private journal should record the way you face up to challenges that beset you."[81]

What does keeping a journal have to do with managing stress? To begin to answer that question, let me share a quote from *The Diary of Anne Frank*. This quote is Anne addressing her diary: "I hope I shall be able to confide in you completely, as I have never been able to do in anyone before. And I hope that you will be a great comfort and support to me... I want to write, but more than that, I want to bring out all kinds of things that lie deep in my heart." Anne knew that in her diary, she could voice her fears, trials, trauma, terror, and complete confusion about the events that kept her and her family hiding in a small attic. Anne was most definitely using a dairy to help her process and cope with her stress.

Writing, whether in a diary/journal or in the form of poetry, songs, or stories, is very cathartic. All of the most quoted poems or most

---

81. Spencer W. Kimball, "The Angels May Quote from It," *The New Era*, February 2003.

popular songs came from someone putting their thoughts, sorrows, and experiences into written words. Writing gives us the opportunity to pour out onto paper our thoughts and emotions. Writing allows us to be completely honest with how we feel. We can write about things that cause us pain and confusion or enjoyment and love. We can spill out the challenges of marriage, parenting, broken relationships, work, spiritual concerns, or events that have affected our lives. Many of these thoughts and feelings are stressful. Many of the topics we write about are things that we do not feel comfortable or confident enough to share with others.

Sometimes, the process of writing is an attempt for us to work out the conflict of emotions that we feel. Perhaps we are trying to gain some clarity of thought or insights about issues that challenge us. Maybe, we write just to vent and get things out. Many therapists suggest that their patients write letters to people who have harmed them in some way so that they can get the anger out of their own hearts. These letters, which are rarely actually sent, still give the writer the ability to say what he has not been able to say before. People can express in writing their thoughts, wounds, fears, anger, damage to their lives, and even how they felt like responding to the other person but could not because it would go against their own personal moral code. Writing the letter has given the writer a release from the emotional pain, trauma, and stress.

Others have used writing as part of their healing from traumatic life events. Writing gets negative emotions and thoughts out of the mind, which automatically reduces stress from those traumatic events. Writing also gives those who write the ability to process how they feel, reduce their depression or fear, and provide a sense of closure.

In addition to the therapeutic effects of writing, keeping a diary/journal allows both the time and the forum to reflect upon our blessings, lessons we have learned, the events in our spiritual journey, and our gratitude. Focusing on all of these positive events helps build our stress capacity and keeps positive thoughts in the forefront of our minds.

Writing in a diary/journal can provide the writer with all of the same stress-reducing, health-promoting benefits of talking with a friend, counselor, or clergy. For some, writing is more beneficial than talking because by writing in a personal forum, the person does not have to be concerned with embarrassment, saying things wrong, figuring out which words are acceptable to use, etc. There is a great deal of research on the mental, emotional, and physical therapeutic effects of writing available on the Internet that might be of interest to you. All of those benefits of writing can help reduce our stress.

CHAPTER 10

Peace

"Peace I leave with you, my peace I give unto you: not as the world giveth, give I unto you. Let not your heart be troubled, neither let it be afraid" (John 14:27). "My son, Peace be unto thy soul: thine adversity and thine afflictions shall be but a small moment: and then, if thou endure it well, God shall exalt thee on high" (D&C 121:7–8).

As you recall from the introduction, I said I received one last principle from the Lord the night before the last day of Brigham Young University Education Week that I needed to include in the Education Week presentation. That principle was supposed to be added to the end of the presentation so that it would be the last lesson from the Savior that the students heard. That principle is peace. The same criteria apply to this book—it needs to be the last principle I present. Perhaps the most precious spiritual concept to help us minimize or manage our stress is the promise of peace from the Savior. It is the last lesson for a very significant reason. The principle of peace can sustain us through very trying times if we ask for that blessing and hold on to it when we receive it.

This prompting regarding this principle came with such love and compassion that it touched my heart. Knowing that it needed to be the last principle I presented so that people could leave feeling peace and love from our Father in Heaven and the Savior confirmed to me that He really does want to bless our lives with peace. Our Father in Heaven wants to bless us with His peace, especially during the severely trying times.

Many people feel that peace and trials are mutually exclusive. This means we think we can only feel peace in the absence of trials, challenges, difficulties, and stress. But think about times when you don't have major stressors surrounding you, do you automatically feel peace then? Not always. The absence of stress does not guarantee that we feel peace nor does the presence of stress require that peace is impossible to feel.

The world may be in turmoil, conflict, and confusion causing a great deal of stress to surround us, but we still can have the blessing of feeling peace. Bishop W. Christopher Waddell tells us "peace of mind, peace of conscience, and peace of heart are not determined by our ability to avoid trials, sorrow, or heartache. Despite our sincere pleas, not every storm will change course, not every infirmity will be healed… Nevertheless, we have been promised peace."[82] We can feel peace at all times—stressful or nonstressful, trials or no trials.

We are instructed in D&C 19:23 on three simple steps to receive the blessing of peace in our lives. We are told, "Learn of me and listen to my words: walk in the meekness of my Spirit, and you shall have peace in me." Three simple steps and a very powerful, much sought after promise of peace. It is important to note that in the promise of peace, the Lord is not promising a lack of trials or stress. Often people believe that the Lord isn't blessing them with peace just because He doesn't make the trial go away. He has told us clearly in John 16:33, "These things I have spoken unto you, that in me ye might have peace. In the world ye shall have tribulation: but be of good cheer; I have overcome the world." Additionally, in John 14:26–27 he comforts us with these words: "Peace I leave with you, my peace I give unto you: not as the world giveth, give I unto you. Let not your heart be troubled, neither let it be afraid." As the Savior promises to leave His peace with us, he further counsels us to not be troubled or afraid. All too often, we focus on the trouble and fear and chase away the peace that has been given. There is great counsel in a quote that is attributed to Joe Stowell, "When we put our problems in God's hands, He puts

---

82. W. Christopher Waddell, "A Pattern for Peace," *Ensign*, May 2016.

His peace in our hearts." Whatever the trial, whatever the stress, the Lord is with us and is ready to bless us with peace if we will receive it and hold onto it.

You may be wondering why I have stated, "if we will receive it" or "if we will hold on to it." Often, the Savior indeed blesses us with peace but we don't allow ourselves to receive it or hold on to it. We might even acknowledge that we feel peace for a moment but then we go back to thinking stressful thoughts, we go back to letting our hearts be troubled and afraid. Then the peace fades away and is replaced once again by stress. We can do the exact opposite, however. Instead of refocusing on stress and letting peace fade away, we can keep our minds focused on peace and let the stress fade away—a much wiser option.

How can we hold onto peace when we are nervous, frightened, or scared of the outcome of a medical procedure or a desperately needed job offer? As we follow the three steps mentioned earlier from the scripture D&C 19:23 to learn of Him, listen to His words, and walk in the meekness of His spirit, we can then pray for that promised peace. When we pray specifically for peace and then obtain it, we can pull that peace into our hearts, focus on gratitude that the Lord has blessed us with peace and then surround ourselves with ways to hold on tightly to that peace. Some ideas for holding on to peace: express sincere and profuse gratitude to the Lord for hearing and answering your prayer for peace, keep your mind focused on peace and refrain from thinking about the stressful event, keep a prayer in your heart, read scriptures or recite memorized scriptures in your mind, write in a journal outlining the feeling of peace and gratitude that you have, play uplifting hymns in your homes, sing hymns and uplifting songs in your minds, think of ways to bless the lives of others, ponder the atoning sacrifice of the Savior, remember that the Savior has promised us peace when we "come unto Him" (Matthew 11:28) so stay as close to Him as you possibly can in thought, word, and deed.

Returning to thoughts of the trial or stressor is extremely easy to do, but remember it will once again send stress hormones out into your body and stir up the feelings of fear and turmoil. How much wiser is it to keep thoughts of peace vigilantly locked in your mind, allowing the spirit to quietly guide your path and whisper words of peace and comfort to your heart? Timber Hawkeye sums up this principle in this way: "You can't calm the storm...so stop trying. What you can do is calm yourself, the storm will pass." Kimberly Jones adds to that, saying, "Don't let people pull you into their storm. Pull them into your peace."

During the horrendous trials that plagued Joseph Smith's life, he begged the Lord for answers and understanding while he was locked away in Liberty Jail (dungeon). The Lord comforted Joseph in words that can be comforting words for us as well, "My son, Peace be unto thy soul: thine adversity and thine afflictions shall be but a small moment: and then, if thou endure it well, God shall exalt thee on high" (D&C 121:7-8). Perhaps this should be the scripture we recite in our minds as we hold on tightly to the peace that we prayed for and received. Now just continue to hold on to that peace. Hold tightly to those precious words of the Savior, "Peace be unto thy soul" (D&C 121:7).

About the Author

Karen Shores learned a great deal about stress and how to manage it when both her parents passed away while she was at Brigham Young University. She was suddenly on her own, trying to work full time and finish a master's degree. She learned more about how to deal with stress when her husband passed away right after she began her doctoral program at the University of Utah. Her doctoral dissertation was on identifying the character traits that help a person become resilient in a life of trials and challenges. In order to help other people learn to deal with stress, she began teaching stress classes at conferences, universities, firesides, and community events. She has had many difficulties in life that have helped her test and refine the stress management principles and skills she has identified.

Notes